...And Always a Detective

Try with me and mix
   What will make a Novel,
All folks to transfix
   In house or hall or hovel.
Put the cauldron on,
   Set the bellows blowing;
We'll produce anon
   Something worth the showing.

     Toora-loora loo,
      Toora-loora leddy;
     Something neat and new,
      Not produced already.

Throw into the pot
   What will boil and bubble;
Never mind a *plot*,
   'Tisn't worth the trouble.
Character's a jest,
   Where's the use of study?
This will stand the test
   If only black and bloody.

     Toora-loora etc.

Here's the 'Newgate Guide',
   Here's the 'Causes Célèbres;'
Tumble in beside
   Poison, gun and sabre.
These Police reports,
   Those Old Bailey trials,
Horrors of all sorts,
   To match the Seven Vials.

     Toora-loora etc.

Crime that knows no bounds,
   Bigamy and arson;
Murder, blood and wounds,
   Will carry well the farce on . . .
Tame is Virtue's school;
   Paint, as more effective,
Villain, knave and fool,
   And always a Detective.

From 'How To Make A Novel'
Blackwood's Magazine, May 1864

...And Always a Detective

Chapters on the History of Detective Fiction

R F STEWART

David & Charles
Newton Abbot London North Pomfret (Vt)

To
ELIZABETH

**British Library Cataloguing in
Publication Data**
Stewart, R. F.
— and always a detective.
1. Detective and mystery stories — History
and criticism
I. Title
809.3'872   PN3448.D4

ISBN 0-7153-7922-4

© R.F. Stewart 1980

Typesetting by ABM Typographics Ltd, Hull
and printed in Great Britain
by Redwood Burn Limited, Trowbridge and Esher
for David & Charles (Publishers) Limited
Brunel House, Newton Abbot, Devon

Published in the United States of America
by David & Charles Inc
North Pomfret   Vermont 05053   USA

CONTENTS

AUTHOR'S NOTE

The titles of full-length books and anthologies are printed in italics, as are names of newspapers, periodicals and magazines. Titles of articles and short stories are in inverted commas.

Unless stated otherwise, a date given against a book is the date of its first publication in volume form, including novels which appeared originally as serials.

Information on sources quoted in the text is supplemented where necessary by footnotes gathered at the end of each chapter and by the bibliography, which should be used in conjunction with the text.

Square brackets round an author's name indicate that the work was first published anonymously. I am indebted to *The Wellesley Index to Victorian Periodicals 1824–1900*, ed. Walter E. Houghton, 3 vols (1966, 1972, 1979), and to *Wilkie Collins: The Critical Heritage*, ed. Norman Page (1974), for the identity of the writers of some of the anonymous articles quoted. A few authors of the invariably anonymous *Saturday Review* articles can be identified from M. M. Bevington's *The Saturday Review 1855–1868* (1941). The majority, however, I cannot identify and I have chosen to name none in the belief that the *Saturday Review* was an institution greater even than the sum of its contributors, or, as Sir Leslie Stephen put it when in later life he searched the *Saturday* for his old articles: 'I was a little startled to discover that I could rarely distinguish them by internal evidence. I had unconsciously adopted the tone of my colleagues, and like some inferior organism, taken the colouring of my "environment." ' (Bevington, p. 381).

ACKNOWLEDGEMENTS

Sincere thanks are due to the following for assistance, advice and, most enjoyable, argument: Professor C. E. Bosworth, Dr. J. S. Brider, Mr. D. S. W. Lumb, Mr. Brian Peters and Mr. Robert Powell.

The author also expresses his thanks to the following for permission to make quotations from the sources named: the City of Edinburgh District Council for an extract from the Council Records; the Controller of H.M. Stationery Office for extracts from Crown-copyright records in the Public Record Office; the *Evening Standard* for extracts from its 'Books and Persons' column by Arnold Bennett; the *Harvard Library Bulletin* for an extract from 'Devoted Disciple' by Robert Lee Wolff; *Punch* for extracts from two articles, 'Sense v. Sensation' and 'The Detective's Rescue'; the *Saturday Review* for extracts from 'Not "Whodunit?" But "How?"' by Jacques Barzun, © *Saturday Review*, 1944, all rights reserved; *The Times Literary Supplement* for extracts from three articles, 'The Literature of Pursuit and Violence' by Norman Shrapnel, 'Fine Knacks' and 'Emile Gaboriau' (both anonymous); The Bodley Head for extracts from *Victorian Detective Fiction;* William Collins Sons & Co Ltd for extracts from *The Rasp* and *The White Crow* by Philip MacDonald and *Masters of Mystery* by H. D. Thomson; Curtis Brown Ltd for an extract from *The First Detectives* by Belton Cobb, published by Faber; Everett/Edwards Inc. for extracts from *Edgar Poe: Seer and Craftsman* by Stuart Levine; Faber and Faber Ltd for extracts from *Bloody Murder* by Julian Symons, *The Dyer's Hand* by W. H. Auden, the Introduction

ACKNOWLEDGEMENTS

by John Welcome to *Best Crime Stories 2* and the Introduction by Ronald Knox to *Best Detective Stories of the Year 1928;* Victor Gollancz Ltd for extracts from *Fletch* by Gregory McDonald, *The American Gun Mystery* by Ellery Queen and *The Puritan Pleasures of the Detective Story* by Erik Routley; Harvard University Press for extracts, reprinted by permission, from *Bloodhounds of Heaven* by Ian Ousby, ©1976 by the President and Fellows of Harvard College, published by Havard University Press; David Higham Associates Ltd for extracts from *Whose Body?*, *Clouds of Witness*, *Unnatural Death*, *The Documents in the Case*, *Murder Must Advertise* and the Introductions to *Great Short Stories of Detection, Mystery and Horror* (1st and 2nd Series) by Dorothy L. Sayers, all published by Gollancz; Hughes Massie Ltd for extracts from *The A.B.C. Murders*, *Appointment with Death* and *Dumb Witness* by Agatha Christie, all published by Collins; John Murray (Publishers) Ltd, Messrs. Jonathan Cape Ltd and Baskervilles Investments Ltd for extracts from *A Study in Scarlet* by Sir Arthur Conan Doyle; and Peter Owen (London) Ltd for extracts from *The Development of the Detective Novel* by A. E. Murch.

Part I
THE FICTION

1
IN WHICH WE BEGIN NOT
TO UNDERSTAND

'The whole affair is a mystery.'
'A mystery?'
'An utter mystery.'

Anna Katherine Green, *The Leavenworth Case* (1878)

When in *Trent's Last Case* the hero is asked if he knows *Huckleberry Finn*, Trent's reply is unequivocal: 'Do I know my own name?' It is with the same certainty that this book can be said to be about detectives of fiction. It is with much less certainty that I approach the sirenic corollary that what follows is about detective fiction. One can point to a character in a book and say that he is a detective, if only in name, and expect a reasonable measure of agreement, but the same consensus is unlikely to follow the claim that the book in which he appears is a detective story, for again as surely as Trent knew his own name I know that someone somewhere is waiting to pounce on a book I mention with a gleeful 'But that isn't really a *detective* story!' Vanity, his and mine, is at the back of this; as Régis Messac points out in his monumental *Le 'detective novel' et l'influence de la pensée scientifique* (1929), those who use such expressions as detective novel and *roman policier* 'are convinced that they know their exact meaning. But words of this kind, especially compounds . . . take on a nuance of individual sense with each person who uses them and each mind that contemplates them'.

Most writers on detective fiction, both before and after Messac, have found themselves faced with this problem and have had recourse to a definition, which seems the commonsense and even necessary thing to do—with the consequent confusion to which commonsense and logic often lead. Thus Messac, unheedful of his own diagnosis, marches on to define a detective novel as *'un récit consacré avant tout à la découverte méthodique et graduelle, par des moyens rationnels, des circonstances exactes d'un événement mystérieux'*. Notice that there is no mention of a detective, while I started off with that gentleman. With the surface of Messac's definition barely scratched, one source of confusion is already revealed: does 'detective' in detective fiction refer to the person of the detective or to the activity of detection or to both in some proportion to be haggled over? The question may seem trivial, but that it has exercised writers' minds and coloured their views can be seen from the varying degrees of emphasis in their definitions.

In *Who Done It?* (1969), an encyclopaedic listing of authors, stories and general detectival bric-à-brac, the compiler, Ordean A. Hagen, settles somewhat abruptly for the primacy of the detective; a detective story, he claims, is one in which 'a detective or detectives solve the crime'. Ellery Queen, as befits that dual personality, plays it both ways, though with a leaning towards the person: 'first, a detective story must contain a detective who detects; second, the detective should be the protagonist; and third, the detective should almost invariably triumph'.[1] With her definition in *The Development of the Detective Novel* (1958) A. E. Murch saves us a struggle with Messac's definition by providing an unacknowledged translation thereof. Stress is now solely on the detection, for a detective story is 'a tale in which the primary interest lies in the methodical discovery, by rational means, of the exact circumstances of a mysterious event or series of events'. Finally, but far from exhaustively, Erik Routley's effort in *The Puritan Pleasures of the Detective Story* (1972) underlines neither detective nor detection, but the solution: 'a detective story, properly so-called, is a story involving crime, a police force, a detective (who may or may not be a member of that force) and a solution. It must evoke a major interest in the finding of that solution'.

Definitions of detective fiction, of which these are but a

sample, and discussions about the distinctions, if any, between detective stories, police stories, crime stories, mysteries, thrillers and the like, are to me at once fascinating and futile; fascinating, because, like a great many more people than will admit it, I am saddled with a pigeon-hole mentality, a bent for casuistry and a healthy dash of masochism, so that the question of what does and what does not constitute a detective story provides an ever splittable hair and a delightful wall on which to bang my head; futile, because at the front of my mind I know that the affair is not one on which the fate of nations hangs, and that even if it were a vital problem demanding immediate attention, no one solution satisfactory to all parties would be forthcoming.

It has been said of definitions that they are as invidious as they are inevitable. Persistence in the habit may be a hangover from the scholastic precept of defining one's terms. In the introduction to one of his anthologies of crime stories John Welcome openly admits this motivation: 'It is, or so I seem to remember having had hammered into me in my youth, essential for an essayist to define his terms,'[2] and he goes on to attempt to distinguish crime stories from detective stories. Those who indulge in definitions of detective fiction—and more seem to have indulged themselves in this than in any other branch of literature—must be blessed with a knowledge and confidence lacking in me, for definitions in this context strike me as occasions of sin, which I seem to remember having had hammered into me in my youth are devoutly to be avoided. It may be that I have already begged the question by seeming to imply above that a work of detective fiction should include a a detective, but the truth is that, given the confusion already surrounding the term 'detective fiction', I do not wish to add to it with yet another *ex cathedra* pronouncement. Invidiousness has for me outweighed inevitability.

This invidiousness becomes increasingly and depressingly apparent the deeper we go into previous efforts. Going back to the four definitions already given (Messac and Murch have been amalgamated), two mention crime and two do not, and as for the detective, both Messac, who does not mention him, and Routley, who plays him down, go on in their books to deal copiously, and at times exclusively, with investigators of all kinds. Now lack of unanimity may be the spice of life and none of these definitions is absolutely and demonstrably wrong. Individually each has something to tell us. Together, however, they are unhelpful to the point of confusion. Does Routley's solution have to be by Messac's rational means, and does Messac's methodical discovery have to be by Queen's detective protagonist? It may be said that the value of each definition must be assessed, can only be assessed, in the context of the book in which it appears, but this places a severe restriction on their general usefulness and even then they can seem inadequate. Routley's definition, for instance, is a reasonable description of *The Moonstone* (1868), but a few lines before promulgating it Routley explicitly, and for his purposes very reasonably, excludes Wilkie Collins' book from consideration as a detective story 'properly so-called'.

This manoeuvre by Routley brings us to another source of confusion. Any definition can be demolished by the production of titles (and a determined producer will always find titles) which fit the requirements of a definition but which are maligned in being classed as detective fiction, or by the production of other titles which have been classed as detective fiction but which do not fit at least some of the requirements of the definition in question.

Fodder for the demonstration of both demolition techniques is afforded by *Victorian Detective Fiction* (1966) which describes itself as 'a catalogue of the collection made by Dorothy Glover and Graham Greene, bibliographically arranged by Eric Osborne and introduced by John Carter'. The criterion for a book's inclusion in this collection, as stated by John Carter in his Introduction, is that, apart from publication before Victoria's death, it 'must be mainly or largely occupied with detection and should contain a proper detective, whether amateur or professional'.[3] If I am ever obliged at gun point to select a definition, this one will tempt me, if only because it most nearly describes many of the books with which I shall be dealing. Self-interest aside, it is in its own right an admirable effort. It is as broad as Hagen's without being as vague, and yet it is sufficiently specific without being dangerously so, like Queen's and Routley's; and it is workmanlike without being overly technical as Messac's seems to be.

Bearing Carter's definition in mind and turning to the contents of *Victorian Detective Fiction*, we find listed *Bleak House* (1853). Granting for argument's sake that this work fits Carter's criteria for inclusion, and that is a charitable concession, it must also be admitted that Dickens' novel goes far beyond these requirements in both content and object; if this is not so, then Dickens, for one, was wasting his time. Definitely unpalatable, however, is the inclusion of *Nicholas Nickleby* (1839) and Jules Verne's *Around the World in 80 Days* (1873), which not only need a mind-bending stretch of the imagination to be deemed to contain a *proper* detective and to be *mainly* occupied with detection, but which are anything but detective stories in anybody's book—and that includes Carter's, who, despite Miss Glover's recorded assurance that 'this collection substantially conforms to [his] terms of reference', confesses to 'a doubtful glance at *Around the World in 80 Days*.'

Coming to the obverse problem of books which are often described as detective fiction but which do not fit the definition, I suspect that the doubtful glance became a polite blind eye when Carter noted the inclusion in the catalogue of such titles as Guy Boothby's *A Prince of Swindlers* (1898) and Grant Allen's *An African Millionaire* (1897). These are also mentioned in Eric Quayle's *The Collector's Book of Detective Fiction* (1972) and La Cour and Mogensen's *The Murder Book* (1971) and I bow to weight of numbers in calling them detective stories, but again neither contains detection in Carter's sense nor that proper detective. These books have rogues for heroes and I suppose that insofar as these gentlemen are pursued by detectives, albeit unsuccessfully, the books in which they appear have come to be classed as detective fiction and hence included in this collection. Similarly, the listing of Rider Haggard's *Mr Meesom's Will* (1888) which lacks even an unsuccessful detective, can be justified, at a stretch, for its court-room scene. Tenuous as this may be, it is no more unreasonable than the featuring in both Quayle and La Cour and Mogensen of the detectivally ir-relevant Dr. Nikola, Boothby's satanic creation whose closest contact with detective fiction was, as Knox/Sauzwasch has pointed out in 'Studies in the Literature of Sherlock Holmes', in *Essays in Satire* (1928), his responsibility for Holmes' stay in Thibet with the Grand Lama.[4] The fact remains, however, that these three books fail utterly to meet Carter's requirements, as do a number of others, such as Max Pemberton's *The Iron Pirate* (1893), Grant Allen's *The Scallywag* (1893) and Eden Phillpotts' *A Tiger's Cub* (1892). The last-named is a particularly inappropriate inclusion as the only claim which Tarrant Tinkler makes to the status of detective allocated to him by Miss Glover is to regret his 'detective efforts' to find out a few facts about the hero at the behest of the villain.

Miss Glover was either over-optimistic or over-enthusiastic in giving her assurance of conformity, and Carter ought perhaps to have known better than accept it, because his definition derives from a twentieth-century concept of detective fiction, a concept which we shall see did not exist for the greater part of Victoria's reign. There are very few novels of the earlier century which are mainly or largely occupied with detection; mystery, secrecy, murder, mayhem, and a sprinkling of detective work, yes; but detection and nothing else, rarely. Many Victorian tales do contain detectives, of course, but again it is doubtful if many are 'proper' in Carter's sense which I take to mean their doing some constructive detective work. Most of the pre-Holmes breed—and not a few after him— either play no more than walking on parts or are, compared with, say, Thorndyke or Father Brown, completely ineffectual. Take Fergus Hume's *A Traitor in London* (1900) as a case in point. Hume provides a murder for which several characters are shown to have a motive, and a scattering of clues from which a detective story in Carter's sense might have emerged, but the author chooses to concentrate on an eternal triangle against the background of the Boer War. The murder and the mystery are resurrected only at the end of the book to be solved, Gordian knot fashion, by the favourite Victorian ploy of a death-bed confession. For *Victorian Detective Fiction* to give Inspector Woke as this book's detective in Carter's sense is quite unrealistic. Woke appears, asks a few questions, gets nowhere and disappears for ever after some twenty pages.

This is the pattern of detective activity in many other items in the Glover/Greene collection simply because this was the pattern of detective writing for most of their period, and one must accept the application in fact of much more elastic terms of reference than Carter's, otherwise the collection would scarcely fill a shelf. The clue to the actual criterion used is the naming of the detective in each book listed, even where fact has to be supplemented by faith on those occasions where 'various police detectives' is the only nomenclature possible. This new criterion is much simpler even than Carter's, namely, the presence in a book of a detective, in the broadest sense of that word and irrespective of his detecting ability and of the length of his appearance. Only on this generous basis can the collection be said to justify its title, the exceptions, such as James Short in *Mr. Meesom's Will*, who starts as a barrister and stays as one, not being worth dispute. The collection now also manages to evade the accusation that detection does not form a principal part of the contents of many of its books, but it is still open to the objection that those same books as before are being maligned or misleadingly pigeon-holed in being called detective fiction simply because they contain a detective.[5]

Adherents of the classic school of detective fiction, with its much tighter concept of the genre as exemplified by Queen's definition, would of course take umbrage at this idea that the mere presence of a detective in a story makes it a detective story. Knox speaks for them in his introduction to *Best Detective Stories of the Year 1928*:

> What is a detective story? The title must not be applied indis-criminately to all romances in which a detective, whether professional or amateur, plays a leading part. You might write a novel the hero of which was a professional detective, who did not

get on with his wife, and therefore ran away with somebody else's in chapter 58, as is the wont of heroes in modern novels. That would not be a detective story.

It would now be possible to continue on this roundabout of confusion by a consideration of Knox's views on detective fiction, but a halt must soon be called before dizziness or boredom or both set in. If it seems that I have been unfair in concentrating on *Victorian Detective Fiction* alone, it is worth remembering that Julian Symons begins his history of the genre, *Bloody Murder* (1972), by pointing to a similar situation of impasse and confusion arising from the very real inadequacies, viewed from today, of the definitions and assertions of Knox, Queen, Haycraft and other heavyweights in the critical world of detective fiction. Symons could indeed be said to take these inadequacies as the basic premiss and starting-point of his history, but his motives are rather different from mine. In the darkness of his perplexity, he believes we should adopt a more 'sensible sort of naming . . . the general one of *crime novel* or *suspense novel*' (his italics). This is an attractive suggestion, pointing as it does to two plausible common denominators— crime and suspense—for all the variations on these themes. Yet it is not the whole truth because it threatens to ignore the very variety of these variations, the historical fact of their existence and influence, and their right, on grounds of quantity and sometimes of merit, to be considered as entities, however fluid their borders. Symons points out that these 'attempts at definition [by Knox and others] . . . apply only to the detective stories written in what is often called the Golden Age between the Wars' and that although many 'books were written within a convention as strict and artificial as that of Restoration plays . . . that does not make the detective story a unique literary form'. Absolutely not, but many people of critical standing— G. K. Chesterton and T. S. Eliot, for example—believed it was just that, and to lump everything under 'crime novel' or 'suspense story' is to do their beliefs and their writings an injustice. The world would be a poorer place without its detective story, whatever it means, and it may be as well to mention here that in what follows the terms 'detective story' and 'detective fiction' refer to writings from Doyle to World War II, particularly those tales of the Golden Age—whatever they are! Moreover, Symons' suggestion seems to throw up as many problems as it solves, as we shall see later.

Suffice it to say here that having propounded his idea Symons almost immediately has to climb down from his platform of generality:

> . . . however unlike Sherlock Holmes and Philo Vance may be to Sam Spade and Superintendent Maigret, and however little any of them may have in common with James Bond and Len Deighton's unnamed hero, they all belong to the same kind of literature. When this has been accepted there are distinctions to be made within the literature too. Spy stories, and thrillers in general, *do* stand apart from books that pose a puzzle to the reader.

Which qualification is not surprising in a book sub-titled 'From the Detective Story to the Crime Novel'. This is not said to put Symons in the pillory, to borrow his own terminology, but to suggest that his broad classification does not in practice work any better than the rigid ones, or, more accurately, that a definition or classification in this context is often the grinding of an axe and hence that it must be assessed in relation to the axe in question.

An interesting example of an early axe and the troubles, indeed sins, to which its honing led is to be found in the first full-length discussion of the detective story, Carolyn Wells' *The Technique of the Mystery Story* (1913). (There, for a start, is an indication of trouble in store: a book on detective fiction with *mystery story* in the title.) In terms of output Miss Wells (1870?–1942) rivals Mary Roberts Rinehart for the title of Agatha Christie of the United States, having over eighty mystery titles to her credit. In terms of quality, however, she falls below her sister writers and her chief claim to fame in this sphere—she was also a well-known anthologist and parodist—is this early critical work. In it her overt task is the instruction of would-be writers of detective stories, an innocuous enough axe. To this end she is at great pains to clear the ground for a definition of the detective story which will distinguish it from associated genres, particularly riddle stories. As distinctive features of detective fiction she selects, very reasonably and very precociously, fair play, intellectual appeal and constructive detective work centred round a crime. Her discussion of riddle stories may be summed up with her comment: 'As a rule, Riddle Stories are not based upon a crime, but on some mysterious situation which is apparently inexplicable, but which turns out to have a most rational and logical explanation'. This seems a needlessly arbitrary basis of segregation, her words on the riddle story being a defensible description of the detective story but for the exclusion of a crime, and as we have seen, even a crime is not considered a necessary feature in some definitions of detective fiction. Miss Wells, however, obviously felt some distinction was essential in order, perhaps, to emphasise to her students the special features of what was in 1913 a relatively new genre, though her book is of more value today as a work of criticism than as a do-it-yourself manual. For example it is interesting to note that many after Miss Wells have pinpointed (I will not say appropriated) these same features of the detective story as grounds not just for its individuality but its superiority. Yet the validity of her distinction between riddle and detective stories is doubtful. One wonders if she has not created a problem where none exists, for it is scarcely contentious to assert that while all detective stories are riddle stories, only some riddle stories are detective stories. Miss Wells herself ends up by admitting the first point: '. . . the plot [of a detective story] must not vary . . . being only the propounding of the riddle and the revealing of its answer'.

Quite apart from this, however, one could regrettably force Miss Wells to admit the unwisdom of her distinction by asking her to account for the following. In her chapter on Riddle Stories she writes:

The distinguishing feature of the Riddle Story is that the reader should be confronted with a number of mysterious facts of which the explanation is reserved till the end. Now this reservation of

20

the final solution, in order to pique the reader's curiosity, excite his ingenuity, and lead him on to an unexpected climax, is a quite legitimate artistic effect. The only question to be asked about it in any particular instance is whether it succeeds, whether the effect is really accomplished? And for its success two primary qualifications are necessary: first, that the mystery should be really mysterious; second, that the explanation should really explain.

In 1906, however, G. K. Chesterton's brother, Cecil, had contributed an article entitled 'Art and the Detective' to the magazine *Temple Bar* in which he wrote:

> The detective or mystery story need not, of course, be primarily concerned with detectives . . . The real distinguishing feature is that the reader should be confronted with a number of mysterious facts of which the explanation is reserved till the end. Now this reservation of the final solution, in order to pique the reader's curiosity . . .

Yes, we have read this somewhere before, right up to the requirement that 'the explanation should really explain'. Miss Wells quotes this article by Cecil Chesterton on three other occasions, mentioning his name though not the source, but on this occasion it appears as her own text.

On the moral issue raised here Miss Wells has long been left to heaven. On the critical side, her wish to apply Chesterton's words on detective stories to riddle stories is more than just a compelling reason for her lack of acknowledgement; the fact that she can do so and that both she and Chesterton can still make sense sets a seal on confusion as the only unimpeachable birthright of detective fiction. The expression has never had a definite, universally accepted meaning, though it is worth noting that this does not stop our using it and being understood in general conversation. Only for critics is there a problem, responsibility for the creation of which must of course be laid at the feet of authors who persist in writing books which refuse to fit into preconceived critical categories. It is not so much that we have, as Julian Hawthorne suggested as long ago as 1909, in his Introduction to *American Stories*, 'something of a misnomer' in this word 'detective', but that we have a superfluity of descriptive terms—crime, mystery, thriller and so on, the existence of which tempts us to differentiate between them and so create a miniature Babel. Detective fiction, whatever it may be, is not a case like the Ten Commandments where the simple, basic principles were set out in tablets of stone only to be chipped and re-shaped by human sophistry until it is no longer clear what is right and what is wrong; for here we could, if we wished, go back to first principles. But it is not so with detective fiction. Despite Knox's detective story Decalogue, laid down in the Introduction quoted earlier, there are no tablets of stone here—and I am remembering Poe.

The controversies and contradictions surrounding detective fiction began with the first stirrings of critical attention around the turn of the century. The following quotations are, I believe, a representative batch of views up to World War II. Taken individually, each seems fair, even persuasive, comment; taken *en masse*, one is glad that the issues are not serious, for these, believe it or not, are the views of writers on the same side. They start with a deliberate repetition of Cecil Chesterton's words; matched against the second passage, it will be seen that he was contradicted before he was plagiarised.

> The detective or mystery story need not, of course, be primarily concerned with detectives . . . The real distinguishing feature is that the reader should be confronted with a number of mysterious facts of which the explanation is reserved till the end.
>
> Cecil Chesterton, 'Art and the Detective',
> *Temple Bar*, 10 October 1906

> In the true detective story . . . it is not in the mystery itself that the author seeks to interest the reader, but rather in the successive steps whereby his analytic observer is enabled to solve a problem that might well be dismissed as beyond human elucidation.
>
> Brander Matthews, 'Poe and the Detective Story',
> *Scribner's Magazine*, September 1907

Which is self-evident:

> Poe is so generally recognised as the father of the detective story that it hardly needs a magazine article by Professor Brander Matthews to recall his services to this branch of the literary art.
>
> *Nation*, 19 September 1907

Or is it?

The typical English detective story is free from the influence of Poe.
T. S. Eliot, New Criterion, January 1927

The situation is really quite simple. Look here:

Of these four kinds of literary entertainment [romantic, adventure, mystery and detective novel] the detective novel is the youngest, the most complicated, the most difficult of construction, and the most distinct. It is, in fact, almost *sui generis*, and, except in its more general structural characteristics, has little in common with its fellows . . . In one sense, to be sure, it is a highly specialised offshoot of the last named [the mystery novel]; but the relationship is far more distant than the average reader imagines.

W. H. Wright, 'The Detective Novel',
Scribner's Magazine, November 1926

Well, not all that simple:

These types [as above] often overlap in content, and at times become so intermingled in subject matter that one is not quite sure in which category they primarily belong.

W. H. Wright, ibid

Optimism:

The expression 'Detective Story', though still loosely used to describe any tale dealing with crime and detectives, has acquired of late years a narrower, specialized meaning. Careful writers now reserve it for those stories of crime and detection in which the interest lies in the setting of a problem and its solution by logical means.

Dorothy L. Sayers, ed., Introduction to
Tales of Detection (1936)

Pessimism:

Even today, few readers and few reviewers attempt to distinguish accurately between the 'detective story', which acknowledges the rule [of fair play], and the 'thriller', which does not.

Dorothy L. Sayers, Introduction to
The Moonstone, Dent (1944)

Now let's get this straight once and for all:

> My friends keep telling me that 'Agatha Christie has written a new one'. They know that I like detective stories and they are surprised when I receive their announcement with a lack-lustre eye. To them, anything with a murder or a detective in it is detection, and nothing I can say in casual conversation can shake their belief. I have long thought I should put something down on paper and distribute copies in self-defense, but now that professional critics have taken up the confusion and made it their own, my half-formed intent becomes a duty . . . A detective story is a narrative of which the chief interest lies in the palpable processes of detection. This sounds like tautology, which it is, and which proves that it is a correct definition. All error comes of forgetting what the definition does and does not imply. Detection does not imply murder, nor the presence of a character called a detective; and this in turn implies its converse, namely that a story containing murders and detectives is not necessarily a detective story—a story of *detection*.
>
> Jacques Barzun, 'Not "Whodunit?" But "How?" '
> *Saturday Review* (American) 4 November 1944[6]

For the moment I offer no comment on this last passage. We will return to it and some of the others in due course. As they stand, they may at least help explain the title of this chapter.

By way of final proof of the continuing confusion and of the hopelessness of seeking any single answer, the first Crime Writers' International Congress in 1975 'grappled', the *Daily Telegraph* tells us:

> . . . with a problem which . . . simply defies solution: how to define the sort of books they write. In America they are called 'mysteries'. Here we play with 'crime novel', 'suspense novel', 'thriller' and various other descriptions, all of them equally unsatisfactory . . . As [the conference] closed one delegate remarked that it had given us — crime writers, mystery writers, writers of the novel of risk — a new sense of identity. Yet no one I met could clearly define that identity. Such confusion is understandable . . . After three days of conference 'mystery writers' remain a mystery, most of all to themselves.

Faced by this disarray within the ranks of the current perpetrators, let alone the contradictions of the last seventy-five years, my reluctance to rush in is understandable, if not forgivable. It may be seen as the reaction of the Frenchman declining a challenge to duel: 'D'abord, je n'en ai pas le temps; ensuite, j'ai peur'. I should prefer to believe that I am sheltering behind the ample form of G. K. Chesterton and his dictum that definitions are for cowards. But the truth is probably that I want to side-step the problem. It seems that no good purpose can now be served by seeking further to define or redefine or even abolish the term 'detective fiction'. If it requires charity to accept *Mr. Meesom's Will* and the Dr. Nikola saga as detective stories, then let us be charitable, keeping smugly to ourselves our infallible system for detecting a *real* detective story; to doubt its meaning is not to doubt its existence.

Something of more value and interest may emerge, I hope, from a consideration of the background to the present confusion, a return, that is, to the origins of the term itself, to the birth, not of the detective story, but of the concept 'detective fiction'. These two—the story and the genre title—are not twins. *Pace* Vidocq, Voltaire, Balzac, Dumas, Cooper, de Beaumarchais, Eastern Mythology, Greek Mythology and the Bible, the detective story began with Poe, although he was ignorant of his invention. The generic term 'detective fiction' is of later and less precise origin, but it is with the situation which caused someone somewhere to institute the expression that I begin. This approach is put forward, not as a solution to any of the problems discussed above, but simply as another, no doubt idiosyncratic, way of looking at detective fiction. I will, however, go so far as to advert my adherence, in contradiction of Barzun (and adding to the confusion), to A. E. W. Mason's assertion:

> All the great detective novels are known by and live on account of their detectives . . . The detective must be an outstanding person, actual, picturesque, amusing, a creature of power and singularity. Without such a being, the detective novel, however ingenious, will pass back to the lending library. With him it may find a permanent place upon the bookshelf.[7]

25

NOTES TO CHAPTER 1

1 Ellery Queen, ed., Foreword to *Rogue's Gallery* (1947). Queen equals Frederic Dannay (1905-) and Manfred Lee (1905-71).

2 John Welcome, ed., Introduction to *Best Crime Stories 2* (1966).

3 This definition was first enunciated by Carter in his chapter on collecting detective fiction in *New Paths in Book Collecting* (1934), edited by him.

4 This particular essay was originally given as a paper to the Gryphon Club at Trinity College, Oxford, in 1911.

5 See Appendix 1, p. 323.

6 This article by Barzun was one of several written in response to the first of Edmund Wilson's three essays against detective fiction which appeared in the *New Yorker* between October 1944 and February 1945. Their titles are: 'Why Do People Read Detective Stories?', 'Who Cares Who Killed Roger Ackroyd?' and 'Mr. Holmes, They Were the Footprints of a Gigantic Hound'.

7 A. E. W. Mason, 'Detective Novels', *Nation and Athenaeum*, 7 February, 1925.

2
DOUBTS AND SUSPICIONS

'Come, we shall have some fun now!' thought Alice. 'I'm glad
they've begun asking riddles — I believe I can guess that.'

Lewis Carroll, *Alice in Wonderland*

One offers one's knuckles for gratuitous rapping in nominating
a candidate as the first user of a particular word or phrase. A
prior claimant, it seems, always manages to appear. Extending
a pre-bandaged hand, however, I should like to propose 1886
as the first written use of the expression 'detective fiction'.

My nominee occurs as the title of an article ('Detective
Fiction') in the *Saturday Review* of 4 December of that year. The
fact that it is the title militates against this being its first appearance. So too, in a way, does the opening sentence of the article
itself: 'Edgar Allan Poe has been commonly reputed the father
of so-called "detective fiction",' implying earlier paternity suits,
and the writer in fact goes on to press the claims of Balzac for
the title. Nevertheless, allowing that the expression must have
been in verbal use before 1886, allowing also that this may well
not be its first written occurrence, there are strong indications
that it is a very early example. Thus the qualifying 'so-called'
and the use of inverted commas round the expression itself
convey the impression of relative newness about the phrase.
This is borne out by the tentative prophesy and persistent
inverted commas of the *Morning Post's* review, just over a year
later, of H. F. Wood's *The Passenger from Scotland Yard* (1888):
'It would seem as if on this side of the Channel we are destined
to have a school of "detective fiction" . . . *The pioneers of this*

class of literature have in Mr. Wood a formidable rival' (my italics).[1] No, Wood was not a nom-de-plume of Doyle's. The reviewer was just plain wrong about his formidability and, for that matter, his ability in any form. The *Athenaeum* set the record straight when it wrote of his next book, *The Englishman of the Rue Cain* (1889), that 'the ornate and spasmodic style in which Mr. Wood writes will weary the lover of simple English, while the riot of his imagination will perplex those who love a simple story . . . this bit of literary rococo'. In the light of which I hope the *Morning Post* reviewer's appreciation of developments in literature exceeded his critical perception, since his remarks support the case for 1886.

'Detective' as both noun and adjective in the context of a criminal investigation became common after the establishment of a detective office at Scotland Yard in 1842, an event commemorated in the *Oxford English Dictionary's* earliest example of the use of the word in this sense: '1843 Chamb. Jrnl. XII. 54 Intelligent men have been recently selected to form a body called the "detective police"'. Over the next few years the word can be found in a variety of compounds. Dickens has ' "Detective" Anecdotes' in his *Household Words* of 14 September 1850; the words ' "Detective" Literature' open *The Experiences of a Real Detective* by Inspector F (William Russell), a *Sixpenny Magazine* serial of 1862, published in volume form in the same year by Ward & Lock. Both instances, however, refer to writings about actual detectives and cases—supposedly actual, that is, in at least the latter case. Of 'detective *fiction*' there is as yet no trace. The *O.E.D.* does not in fact vouchsafe an example of the expression from the nineteenth century, but it does give 1883 as an early use of 'detective story' from Anna Katherine Green's *X.Y.Z.* which is so sub-titled. In *The Development of the Detective Novel* Murch claims that Green's first novel, *The Leavenworth Case* (1878), has 'detective story' on its title page. This would, if correct, advance the use of that term by five years, but I suspect that Murch has confused Green's two books. *The Leavenworth Case* is sub-titled 'A Lawyer's Story', though there is an edition of 1895 by W. Nicholson of London with the title 'The Great Detective Story: The Leavenworth Case', a reflection, perhaps, of the growing sales value of books clearly associated with detectives and detection.

Confining the search to 'detective fiction', Murch in *The Development of the Detective Novel* states that by 1883 'the *Saturday Review* was frankly discussing the general popularity of detective fiction in England'. This is misleading on two counts. First, and of relative unimportance except in the present game of dating, the expression 'detective fiction' is not used in the article mentioned by Murch.[2] There is reference to 'fictitious detectives'—not uncommon at the time—but only as a preamble to the burden of the article which is a comparison of French and British police methods. Secondly, and much more significantly, the *Saturday Review* had mentioned the popularity of 'the romance of the detective' nearly twenty years earlier at least (11 June 1864) and had continued to discuss it at regular intervals thereafter, for example in the issues of 11 February 1868 and 18 May 1878. So too had other periodicals and newspapers, though the *Saturday* seems to have had more to say more often. It may be that 'romance of the detective' and 'detective fiction' are roses of equal bouquet and that Murch is guilty of nothing more than a technical and unimportant inaccuracy when she implies the frequent use of 'detective fiction' before 1883. Technical, perhaps; unimportant, the reader can judge for himself at the end of this book. Certainly, something bearing a remarkably close resemblance to detective fiction was in existence long before the 1880s. Anyone who has heard of 'The Murders in the Rue Morgue' and *The Moonstone* does not need obscure references to the romance of the detective to tell him that. But, accepting for the moment on faith that there is significance in the origins of 'detective fiction' as the enduring genre term, however difficult to define, for a certain type of story, there does seem to be the sort of progression in its institution that we might expect—from the elaborate, even condescending 'romance of the detective' in the 1860s to the more mundane 'detective story' in the early 1880s and thence to the collective term 'detective fiction' in the mid-1880s. Thus it is worth noting that *X.Y.Z.* can be sub-titled 'a detective story' in 1883, while five years before the same author's *The Leavenworth Case*, equally if not more deserving of the title, rated the much less indicative 'lawyer's story'. Similarly, the author of that article on 'Detective Fiction', published in the *Saturday Review* in December 1886, was very diffident about using 'detective fiction' as a genre title, for he also speaks of 'the modern Gaboriau novel, to adopt the generic, but by no means exact, expression by which this kind of literature is now generally known'. But Gaboriau is now only a name, and 'detective fiction' has won the day, though affording, as we have seen, no more precision than its predecessors.

That something had occurred which further justifies and explains the case for 1886 or thereabouts will be argued later. Accepting the case as it stands at the moment for argument's sake, the situation has arisen that here we are in the mid-1880s, forty years after Poe's short stories about Dupin, nearly twenty years after Wilkie Collins' *The Moonstone* (1868), Doyle in labour with Holmes, and yet what was to become the accepted genre title covering these landmarks in that genre is so new that it has to be qualified in one way or another, so tentative that some half-remembered Frenchman could take precedence over it.

Accordingly it is now tempting to throw a minor squib into the history of detective fiction by concluding from this alarming state of affairs that Poe and Collins did not write detective fiction. Tempting but suicidal, I suppose. Perhaps wrong even, because it is obvious, it will be argued, that a thing must exist, if only in men's imagination, before a name is needed for it, and Poe's stories and *The Moonstone* more than adequately fulfil the criteria of the genre as it came to develop. For me to say that this seems a case of *post hoc ergo propter hoc* would be to go by the sound of the argument rather than its good intentions.

What may more safely be concluded is that Poe and Collins did not know they were writing detective fiction, and this less controversial conclusion may at least serve as a corrective to the assertion, assumption or implication in many commentaries on detective fiction that Poe and Collins were deliberate founders of the genre. In *Murder for Pleasure* (1941), Howard Haycraft has Poe writing the 'first avowedly fictional detective story'; and E. A. Seaborne in his introduction to a short story collection, *The Detective in Fiction* (1931), claims that 'Wilkie Collins proved . . . that there was a ready and apt public for the detective novel'. As if, in the case of Poe, there was, prior to 1841, a neat bundle of non-fictional or pseudo-factual detective stories which led Poe to take thought and pen to produce a fictional version; and as if, in the case of *The Moonstone*, Collins espied a ravening public and forthwith set out to feed it, speculatively, with a detective novel. Now Poe did have Vidocq and Collins did have a ravening public, but only Holmes could deduce from this that they were writing detective fiction in any deliberate sense.

This is perhaps an over-harsh reaction to the remarks of Haycraft and Seaborne, which after all have been quoted out of context. Yet it is interesting to note that one leading historian of the genre, H. D. Thomson, in *Masters of Mystery* (1931), while accepting *The Moonstone* as a classic, does not think much of it as a *detective* classic: 'Sergeant Cuff, the detective, makes the deplorable mistake—the mistake of the Lestrades and the stern police—of suspecting the heroine. That is in the extreme of bad taste'. But Thomson's was a none too serious voice crying in the wilderness, and the attitude of Haycraft and Seaborne is typical of the approach of the majority of their contemporaries. Duplicate examples of comments like theirs abound, most stemming from the period between the Wars (1918–39) when the search was on to find detective fiction a pedigree.

Indeed, it is to this search, and to T. S. Eliot and Dorothy L. Sayers in particular, that we owe the rescue of Collins from threatened oblivion; and if at first he was rescued as a writer of detective-cum-mystery stories alone, this led in turn to his re-assessment as a major Victorian novelist writing, to his misfortune, in days when there was a glut of giants. Not that Eliot and Sayers were unaware of the true status of their

31

protégé and his detective stories. Eliot's much-quoted opinion, from his Introduction to a 1928 edition, that '*The Moonstone* is the first, the longest, and the best of modern English detective novels', is immediately followed by: 'but it is something more important than that . . .' and Eliot goes on to stress the influence of Dickens and Collins on each other. In much the same way, Sayers' 1928 assessment of the book almost exclusively as a detective story in her Introduction to *Great Short Stories of Detection, Mystery and Horror* was modified, in her 1944 introduction to *The Moonstone*, to:

> Collins . . . has always been very much under-rated as regards his competence to create living character, and to handle social themes . . . We are accustomed to read such books [as Collins'] merely with an eye to their detective plot, and not to look to them for a serious commentary on life. This point of view would have surprised and distressed him [because he saw himself as a novelist] working in the main tradition of the novel.

Nevertheless, in their enthusiasm for their discovery of *The Moonstone's* consistency with their Platonic form of the detective story, these twentieth-century excavators, of whom Eliot and Sayers were but two, emphasised the detective features of the book—Cuff, clues, conundrum, culprit—at the expense of its claim to be a typical novel of the period, and it was as a detective story that *The Moonstone* was initially unearthed and it is as a detective story that it is still best known today.

G. D. H. and Margaret Cole tried to reverse this viewpoint, perhaps a shade too forcibly, in 1953 in their Introduction to yet another edition of *The Moonstone*: '[It] is a Victorian novel, and not a detective story' and while 'there are, of course, elements in *The Moonstone* which have since become classic detective-story-components . . . [it] cannot be regarded as the master-pattern of the modern detective story'. Oddly enough, in 1929, the very time when Collins was enjoying a second, if posthumous, heyday at the hands of English commentators, Messac was giving France the opposite impression about him by suggesting that Collins specifically rejected the idea of writing mystery novels and supporting this contention with the following extract from Collins' preface to *No Name* (1862):

. . . it will be seen that the narrative related in these pages has been constructed on a plan, which differs from the plan followed in my last novel, and in some other of my works published at an earlier date. The only Secret contained in this book, is revealed midway in the first volume. From that point, all the main events of the story are purposely foreshadowed, before they take place — my present design being to arouse the reader's interest in following the train of circumstances by which these foreseen events are brought about.

'In this way', concludes Messac, 'Collins repudiates the principle of the mystery-novel', but Collins' next words, not quoted by Messac, cast some doubt on the nature of this repudiation:

In trying this new ground, I am not turning my back on the ground which I have passed over already. My one object in following a new course, is to enlarge the range of my studies in the art of writing fiction, and to vary the form in which I make my appeal to the reader, as attractively as I can.

That Collins was simply experimenting and had not permanently turned his back on old stamping grounds is sufficiently borne out by the existence of *The Moonstone*, a book which Messac subsequently and consequently is obliged to play down as a detective story. It might be more accurate to see in this preface Collins' repudiation of the idea of a story based on a secret or a mystery and on nothing more, a principle unfortunately abandoned by much twentieth-century detective fiction, rather than his total rejection of a principle which, at most, was only beginning to form in the 1860s. Overall, Kenneth Robinson's middle-of-the-road view of *The Moonstone* in his 1951 biography of Wilkie Collins is perhaps to be preferred: 'In this, above all his books, he achieved precisely what he set out to do—and more—for it is unlikely that he intended to produce the archetype of a new branch of English fiction.' But whatever the degree of emphasis we place on it, the fact is that there was no conscious effort on Collins' part to write detective fiction as we know it.

There remains Poe. The Coles, having demolished *The Moonstone* as a detective story, seemed nevertheless unwilling to query the existence of detective fiction as a genre in the mid-nineteenth century. Poe had written his stories about Dupin which dovetailed with the post-Doyle development 'of the solution of a crime by the exercise of pure ratiocination' and therefore according to the Coles 'the genre had . . . come into existence'. But if *The Moonstone* goes, so too must *Bleak House*, *East Lynne*, *Wylder's Hand* and all similar works of the period which are advanced from time to time by detective genealogists in search of a family tree. This in turn leaves an alarmingly wide gap between Poe and the 1880s when I have suggested detective fiction began to be written as a deliberate form under that name.

Historians of the genre openly acknowledge the gaps between Poe and Collins and between Collins and Doyle. In *Murder for Pleasure* Haycraft actually entitles his chapter covering the period from Poe to Collins 'The In-Between Years', while Symons in *Bloody Murder* favours 'Interregnum' for his chapter on the years between Collins and Doyle. Explanations, however, are sparse. In *Masters of Mystery* Thomson gives a verbal shrug—'The detective story [Poe's] did not apparently stagger the world'—and jumps twenty years to Gaboriau. Haycraft chooses not to investigate the causes of his chapter title.

Symons does offer something concrete. Referring to the gap between Collins and Doyle, he writes:

> The explanation is simple. The history of the crime story up to the end of the nineteenth century is linked chiefly with the few writers of talent who were interested in police work, and the form itself was not sufficiently attractive to the public, or sufficiently well-defined, to receive much attention from the hacks.

This statement requires elucidation, for Symons seems to be saying that the crime story, whether well or badly written, was a relative rarity in the nineteenth century. Yet novel after Victorian novel hinges on a crime in Symons' own sense of a crime book as one 'in which interest in the nature of, motives for, and results of, a crime are at the heart of a story'. Miss Braddon and her monstrous regiment of imitators alone bear witness to this development in Victorian fiction, as does the eventually monotonous inveighing of critics against it, points dealt with more fully in the next chapter. These writers may not treat crime in the social and psychological setting that Symons might prefer, but crime—fraud, bigamy, murder, robbery—is the mainspring of their works, and 'criminal romance' was one of the critics' favourite terms for it. Certainly few writers of enduring reputation indulged in it, but many minor novelists, let alone the hacks, wrote nothing else. Certainly these books may contain only a passing reference to the police, if at all, but this casts doubt, not on their right to be called crime stories, but on Symons' implication that there is a necessary connection between a crime story and police work. The works of one of his own favourite crime novelists, Patricia Highsmith, testify to the non-essentiality of the link, as does his own description of the modern crime story as emphasising character and the crime itself with its causes and repercussions, often at the expense of a detective, professional or amateur. Symons' explanation makes sense only if we substitute 'detective story' or 'police story' in the sense of stories specifically about detectives and police for 'crime story'. He is hoist with this petard of using 'crime novel' or 'crime story' as his general descriptive term; he is less than one hundred per cent faithful to its use himself, but we have here a prime example of the possible misunderstandings to which the use of his terms can lead, misunderstandings as confusing as those which follow from the use of 'detective story' in a rigid and restrictive sense.

If my amendment is accepted, Symons' explanation can be seen as confirmation of the failure of both Poe and Collins to make any impression on their contemporaries as specialists in what came to be called detective fiction. His remarks are directed at the post-*Moonstone* period, but apply even more appropriately to the preceding quarter of a century and are particularly relevant to Poe in that the latter's so-called detective stories were not motivated by an interest in police work, but by a preoccupation with crime and violent death on the one hand and by curiosity about reasoning and logic on the other. It was happy coincidence that his acquaintance with the writings of Vidocq led him to give his tales of ratiocination a background of police and crime, but he would probably have written them anyway. The police and the detective have no monopoly on deduction and analysis. All kinds of problems —mathematical, historical, literary and the like—are being probed every day by thought and reasoning. Criminal problems, offering the built-in dramatic advantages of violence and sensation, are the more obvious choice for a writer concerned also with the reasoning processes, but there is no necessary connection between the two. It was as recently as 1972, however, that a critic of detective fiction (who but Symons in *Bloody Murder*!) dared to emphasise the coincidentally detectival nature of some of Poe's stories:

> In the pursuit by this figure of unmistakable genius of some completely original form, the detective and puzzle stories played a small part. Poe's paternity of the detective story is not in dispute, but his fatherhood was unintended.

This mildly debunking appraisal must have caused a flurry of rotations in cemeteries throughout the world, for while most detective fiction commentators might acknowledge, as we have seen with Eliot and Sayers, the coincidental aspect of Collin's contribution to detective fiction, albeit sometimes back-handedly, none, as far as I am aware, has ever said the same about Poe as explicitly as Symons does above. For my case, of course, it is this 'accident' of their being detective stories that is the interesting and important feature of Poe's tales of ratiocination, since it confirms what was suspected from the gap in detective fiction between Poe and the 1880s—and the dearth of explanations for it—namely, that Poe cannot be credited, any more than can Collins, with a conscious role in the creation of the genre. At this stage the gap is most easily accounted for by denying its existence.

None of this is to deny the ultimate influence on detective stories of either Poe or Collins, but to stress this very point that their influence was not immediate and to correct the impression conveyed by most histories that detective fiction was a deliberate innovation by Poe and that it then moved in smooth, organised progression or, rather, bounds, through Dickens, Collins and Gaboriau to Doyle. Certainly Poe and Collins wrote detective stories, but this is known only by hindsight, the same hindsight which enabled Thomson to question the detective qualities of *The Moonstone*, the hindsight granted by knowledge of detective fiction as it developed after Doyle and particularly between the two World Wars, and by that token an unknowable concept in the middle of the nineteenth century. Stuart Levine makes this point in *Edgar Poe: Seer and Craftsman* (1972):

> One might, for example, expect the detective tales to be far removed from the pattern of complex vision and perception because they seem like logic-games. I think we feel this way partially because of certain preconceptions we have regarding detective tales. We know what the modern whodunnit is like; we see similar features in the Dupin stories, and we conclude that the significant thing about Dupin is that he is a precursor of Sherlock Holmes and Perry Mason. Well, that is true enough, but it is not the whole truth.

The probable injustice done to Collins by the modern tendency to rate his novels as detective stories has been noted. Levine goes on to suggest a rather similar situation with Poe's tales of ratiocination. Accepting the debt of detective fiction to Poe, he adds: 'The Dupin tales have all these elements which by now are traditional, but they have something else, which becomes apparent when one examines the language with which Poe describes Dupin's methods.' Levine then suggests that 'Poe's detective succeeds not because of a superior mechanical ability to piece facts together, but because he is an artist', and after discussing this Levine makes his 'main point' which is:

> that the detective stories should not be considered as an isolated handful of experiments in a totally different genre. Rather, they fit in perfectly well with the pattern which we have seen operating in so many of Poe's stories . . . I do not think that it is overstating the case to claim that Dupin can be understood not merely as the prototype for a large number of whodunnit heroes, but also as an example of the transcendental hero, the

character whom the author uses to show the transcendental way, or to demonstrate its hazards.

Whether or not we agree with Levine's view of Poe and Dupin's place within it, it *is* true that many detective fiction critics have tended to isolate Poe's tales of ratiocination and, because of the preconceptions which Levine mentions, to make rather exaggerated claims for them; such remarks, for instance, as Haycraft's in *Murder for Pleasure*: 'As the symphony began with Haydn, so did the detective story begin with Poe.' But at least the term 'symphony' existed in Haydn's time; Poe managed to write his stories without using the word 'detective'. Or there is Brander Matthews': '. . . the history of the detective story begins with the publication of the "Murders in the Rue Morgue" . . . and Poe, unlike most other originators, rang the bell the very first time he took aim',[3] but was unaware of the nature of the target, or was, as Levine says, aiming at a different target. These examples and many more like them are probably no more than the enthusiast's careless way of talking, but the result has been over-emphasis on Poe as the inventor of the detective story to the exclusion or underestimation of other influences, and to his treatment in grand isolation from these influences; as Edward Wagenknecht says in *Edgar Allan Poe* (1963):

> I do not believe, however, that, having paid tribute to Poe's creativity, we are well advised to follow those critics who seem to feel it necessary to deny that others have made later important contributions to the detective story.

Thus Matthews might have taken more to heart the words of M. Jules Lemaitre whom he quotes:

> Nothing is more difficult than to discover who have been in literature the first inventors of a new form, so M. Jules Lemaitre once asserted, adding that innovations have generally been attempted by writers of no great value, and not infrequently by those who failed in those first efforts, unable to profit by their own originality.

That last phrase seems particularly appropriate to Poe's situation, not because he 'failed', but because neither he nor anyone else at the time knew in what he had succeeded. The best proof of this is not so much that he himself did not follow up the pattern of his own detective short stories, but that no one else did. The problem facing Doyle's contemporaries was, 'Follow that!'. The attitude of Poe's contemporaries was, I suspect, 'Who wants to follow that?'. The solemnity of these tales must have struck any intending imitator much more forcibly than their potential goldmine as patterns for a new genre. From the blueprint of 'Marie Roget' in particular, but also from 'The Murders in the Rue Morgue' and 'The Purloined Letter', one wonders whether an imitator would have produced a detective story or a treatise, and even if this would-be disciple had been able to filter out the detective element in these stories, little of immediately obvious saleable value would have rewarded his efforts. The detection from which we have come to expect an active thrill is stifled by the didactic, even pedantic, process of exposition, and the deductions, by which we should be startled, are all too often laid out as philosophical —and hence, as detective fiction, boring—arguments. Dupin is less a detective than a rationalistic philosopher. In 1874, referring to 'Marie Roget', the *Saturday Review* in an article on 'Edgar Allan Poe' commented that he covered 'obvious inferences with . . . a mass of ingenious remarks about logic in general, and . . . elaborate refutations of silly newspaper guesses'. That was in 1874. Nearly a century later Wagenknecht seems to go even further:

> Interesting as 'The Mystery of Marie Roget' is as a careful piece of reasoning . . . judged by Poe's own standards it is a very bad story; long before he has finished, the author abandons narrative altogether for ratiocination *per se* . . . 'The Purloined Letter' is much better, but even here the story fairly stops so that we may follow the workings of Dupin's mind, much as we might do in an article.

The sensational wood is hidden by the syllogistic trees. Only later, when fiction had behind it fifty years of development during which others made their contributions to the evolution of something that merited the invention of the title 'detective fiction', could the invaluable contribution of Poe begin to be appreciated. As Padraic Colum wrote in 1908 in his Introduction to Poe's *Tales*: 'In "The Murders in the Rue Morgue" and in "The Gold Bug", Poe brought a new and fascinating method into the narrative—a method which has been *rediscovered in our own day* and used with much public success' (my italics).

It is in this intervening period, beginning about the time when Poe was writing, but involving much more than his brilliant pieces of anticipation, that the origins of detective fiction lie: in this period the 'gap' is filled in.[4]

NOTES TO CHAPTER 2

1 Quoted from advertisement in H. F. Wood's *The Englishman of the Rue Cain* (1889).

2 'Detectives', *Saturday Review*, 5 May 1883.

3 Brander Matthews, 'Poe and the Detective Story', *Scribner's Magazine*, September 1907.

4 See Jerry Palmer, *Thrillers* (1978), Part III Chapters 1 and 2, for a discussion of the topics of this chapter and the remainder of Part I of this work. Unfortunately, Palmer's book appeared too late to be considered here.

3

SIGNIFICANT INFORMATION

It would be absurd to conclude that every English family circle must include at least one murderer or murderess, and one maniac, because Wilkie Collins and Miss Braddon have found it convenient thus to represent the social existence of English people.

'Novels With A Purpose', *Westminster Review*, July 1864

If, then, Poe and Collins—and Dickens and Miss Braddon and Mrs. Henry Wood and many others—were not writing detective fiction in so far as that term did not exist, let alone the modern conception of it, what were they writing? The question is unanswerable today since these authors' works cover the whole range of fiction from classic to penny dreadful. To the Victorians, however, the answer was easy: 'sensation fiction'.

'Sensation' was the 'in' word of the late 1850s and the 1860s. It was used to describe everything and anything in the least out of the ordinary, from the feats of Blondin to the melodramas of Boucicault, from the chess-playing dog and the singing mouse to murder most foul. Judging by the poetic protest which it drew from Mr. Punch, in 1861, in a poem called 'Sense v. Sensation', it seems to have been an import from the United States:

> Some would have it an age of Sensation,
>   If the age one of sense may not be —
> The word's not *Old* England's creation,
>   But New England's, over the sea, —
> Where all's in the high-pressure way,
>   In life just as in locomotion,
> And where, though you're here for today,
>   Where tomorrow you'll be, you've no notion.

Three verses follow, showing the word at work in America, then:

> And now that across the Atlantic
> > Worn threadbare 'Sensation' we've seen,
> And the people that lately were frantic,
> > Blush to think that such madmen they've been;
> *Mr. Punch* sees with pain and surprise,
> > On the part of this commonsense nation,
> Every here and there, on the rise,
> > This pois'nous exotic 'Sensation'.

Another verse and the poem concludes:

> *Mr. Punch* 'gainst the word and the things
> > It applies to, his protest would enter;
> For the vulgar excitement it brings
> > May England ne'er prove fitting centre.
> If you've got something good, never doubt it
> > By deeds will avouch its vocation;
> And be sure that not talking about it,
> > Is the true way to *make* a 'Sensation'.

Mr. Punch's protest was unavailing, however, and his advice went unheeded, nowhere more so than in literature where the word was seized upon, almost thankfully, one feels, to label a type of fiction which was beginning to enjoy a boom at this period. 'Sensation' and its derivatives became key words in the literary critics' jargon.

Who and what started it all? If the *Saturday Review*, writing as close to the event as 1874 had to admit, in an article on 'Sensationalism', that 'we do not know who was the inventor of the new popular word "sensational" ', then it seems useless for us to try. Probably no one book was responsible, but, although there are obvious earlier examples, the two novels most frequently mentioned by critics as brand leaders are Wilkie Collins' *The Woman in White* (1860) and *Lady Audley's Secret* (1862) by Mary Elizabeth Braddon (1835–1915). The titles alone give a good intimation of the content of sensation fiction, though in scope it is as difficult to pin down as detective fiction. Both terms are convenient handles to colanders. With sensation fiction perplexity set in very early, as can be seen from the way in which the *Athenaeum's* reviewer of Miss Braddon's *John Marchmont's Legacy* (1863) tries to grope his way through the maze already well established, it seems, by that year:

> In the absence of an accepted definition of the word 'sensation' as applied to prose tales, it is difficult to say whether this novel belongs to sensation fiction. If that strong element of mystery which marked *The Woman in White* and *Lady Audley's Secret* be a necessary feature of a sensational novel, Miss Braddon has in her present work left that field in which she achieved her first success. *John Marchmont's Legacy* has no vague secret hinted by the action of its principal characters, and this absence of imperfectly shrouded horror offers the author's admirers an opportunity of judging how far she is readable when she neglects to stimulate curiosity by placing in Volume I a puzzle, the solution of which is not given till the close of Volume III. But those who apply the word 'sensation' to every tale which relies for effect on startling positions, sudden surprises, and a series of incidents causing painful emotions, will hold that the novel may be fairly classified with the author's preceding works.

Almost at its inception, then, Victorian sensation fiction was a victim of careless talk, and capable of bearing either a narrow or a broad meaning. In the latter sense it is the ancestor of the whole gamut of popular fiction and it is in this sense that the term is used today. The narrower sense, however, as given in the *Athenaeum* is the more interesting in the present context, evocative as it is of detective fiction, whose link with vague secrets and shrouded horror is more substantial than many writers have allowed. A consideration of nineteenth-century sensation fiction in general bears this out. Three broad features seem to have marked this genre to judge from contemporary attitudes: it was new; it was popular, formula-writing; and it was second-rate. In looking at these, the detailed characteristics of sensation fiction will appear, as will unexpected and sometimes disconcerting affinities with detective fiction.

It is possible to trace aspects of Victorian sensation fiction back in a direct line through Poe's *Tales* and Mary Shelley's *Frankenstein* to the Gothic romances of Mrs. Radcliffe and

Walpole, and on this approach it was not new. Yet, due to some combination of quantity, quality, content and technique, the sensation novels of the 1860s were regarded by commentators as breaking fresh ground. In an article entitled 'Literature of the Month' published in September 1861 and containing perhaps the earliest reference to sensation novels,[1] the *Sixpenny Magazine* sees these earlier examples as 'obsolete among fashionable readers', and goes on to suggest that 'if "they are gone where the good niggers go", they had better keep there, for there is no probability of their being wanted here. The works now in request, by comparison make them "pale their ineffectual fires", till they enjoy but a rushlight existence, which, moreover, threatens speedy extinction'. This flowery prediction was unfulfilled but it is indicative of the impression of novelty about the sensation fiction then current. Writing in *Blackwood's Magazine* (May 1862) on sensation novels in general and referring to *The Woman in White* in particular, Mrs. Oliphant is more explicit:

> . . . the well-known old stories of readers sitting up all night over a novel had begun to grow faint in the public recollection . . . Now a *new* fashion has been set to English novel-writers [and] a most striking and original effort, sufficiently individual to be capable of *originating a new school of fiction*, has been made . . . (my italics).[2]

A year later, H. L. Mansel, Dean of St. Paul's, writing on 'Sensation Novels' for the *Quarterly Review*, refers to sensation fiction as 'a class of literature that has grown up around us', and he lists the chief causes of 'this phenomenon of our literature' as 'periodicals, circulating libraries and railway bookstalls', all of which were at the dawn of their heyday at the beginning of the second half of the nineteenth century. Mansel also picks out 'proximity' and 'personality' as features peculiar to sensation fiction. By the former he means that much of the spice of these works comes from their contemporary setting, with characters of the type we might expect to recognise in our own lives—in his own expressive phraseology, 'It is necessary to be near a mine to be blown up by its explosion.' 'Personality' is the sensationalist's custom of taking actual scandals and crimes in high life and weaving 'the incident into a thrilling tale, with names and circumstances slightly disguised, so as at once to exercise the ingenuity of the reader in guessing the riddle and to gratify his love of scandal in discovering the answer'. In these respects sensation fiction was at least up-to-date, if not new.

Henry James is also convinced that sensation fiction is a departure, going so far as to bestow on it a specific christening day—1862, *Lady Audley's Secret*. He acknowledges the influence of Collins, however, and his comments here, taken from an article on Miss Braddon in the *Nation*, reinforce Mansel's idea of proximity and the novelty of these tales in general:

> To Mr. Collins belongs the credit of having introduced into fiction those most mysterious of mysteries, the mysteries which are at our own doors. This innovation was fatal to the authority of Mrs. Radcliffe and her everlasting castle in the Appenines. What are the Appenines to us or we to the Appenines? Instead of the terrors of *Udolpho*, we are treated to the terrors of the cheerful country house and the busy London lodgings.

There seems little doubt in the minds of those who survived the explosions that the mines were a new mark. Of special interest in what they have to say is their mention of features more often associated with detective fiction in this century. There is the contemporary setting, for example; until recently, historical detective stories were as snow in June. It is the same with local settings; when in 1926 W. H. Wright wrote that a castles-in-Spain atmosphere was not suitable for detective stories, he was simply amending Jamesian geography. Again, where would later writers be without real life crime for their *romans à clef?* The predilection of the 1920s and 30s for settings in high life and the snobbery ascribed thereto has provided material for a book on the subject—Colin Watson's *Snobbery With Violence* (1971). And could M. Poirot be a guest at that country house? And who was it had lodgings in London?

Alongside novelty, no doubt to some extent because of it, came popularity. 'These books', sniffs Mansel, 'would certainly not be written if they did not sell; and they would not sell if they were not read; *ergo*, they must have readers, and numerous readers too'. And these works *were* the best-selling as serials and the most-borrowed as three-deckers. People read *All the Year Round*, Dickens discovered, not for its articles, but for its sensational serial, and if the story was not up to the standard set by *A Tale of Two Cities* and *The Woman in White*, sales fell away. Moreover, a popular serial, besides being a tonic for sales, could on occasion administer the kiss of life to an ailing magazine. Collins' *Armadale*, as Kenneth Robinson tells us, revived the sinking *Harper's Monthly* in 1866, and in the same year in France, Gaboriau's *L'Affaire Lerouge*, although it had come too late to rescue *Le Pays*, did restore *Le Soleil* to excellent health after the near-mortal wound inflicted on it by Hugo's *Les Travailleurs de la Mer*.[3] When published in volume form these serials lost nothing in popularity. Mudie's stock of fiction in the 1860s averaged one-third of his total and the major part of that was in the 'class whom nearly all critics condemn, and nearly all readers now run after—the Sensation Novelists'.[4]

The condemnation was tempered only with despair:

> There is no accounting for tastes, blubber for the Esquimaux, half-hatched eggs for the Chinese, and Sensational novels for the English . . . Just as in the Middle Ages people were afflicted with the Dancing Mania and Lycanthropy, sometimes barking like dogs, and sometimes mewing like cats, so now we have a Sensational Mania . . . its virus is spreading in all directions, from the penny journal to the shilling magazine, and from the shilling magazine to the thirty shillings volume . . . to attempt to put down Sensationalism by words, is like trying to remove the lump off a camel's back with a poultice . . . Sensationalism must be left to be dealt with by time, and the improvement of public taste. But it is worth while stopping to note, amidst all the boasted improvement of the nineteenth century, that while Miss Braddon's and Mr. Wilkie Collins' productions sell by thousands of copies, *Romola* with difficulty reaches a second edition.
>
> Review of *Armadale*, in *Westminster Review*, (October 1866)

And Mr. Wilkie Collins could and did gloat over his receipts. Referring to his income from *No Name* (1862), he wrote to his mother: '. . . the amount reaches Four thousand, six hundred. Not so bad for story-telling!'[5] While George Eliot wept: 'I sicken with despondency [she wrote in 1866 to her publisher, Blackwood] . . . that the most carefully written books lie . . . deep undermost in a heap of trash . . . my 6/- editions are never on the railway bookstalls . . . They are not so attractive to the majority as "The Trail of the Serpent" '.[6] Crocodile tears these, really; in 1863 *Romola* had brought her a near-record £7,000 with reversion of copyright. But George Eliot was right about the popularity of the author of *The Trail of the Serpent* (1861)[7]— none other than Miss Braddon, who certainly seems to have deserved her title of 'Queen of the Circulating Libraries'. The *Westminster Review* was only just guilty of exaggeration in saying that her 'novels must appear in a second edition the very day after [their] first publication and . . . a third follow the second before the week is well out'. Keeping strictly to facts, however, the story of crowds queuing for the *Strand* with the next Sherlock Holmes story is well-known; less remembered is the fact that their fathers had done the same for the next episode of *The Moonstone*, and when published in book form, having already been serialized, the first impression of 1,000 copies of *The Woman in White* sold in one day. George Eliot could perhaps draw some consolation from the admission of an American pirate-publisher that he had sold 126,000 copies of the latter book and paid Collins not one penny.

Who read these stories? Not the working classes, who could not afford them even in serial form and who were catered for, sensation-wise, by the penny dreadful. There was of course, as the *Westminster Review* pointed out in the passage quoted above, an overlap between the sensation fiction of the 'better' magazines or three-deckers and that of penny fiction. Some authors, Miss Braddon for one and Charles Reade for another, straddled both categories. Similarly, some penny stories reached the dignity of three volumes—*The Flower of the Flock*, for example, by Pierce Egan, 'that mighty potentate', as *Macmillan's Magazine* describes him in a none too favourable article on 'Penny Novels' in June 1866. There was traffic in the other

47

direction, too, with varying success. One can understand the ebbing sales of the penny production which published a run of Sir Walter Scott's novels, but we can join with Wilkie Collins writing on 'The Unknown Public' (*Household Words*, August 1858) in his surprise that Dumas, Sue and Reade should have met with similar receptions. However, the fiction of Collins' 'unknown three million' would require a separate book. The readers of the sensation fiction with which we are concerned here were mainly of the expanding middle class and the upper class right up to Prince Albert who is said to have presented a copy of *The Woman in White* to Baron Stockmar; Queen Victoria's amusement or otherwise is not recorded. That same book kept Gladstone from the play, and Miss Braddon was a great favourite of Tennyson and Thackeray. Here perhaps we have the beginning of that pastime popular with detective fiction commentators of pointing proudly to its elevated readership, for Justin McCarthy remarks in 1864 that 'only of late years have cabinet ministers ventured to quote from popular stories', a trend which only this cynical age might regard as detracting from the politician or the story or both: writing of Anna Katherine Green's *The Leavenworth Case* in *Bloody Murder*, Symons comments that 'the book was the favourite detective story of Prime Minister Stanley Baldwin, a fact tending to confirm one's gloomy view of politicians' literary taste'. Unless, of course, the politician happens to agree with one. Symons goes on in his history to single out for praise the writings of John Franklin Bardin and in his Introduction to *The John Franklin Bardin Omnibus* (1976) one can read: 'Denis Healey was the guest of honour at a Crime Writers' Association dinner a few years ago . . . In the course of his speech Mr. Healey showed a considerable, almost a dazzling, knowledge of crime fiction . . . [and] picked out for special praise the crime novels of John Franklin Bardin . . . Our present Chancellor of the Exchequer is not Bardin's only English admirer . . .'

What sensation fiction and the tales of the penny dreadfuls do have in common is the fact that both were written to formulas. This was a feature of sensation fiction against which the critics ranted, just as it was a source of its popularity. Many people feel happier with familiar things, be it clothes or plots. Let an easily assimilated, easily imitated story be once successful and there will be no standing room on the bandwagon. Spy story, western, science fiction—each has its wave of popularity following some outstanding success. Sherlock Holmes and detective stories is the obvious example, but there is John Buchan and the *pro patria* thriller, James Bond and the spy story, then Alistair MacLean refurbishing Buchan and so on, not forgetting Collins and Miss Braddon with the precursor and the progenitor of them all, sensation fiction.

The formula for sensation fiction has already been given at the beginning of this book with the poem from *Blackwood's Magazine*. Eleven years later, in 1875, in an article called 'In a Studio' by W. W. Story, the same magazine repeated the recipe in prose:

> Take a number of characters, some supernaturally good, some supernaturally bad, and roll them up in a mass of mystery and crime. Dash in murder, and poison, and secrecy *ad libitum* . . . add a weak-minded clergyman, a helpless girl, and a detective who sees through everything with supernatural acuteness.

But verse or prose, it adds up to Edgar Wallace and, if we are honest, to Dorothy Sayers as well.

The third characteristic of Victorian sensation fiction is that it was second-rate. As with its novelty, this is a generalisation requiring immediate qualification.

In his 'Preliminary Word' to *Uncle Silas* (1864) Joseph Sheridan Le Fanu (1814–1873) wrote:

> May [I] be permitted a few words . . . of remonstrance against the promiscuous application of the term 'sensation' to that large school of fiction which transgresses no one of those canons of construction and morality which, in producing the unapproachable *Waverley Novels*, their great author imposed upon himself? No one, it is assumed, would describe Sir Walter Scott's romances as 'sensation novels', yet in that marvellous series there is not a single tale in which death, crime, and, in some form, mystery have not a place.

Taking a sensation novel in Le Fanu's terms as a tale involving death, crime and mystery, there is, on the face of it, almost no limit to the literature that can be included—Greek tragedy, Shakespeare, Fielding and Scott, to name but a few. This indeed was the first line of defence of Victorian sensation writers. It is still a line of defence today, offered humorously by some: 'If there had been a Mystery Writers of America in 1610, we would have given Shakespeare a prize for *Hamlet* as the best mystery of the year,' remarked Richard Martin Stern at the Crime Writers' International Congress in 1975. On the same occasion, as reported in the *Daily Telegraph*, Eric Ambler was perhaps half-serious when he said: 'Mystery writing really is a "catch-all". *Jane Eyre* is a mystery! So is *War and Peace*.' But the point has been urged seriously more than once, for example in 1941 by Philip Van Doren Stern in an article entitled 'The Case of the Corpse in the Blind Alley':

> There is nothing inherent in the mystery story that limits it as literature. Its central core is almost always premeditated murder . . . and premeditated murder is one of the greatest themes in all literature: witness such works as *Electra*, and *Crime and Punishment*. If it is true that the average mystery story makes little attempt to deal with the great drama of life and death, that is because it is an average mystery story, written by a hack. There is no reason why a tale concerning itself with the most soul-racking deed a human being can undertake should be a silly, mechanically contrived affair. The writer of murder mysteries holds high cards in his hands; if he does not know how to play them, that does not lessen their value.

And in his review in the *Daily Telegraph* of Gavin Lambert's *The Dangerous Edge* (1975) David Holloway tells the story of how 'in a misguided moment I once wrote that a book was "only a thriller" and received a stern rebuke from its author saying that a thriller had just as much right as anything else to be considered as literature. He added words to the effect that "Some of us are trying to say something quite important in the thriller form." ' Holloway adds significantly: This is quite true but because many thrillers are so entertaining and so commercially successful, their other merits tend to be forgotten', a kinder let-down than that meted out to Le Fanu at whom the *Saturday Review* came back with the obvious retort in its review of *Uncle Silas*:

> . . . that a novel may contain incidents of a very startling kind without thereby incurring the imputation of being a 'sensation' novel . . . is a proposition which no one probably would think of questioning . . . To be sure, there is no stint of this sort of interest in *Uncle Silas* . . . but these things do not make this a sensation novel. It is the volcanic phrases which stud its pages, and the lurid medium through which every incident and personage, whether commonplace or extraordinary, is seen, that appear to us to take it out of the category of the Waverley Novels.

Or, more briefly—and crudely—it's not what you write about, it's how you write about it.

All this verges on the trite. Obviously, Shakespeare and Scott were not sensation writers in the same sense as, say, Miss Braddon, but this does lead to the perennial problem of where and how to draw the line. Le Fanu wanted to be included on the side of the gods, but most critics followed the *Saturday Review* in refusing him a visa. Kathleen Tillotson, on the other hand, issues him one with little ado, believing him justified in his claim to belong to the 'legitimate school of tragic English romance'. Collins is another linesman. Norman Page puts the problem neatly in his preface to *Wilkie Collins: The Critical Heritage* (1974):

> In [Collins'] hands, fictional sows' ears were apt to turn out as silk purses; and the reviewer was faced with a problem which may be put briefly in some such form as 'Under what circumstances can a third-rate literary genre accommodate a first-rate work?' . . . Victorian men of letters felt a genuine puzzlement at the difference between the kind of novel Collins appeared to be writing and the powerful and unignorable response of the reader.

We have already seen one expression of this puzzlement in the *Westminster Review*'s sad shake of the head that despite all the advances in other directions, the nineteenth-century reader could still prefer Collins to Eliot.

The problem remains, and I draw attention to it, not to proffer an answer, but to emphasise that sensation fiction is here being limited to novels so designated by the critics of the 1860s and 1870s, and to authors seen by these critics as sensational writers; and this must include Dickens and Collins. That certain of these writers or certain of their works have since been elevated above the ruck of sensationalists, or out of the class altogether, is not in dispute (though which ones, may be), but the concern here is with contemporary opinion as voiced by a majority of critics. Page points out that 'the modern reader, trained by such modern instances as the thrillers of Graham Greene, takes the paradox in his stride', and perhaps the partitions between genres built by the Victorians are beginning to break down as new writers and new criteria emerge. Or should we be content with G. K. Chesterton's division of books into 'good' and 'bad' with the further sub-division of each category into both 'good' and 'bad' again? If so, then it is almost exclusively with the 'good bad' and the 'bad bad' that this book deals.

This begs the original question, however, which was the assertion that sensation fiction was second-rate. This remains to be proved, or rather explained, since the proof was in your reaction to the first mention of the expression a few pages back.

Sensation fiction got off to an unpromising start in life in that any purely descriptive meaning it may have had was almost at birth displaced by a pejorative connotation, just as Mr. Punch saw the more general application of the word 'sensation' worn threadbare through over-use. This was precisely Le Fanu's point, and the beginnings of this automatic association of sensation fiction with the second-rate can be found as early as that *Sixpenny Magazine* article of 1861 containing that nominee for the first use of the term:

There are three kinds of works of fiction, each with strongly marked characteristics — the first, in which acknowledged fidelity to nature is a marked feature; as examples we may instance the earlier works of Dickens, *The Caxtons* of Bulwer, and *Adam Bede*. The second, in which there is an evident element of ex-aggeration, treated with more or less artistic merit, such as the later works of Dickens, *Jane Eyre*, *John Halifax* and *The Woman in White*. In the third, nature is entirely disregarded, and the author contents himself with repeating old forms of melodramatic narrative.

'Literature of the Month', *Sixpenny Magazine*, September 1861

The article goes on to allow that individual authors can be promoted or demoted from one division to the other, its own duplicate example of Dickens being an instance of this, but the implications are clear. It is the Dickens 'A' team in the first division, and Dickens 'B' in the second. We may disagree with the placement of some of the examples, but the concept of a hierarchy of genres, classes, types—call them what you will— within fiction is here proposed as a feasible, if not already established, critical principle; and sensation fiction with its exaggerations is at best in the second group. The author of the article would, I think, have admitted that there was nothing absolutely or necessarily derogatory in a novelist's being placed in the second category. As long as there is 'artistic merit' the 'element of exaggeration' is acceptable, and writers working along these lines were taking the novel down a perfectly respectable and legitimate path—not the main road, to be sure, but a good B road with its own special attractions. The idea of sensation fiction as secondary is explicit; it can only be a short step to the idea of it as second-rate.

At this time the theory of the novel was at an elementary stage of evolution, but the increase in the quantity of fiction being produced, quite apart from its content and influence, was forcing critics to have more regard to it. As late as 1864, however, Justin McCarthy could write:

> If a man or woman attempt to be a novelist and fail, the blame cannot be laid to the account of pedantic critical legislation. Perhaps this happy freedom was greatly owing in the first instance to the fact that criticism deliberately ignored the novelist altogether, and regarded him as a creature outside the pale of art . . . It is only of recent days that critics have begun seriously to occupy themselves in the consideration of prose fiction. It forced itself on them by its popularity and influence . . . It was, then, however, too late to set about laying down laws, and forming schools, and prescribing this and proscribing that, and attempting all the freaks of pedantic power in which criticism delighted to indulge.[8]

That this talk of 'happy freedom' and absence of laws and schools was more than a little naive is too obvious to require

53

comment; in the context of sensation fiction it was naive even at the time of writing, for that class at least was already proscribed in many critics' opinion. The article does, however, bear out the fluid situation in the critical world of the 1860s.

The main justification for the existence of the novel in general, in so far as one was necessary, had been that it afforded amusement. When the Victorian critics began to turn their attention to fiction, this seemed to them altogether too frivolous a purpose, and the main objection to novels in general became that they could only entertain. Hence, as Kenneth Graham has pointed out, in *English Criticism of the Novel, 1865–1900*, those 'anxious for their subject's prestige could hardly be expected to stress its doubted ability to entertain'. If this was true of fiction as a whole, what price the sensational variety? Really, the first question many critics were asking was not how fiction should be written, but whether it should be written at all. Criteria other than entertainment value alone had therefore to be sought, criteria for commendation and for condemnation, and these are seen in embryo formulation in the *Sixpenny's* divisions. A consensus of critical opinion confirmed them until the situation here described by Graham was reached:

> Truth to human nature is one of the most widespread and durable critical principles of the age. 'Not true-to-life', 'blurred', 'indistinct', and 'caricatures' are perpetually recurring phrases of condemnation; and 'mixed' or 'well-rounded' characters become a reviewer's fetish. Dickens . . . is often in the pillory. His characters are criticised as 'speaking abstractions or animated machines', compared with Jane Austen's or Mrs. Gaskell's, or with the more accurate 'photography' of Thackeray, or the 'sound, detailed, substantial completeness of sculpture' of Trollope. And his influence is blamed for the way the 'Sensation School' draws 'characteristics' rather than 'character', mere puppets instead of 'living' figures like George Eliot's Tito Melema.

Following on from this we have the story of the controversies which enlivened nineteenth-century criticism—plot versus character, for example, domestic story versus realist and realism versus escapism, with all their permutations and shadings. Going back to 1861 and the *Sixpenny Magazine*, however, it would be broadly true to say that its proposition of the primacy of 'fidelity to nature' over the 'element of exaggeration' was still by no means the established fact of critical life that it was to become. The writers in the *Sixpenny's* second division were unlikely to, and indeed did not, meekly accept this arbitrary arrangement. But almost before discussion could begin, events took theory by the forelock and confirmed sensation fiction not only as secondary but as second-rate.

Within three months of that article in the *Sixpenny Magazine*, the *Spectator*, in an article on 'The Enigma Novel', 28 December 1861, was pointing to the all too obvious links between the second and third divisions in terms not inapplicable to detective fiction:

> We are threatened with a new variety of the sensation novel, a host of cleverly complicated stories, the whole interest of which consists in the gradual unravelling of some carefully prepared enigma. Mr. Wilkie Collins set the fashion, and now every novel writer who can construct a plot, thinks . . . he may obtain a success rivalling that of *The Woman in White* . . . but there is not the slightest probability that the swarm of imitators will construct plots nearly so good, or achieve any result except that of wasting very considerable powers upon an utterly worthless end.

Mrs. Oliphant, too, could read the writing on the wall: 'What Mr. Collins has done [in *The Woman in White*] with delicate care and laborious reticence, his followers will attempt without any such discretion', though I doubt if even she realised the enormity of the iceberg from the tip she was seeing. Her warning, coming after the *Spectator's*, was already too late. Even as she wrote her forebodings were materialising in the shape, not only of *Lady Audley's Secret* then being serialised in none other than the *Sixpenny Magazine*, but of the following selection for 1862 from what Le Fanu called the 'three volumed gospel of the circulating library': *Recommended to Mercy; Such Things Are; Passages in the Life of a Fast Young Lady; The Woman of Spirit; Spurs and Shirts; The Last Days of a Bachelor; Ashcombe Churchyard;* and last but obviously far from least, *Clinton Maynard, a Tale of the World, the Flesh and the Devil.*

The forecast flood was now in full spate. The raw sensational ingredients of Dickens' and Collins' works were fallen upon by an army of carrion who began what was perhaps the first example of mass-production of literature outside penny fiction. Faced with what must have seemed to them a mountain of unrelieved trash, most critics—and who can blame them—failed to pick out the nuggets. Most of what they read *was* bad, and they condemned virtually all, on a variety of grounds—religious, ethical, aesthetic, depending on their point of view.

The ideals and objects of the Dickens school of applying to fiction the conventions of drama by stressing incident and dialogue while still adhering scrupulously to truth went unheeded or unnoticed by the imitators and proved either too strong a mixture or too wrong a concept for most critics. 'In this novel', opines the *Dublin University Magazine* of *The Woman in White* in an article of 1861 on 'Recent Popular Novels', which claims a passing notice from the marked disproportion of its actual merits to its seeming popularity, the spirit of modern realism has woven a tissue of scenes more wildly improbable than the fancy of an average idealist would have ventured to inflict on readers beyond their teens.' And Mrs. Oliphant reluctantly admits of Dickens that 'Whenever he aims at a scene, he has hurried aside into regions of exaggeration, and shown his own distrust of the common and usual by fantastic eccentricities, and accumulations of every description of high-strained oddity.' If Dickens, then, could nod and sometimes slip from dramatic representation into melodrama, what could be expected of lesser writers? Certainly nothing from Miss Braddon, according to the *Eclectic Review* (January 1868):

> She undoubtedly possesses strong theatrical — using the word in contradistinction to dramatic — proclivities. Her method in arranging the scenes and incidents of her stories is . . . excessively 'stagey'. They remind us very forcibly of the manner in which a farce or melodrame is placed upon the stage, the main object of which consists in procuring any number of sudden interviews, abrupt confidences, and startling revelations, all of which are supposed to add intensity and interest to the story.
>
> 'Miss Braddon. The Illuminated Newgate Calendar'

The influence of drama is also seen in the emphasis in sensation fiction on plot. The *Blackwood* recipe, accurate in all other ingredients, seems to have miscalculated in its injunction to 'never mind a plot', though in fairness it may have had in mind the episodic approach of certain authors to the sensational mixture, for example G. A. Sala in *The Seven Sons of Mammon* (1862) and *The Baddington Peerage* (1860), quickly re-designated 'The Paddington Beerage' and 'The Badly-Done Peerage'. In the eyes of the critics, however, the omnipresence of plot, to the exclusion, as they saw it, of all else, was the greatest single factor contributing to the downfall of sensation fiction: 'Those who make plot their first consideration', thundered H. F. Chorley in his review of *Armadale* in the *Athenaeum* of 2 June 1866, '. . . have placed themselves in a groove which goes, and must go, in a downward direction, whether as regards fiction or morals.' These opponents saw the undeniable emphasis on plot as over-emphasis, decried the improbabilities of each sample that came before them, and on occasion took a sadistic delight, emulated in this century by Howard Spring, in revealing the ending, despite or perhaps because of the protestations of authors such as Collins. The *Dublin University Magazine* even contrived to put Collins in a 'heads-I-win-tails-you-lose' situation on this issue:

> A novel that cannot bear a slight rehearsal must be either wholly unreadable, or, at best, belong to a low type of literary art whose whole merit lies in the production of clever puzzles and startling metamorphoses. To which of these classes *The Woman in White* may be assigned we shall leave others to settle for themselves, only asking, for our own part, how it is possible to criticize a book of this sort without a continual reference to the plot.

How many subsequent reviewers of detective fiction have felt the constraint 'not to give it away', and how much, in obeying it, have they contributed to the relegation of detective fiction to a cramped corner of their paper's book page? Or have the books themselves brought about their own damnation by containing nothing of interest save their dénouements?

Today we do not usually think of sensation fiction as having a didactic face, but most 'novels with a purpose', as they called them, were often so classed by Victorian critics. One reason for the proliferation of novels as 'engines of controversy' may have been that since amusement alone was deemed an insufficient justification for writing fiction, authors hoped that by founding tales on topical issues they might avoid accusations of frivolousness and sensationalism in its immoral sense. 'Sensation novelist' in the sense of one who uses dramatic means to draw attention to abuses still survives today. Thus Tillotson, again in the role of mother confessor, is willing to absolve Charles Reade from the charge of sensationalism by regarding him as 'sensational in the traditional sense and in the service of his social purpose'. In *Bloody Murder*, Symons also makes the point that the 'social attitude' of the modern crime novel varies, but is 'often radical in the sense of questioning some aspects of law, justice, or the way society is run'. Perhaps the sensational clock has taken a century to turn full circle. Murch, however, seems to carry this link between moral purpose and sensationalism a step too far when she says of Dickens and Collins (in *The Development of the Detective Novel*) that they 'were, in the phrase of the period, "sensation novelists", satirizing social evils, attacking legal anomalies and championing the cause of those who seemed to them victims of injustice '. That the link mentioned does exist cannot be denied, but to equate Victorian sensation fiction with moral purpose alone is at once to exaggerate the didactic and reformatory elements which occur only in some of these books, and then only in part, and to underestimate and gloss over other, more obvious, features of sensationalism. Perhaps this particular aspect of sensational literature has been revived by the academic ladies in order to rescue Dickens and Collins and Reade from being branded as sensational in the disreputable sense. Ironically, this would leave Collins high and dry, for the more his books have a message the less they are remembered. A far better epitaph for Collins than his crusades against athleticism and the Jesuits is his own phrase: 'make 'em laugh, make 'em cry, make 'em wait', though I bow to his own choice: 'the author of *The Woman in White* and other works of fiction'. . . *The Woman in White*, notice, in which his tiltings at the mental asylum system go virtually unremarked. In the light, then, of the actual scope and development of sensation fiction it seems inadequate and artificial to define it solely in terms of reformatory zeal.

Mansel, in the *Quarterly Review* for April 1863, had no doubts that this didactic element was only half the story, and so far from giving it credit for being at least well-intentioned, he saw in it the variety of sensation fiction to be most deprecated, worse even than the variety which sought only to amuse. He prefers the latter, 'as a fly, though a more idle, is a less offensive insect than a bug'. And the bugs were treated to a large dose of disinfectant:

> Let a writer have a prejudice against the religion of his neigh-bour, against the government of his country, against the administration of the law, against the peerage, against the prohibition that hinders a man from marrying his grandmother . . . forthwith comes out a tale to exhibit in glowing colours the evil which might be produced by the obnoxious object in an imaginary case . . . The method is thus far perfectly impartial that it may be applied with equal facility to the best things and the worst . . . Mr. Dickens, we regret to say, is a grievous offender in this line; and, by a just retribution . . . he never sinks so nearly to the level of the ordinary sensation-novelist as when he is 'writing with a purpose'. Unfortunately . . . the vice of a great writer has been copied by a hundred smaller ones, who, without a tithe of his genius, make up for the deficiency by an extra quantity of extravagance.

Mansel's last words confirm the general point being made here —how, by sheer weight of imperfect imitations, sensation fiction lost whatever chance it may have had of surviving as an unemotive descriptive term, and took on the disparaging overtones that are with us today.

It should not be thought, however, that it was all one-way traffic against sensation fiction. Dickens, Collins and Reade were more than capable of propounding and defending their ideas, and often did so—too often, perhaps, in the case of

Collins, whose contentious prefaces were a source of his disagreements with Dickens.

> What brought good Wilkie's genius nigh perdition?
> Some demon whispered — 'Wilkie! have a mission.'

Swinburne's couplet neatly explains Collins' failure to maintain the standard of his novels of the 1860s, for after *The Moonstone* his missions and self-justifications loom much larger in his books. Similarly, when George Augustus Sala entered the lists in verbose defence of sensationalism in a contribution to the *Belgravia* magazine, edited by Miss Braddon, the reaction of the Dickens school may have been a silent prayer to be saved from friends; as the *Saturday Review* remarked:

> Bad as is the case for sensationalism, we are unwilling to believe that Mr. Sala has made the best of it. We would rather hope that, having seen the error of his ways, and having determined upon dealing his school a deadly blow in the pages of the magazine most devoted to its support, he has deliberately written the farrago of illogical nonsense before us with the intention of disgusting Miss Braddon's most persevering admirers and inducing them to turn their backs upon her once and for all.[9]

Unknown to the *Saturday*, this is precisely what Miss Braddon feared. She had commissioned Sala to write a defence of sensationalism in response to an anonymous attack on her in *Blackwood's* of September 1867—actually by Mrs. Oliphant. In his article Sala sullied some of the works of Bulwer-Lytton, Miss Braddon's friend, hero and almost father-figure, which put her in something of a quandary. 'This passage I have begged him to suppress,' she wrote to Lord Lytton, '. . . but he refuses, and dares me to tamper with his proof. What shall I do? If you have any objection to the passage, it shall go out—come what may. I would much rather offend Sala than offend you.'[10] Bulwer-Lytton apparently did not object for the article was published in full in November 1867.

Bulwer-Lytton indeed was a much-needed pillar of support for Miss Braddon till his death in 1873 and it is also true that not all critics joined in what may seem from the foregoing

pages to have been the universal condemnation of all sensation
fiction. 'More claymores, less psychology', says Andrew Lang
in support of the telling of a story as the *raison d'être* of fiction,
and it is possible to unearth favourable reviews and comments
about sensational works; but easier to fall over unfavourable
ones. The immediate relevance of these, as may be becoming
clear and will become clearer still, is how the case against
sensation fiction resembles the case against detective fiction yet
to be.

The broad trend was unmistakably against sensationalism
in fiction, and a feature of complimentary and moderate
opinions is that even they are often tinged with a suspicion of
the secondariness of the novels they commend or defend. For
example, McCarthy has this to say about sensation fiction in
1864:

> There is something to be said in defence of that most popular
> section of our romanticists [Sensation Novelists] too . . . they
> are an inevitable reaction against the realism of far greater
> authors . . . Considering the facility with which novels are
> written, published, and read in our day . . . it is really much
> to the credit of the age, and testifies highly to the progress of
> public education, that so many books of this class are produced
> which deserve to be read, and that so small a number, com-
> paratively, are worthy only of utter contempt or positive
> condemnation.

In other words, it could have been worse; a good example of
Victorian self-satisfaction.

One of the most notable outbursts against sensation novels
was a speech by the Archbishop of York, Dr. Thomson, de-
livered at the Huddersfield Church Institute in November
1864. He decried these 'stimulating narratives' at length,
threatening addicts amongst the laity with the loss of their souls
and addicts amongst the clergy with the loss of preferment. In
their place he urged the study of history and novels portraying
'the larger chapter of homely sympathies'. Critics were not slow
to take him up for their own purposes, but in disagreeing with
him about the evil influences of sensation novels the *Saturday*

Review, writing on 'The Perils of Sensation', in November 1864, produced less a defence of the indicted party than a gentle and light-hearted hint to archbishops to eschew literary criticism. There are no grounds, the *Saturday* assures us, for Dr. Thomson's belief that sensation fiction corrupts the citizen and actually makes him behave as sinfully as the sensation characters he reads about: 'the horrors of these stories have just as little practical effect upon [people's] conduct in making them better or worse as the horrors threatened in fanatical sermons and religious journals. They may look at crime or misery through the sensation microscope for an hour, but on leaving it the natural aspect of things instantly recurs with unweakened form'. Under the heading 'The Sin of Light Reading', the *Saturday* returned to the Archbishop in September 1865—almost a year after the speech and an indication of its impact—to point out to him the 'sad piece of news' that demand in the libraries for Miss Braddon's *Only A Clod* was seventeen times that for Froude. The writer goes on to tease the Archbishop with the thought that Henry VIII's 'excellent principle that it is possible for a man to get tired of his wife, and that in such a case it is right for him to make away with her and to take another, is not illustrated in fiction on so large a scale as in fact'. None of which helped sensation fiction; on the one hand it is deemed so improbable that no one really pays it permanent heed, and on the other hand it may be less gruesome than reality but this earns it no laurels in its own right.

It is a similar helping backhand which Henry James, writing on Miss Braddon in the *Nation*, offers Collins:

> Mr. Collin's productions deserve a more respectable name [than sensation novels]. They are massive and elaborate constructions — monuments of mosaic work, for the proper mastery of which it would seem, at first, that an index and a notebook were required. They are not so much works of art as works of science. To read *The Woman in White* requires very much the same intellectual effort as to read Motley or Froude.

The *Saturday Review* on Collins' *Man and Wife* (1870) is interesting as reflecting the puzzlement mentioned earlier:

'Why, being so good, is it not a little better?', and the same magazine's verdict on *East Lynne* (1862) sums up both this particular point that sensation fiction received but qualified support at best and the general contention that it was second-rate: 'This is a really good novel. It is not, indeed, a novel of much pretension, and it is unmistakably a novel of the second class . . .'

Alongside this lukewarm patronage one can detect an air of battle fatigue beginning to pervade criticism. 'Sensation novels have become a weariness to the flesh', sighs the *Cornhill* in 1869. One senses that the doves would be willing to accept the surrender of sensation fiction on terms allowing it to continue as a sort of inevitable sub-literature. This parallels the growing acceptance of prose fiction in general as part of literature. Adverse criticism of sensation fiction, particularly on Mansel's virulent lines, grows less common, though without ever disappearing. The grounds of objection also shift away from the moral and aesthetic to an emphasis on the technical problem thought to be facing this type of book. That sensation fiction was all plot and no characters and therefore defective had always been the cry of its opponents, but as the formula behind the books became apparent from the mass production, there is now added the charge that the plots themselves are repetitive and boring and hence that the genre will play itself out. There also insinuates itself into critics' parlance that tone of amused tolerance and condescension which was to mark their approach to detective fiction, instanced specifically by the *Saturday* on *East Lynne*, and more generally by that gentle but nonetheless fatal stab in the back—'good of its kind'—applied by countless critics to endless books.

In 1868 the *Saturday Review* could claim that 'sensationalism . . . has not so much been written down as written out. People have not so much protested against it as turned away from it in sheer weariness . . . an ordinarily intelligent person is not to be excited or astounded in precisely the same manner for an indefinite number of times.'[11] If only the writer had known . . . D. E. Williams, reviewing Collins' *Poor Miss Finch* (1872) in the *Athenaeum*, could afford to dispose of it light-heartedly: 'It is a sensation novel for Sunday reading, and, as such, can be confidently recommended to the notice of parents and guardians . . . [Collins] has certainly no right to expect immortality for Miss Finch. But it is something to be *facile princeps* even in a transient school.' A note of nostalgia, no less, creeps into *Blackwood's Magazine* in 1879:

> . . . if we were driven to choose . . . we should decidedly prefer the modern sensation school. There at least you have brightness, and, occasionally, fun; and at one time it could boast a certain originality. It was rather a happy thought . . . when it was suggested that in the sylph-like form of a shrinking maiden or a blushing bride, there might lurk the passions and callous cruelty of a Brinvilliers . . . Murder stalked with stealthy tread up the back staircases of the most highly-rented houses . . . mothers made away with their children as if ordering the execution of a litter of puppies . . . but as bold conceptions of this sort began with a climax, it was difficult, or rather impossible, to cap them.[12]

Even Trollope put out peace feelers in his *Autobiography* (1883):

> There are sensational novels and anti-sensational; sensational novelists and anti-sensational; sensational readers and anti-sensational. The novelists who are considered to be anti-sensational are generally called realistic. I am realistic. My friend Wilkie Collins is generally supposed to be sensational . . . All this is, I think, a mistake — which mistake arises from the inability of the imperfect artist to be at the same time realistic and sensational. A good novel should be both, and both in the highest degree.

and then stabbed sensation fiction in the back:

> [Its] construction is most minute and wonderful. But I can never lose the taste of the construction . . . Such work gives me no pleasure.

apologising all the while:

> I am, however, quite prepared to acknowledge that want of pleasure comes from fault of my intellect.[13]

By this time, however, the major critical battle was over. Sensation fiction was as popular as ever. Late in his life and despite poorer works Collins could still top the polls[14], but the mainstream discussion and controversy about the novel had gone off in other directions, leaving sensation fiction to pick its own way through its self-generated undergrowth.

For detective fiction, of course, the war was just beginning, because here we are, back in the 1880s when the term was coming into use. Is it a coincidence that detective fiction comes in just as sensation fiction seems to be running out of steam?

NOTES TO CHAPTER 3

1   In 'The Lighter Reading of the Eighteen Sixties', her Introduction to *The Woman in White*, Houghton Mifflin (1969), to which I am indebted, Kathleen Tillotson mentions this *Sixpenny Magazine* article and points out that it appeared three years before the *Oxford English Dictionary*'s earliest reference to 'sensation novel', which is taken from the *Edinburgh Review* of 1864. Tillotson quotes this in support of the newness of sensation fiction and it is worth another airing: 'Two or three years ago nobody would have known what was meant by a Sensation Novel; yet now the term has already passed through the stage of jocular use . . . adopted as the regular commercial name for a particular product of industry for which there is just now a brisk demand.'

2   [Margaret Oliphant], 'Sensation Novels', *Blackwood's Magazine*, May 1862. Mrs. Oliphant (1828-1897) was a prolific author of both fiction and non-fiction and a regular contributor to *Blackwood's*.

3   See Valentine Williams, 'Gaboriau: Father of the Detective Novel', *National Review*, December 1923.

4   [Justin McCarthy], 'Novels with a Purpose', *Westminster Review*, October 1866.

5   Quoted in Kenneth Robinson, *Wilkie Collins* (1974), first published 1951.

6   Quoted in Tillotson, 'The Lighter Reading of the Eighteen Sixties', *op. cit.*

7   For the curious publishing history of this work, see Appendix 1, p. 323.

8   [McCarthy], 'Novels with a Purpose', *op. cit.*

9   'Mr. Sala on Sensationalism', *Saturday Review*, 15 February 1868.

10 Miss Braddon to Lord Lytton, 10 October 1867, quoted from R. L. Wolff, 'Devoted Disciple: The Letters of Mary Elizabeth Braddon to Sir Edward Bulwer-Lytton, 1862-1873', *Harvard Library Bulletin*, April 1974.

11 'Mr. Sala on Sensationalism', *op. cit.*

12 [A. Innes Shand], 'Contemporary Literature: IV. Novelists', *Blackwood's Magazine*, March 1879.

13 Trollope completed his autobiography by 1876, but it was first published posthumously in 1883, a year after his death.

14 Robinson, *op. cit.* mentions that 'in a ballot organised about this time [mid-1880s] by the *Pall Mall Gazette* to decide the most popular author, Wilkie Collins outdistanced all his competitors'.

4

A CORNER OF THE VEIL
IS LIFTED

Works answering all the purposes of lengthened Police reports . . .
'Miss Braddon', *Eclectic Review*, 1868

In discussing sensation fiction I have pointed in passing to
certain similarities between it and detective fiction. None of
these is in itself significant, affording perhaps no more than
confirmation of the commonly received opinion that there are
vague links between the two with occasional glimpses, particularly in Collins' works, of what was to come. Taken *en
masse*, however, one wonders if there is not more to these links
than just a borrowing here and a crossover there. The contemporary setting, usually in high life; the class of reader; the
improbabilities or, if you prefer, the 'element of exaggeration';
the drama; the melodrama; the puppet-like characters; the
plot-bias and the mass-production to a formula—all point to a
possible closer relationship between sensation fiction and
detective fiction than is usually entertained. With those last
two points especially—plot and formula—the links seem to go
beyond features shared to features merged. Both types of story
not only emphasise plot but reveal, on investigation, the same
kind of plot, the same kind of formula, sometimes in detail,
always in principle.

Remember Le Fanu on sensation fiction: 'death, crime and
mystery'; then take Thomas Hardy's description of it: 'mystery,
entanglement, surprise and moral obliquity'.[1] Add the
Athenaeum's approach to a definition, quoted earlier in full:
'strong element of mystery . . . vague secret . . . in Volume I a

puzzle, the solution . . . [at] the close of Volume III'. Note the common factor—mystery. Tillotson aptly expresses the conclusion to be drawn from this:

> Especially mystery. The purest type of sensation novel is the novel-with-a-secret; a secret of whose effects the reader is made aware just so far as to excite his continued curiosity, and which when finally disclosed should both surprise and gratify his expectation. It is no accident that the prototype should be called *Lady Audley's Secret* . . . The 'secret' is the dimension added by the sensation novel to the novel of exciting incident and suspense; to the question 'What will happen next?' it adds the more interesting question 'What has happened?'—whether, as often, before the action ever begins, or kept out of sight of the reader during its course and gradually discovered.

Tillotson then adds, 'the link with the detective story, an obvious descendant, is substantial.' Very substantial indeed, more so than she herself may realise. Here is Ronald Knox in 1929 in his Introduction to *Best Detective Stories of the Year*:

> It will be seen, therefore, that the detective story differs essentially from every other type of fiction. For the interest of the ordinary romance centres in the question, 'What will happen?' — unless you include the modern sex novel, where the interest centres in the question, 'Will anything ever happen?' But the interest of the detective romance centres in the question, 'What has happened?' It is a *hysteron proteron* in the Homeric manner.

Hysteron proteron it may be, but the passage is no *hapax legomenon*. This must be more than just one of those coincidences that happen in real life but are barred from mystery fiction, for here we have an authority on nineteenth century fiction talking of sensation fiction in terms identical with a noted detective fictioneer of the Golden age writing on his part-time specialty. And the aspect on which both fasten—the secret in the past and the plot worked backwards from the results of that secret to its disclosure—is one of the few aspects of detective fiction which a majority of commentators agree is a distinguishing one.[2] It may be argued that Tillotson, having experience of both genres, has unconsciously interpreted sensation fiction in terms suggested by her knowledge of detective fiction, imposing on sensation fiction a pattern that is not there. But the nineteenth century refers to sensation fiction in much the same terms, highlighting too often for comfort the same general and detailed identifying features as the twentieth century attaches to detective fiction. The *North British Review* specifically equates secrets with sensation: '*Lady Audley* contains one secret only: this one [*Eleanor's Victory*] contains three . . . Thus there is abundance of "sensation" in this novel also.'[3] And many of the passages already quoted remind us of detective fiction in no uncertain way—'. . . the gradual unravelling of some carefully prepared enigma'; James' request for an index and a notebook, to be more than adequately gratified in the years to follow by way of maps, diagrams and tabulations; the addiction to 'sudden interviews, abrupt confidences, and startling revelations'. Going beyond the odd phrase, however, doubting Thomases may like to compare the following passages. The first is from *The Times*' review of *The Moonstone* (1868):

The essence and secret of sensational novel-writing is to keep flashing a metaphorical bull's eye up the particular dark archways where the thief is not lurking; to make the circumstances agree with one given explanation, which is not the true one; and to disguise as long as possible the fact that they agree also with a perfectly different conclusion. It is to present a real clue and a pseudo, and tempt the reader on to follow the pseudo clue till past the middle of the third volume. The whole school has this habit of laying eggs and hiding them. But Mr. Wilkie Collins has a complex variety of this propensity for secretiveness. He is not satisfied with one false clue, but is perpetually dropping clues, and, like a bird, by his demonstrative employment of various arts to lead his readers elsewhere, away from the spot where he originally induced them to fancy the nest was, only makes them more bent on keeping the old path. Every character in the book has his or her theory as to the mystery, and each of the theories is partly true. But then it is also partly, and that manifestly, false. So, when, as often, a hint of the truth is let fall by one of them, the reader has by this time grown so suspicious that he refuses to accept it.

It hardly needs an equivalent modern quotation to drive home the fact that this writer, in talking of sensation novels and of *The Moonstone* in particular, has described the detective story, but the following from Dorothy L. Sayers, in her Introduction to a second series of *Great Short Stories of Detection, Mystery and Horror* (1931), is remarkable if only for its similarity of metaphor:

> The reader we mystery-mongers really like to lead for our little walk up the garden, comes out like an intelligent terrier . . . ready to run after what is thrown to him . . . we show him the ball and feint to throw it towards the old summerhouse. He darts off in that direction — then stops, puzzled and amused. No; we are fooling him again. That stuff about the summerhouse is only poppycock. He was nearly taken in that time, but he has seen through us and awaits the next throw without bearing malice for the deception. At last he is off! That was a real ball — it has disappeared behind the water tank. He grubs away energetically. There is some difficulty. He looks around deprecatingly. He feels sure the ball is there but he cannot get it out for himself. It has gone to earth behind a large immovable stone. (How could Jones possibly have committed the murder, when he has that impregnable alibi.) We walk up — we lift the stone — yes, indeed the stone only appeared to be the immovable fortress that it seemed. If he had only just known how, he could have shifted it for himself.

But *The Moonstone*, it will be objected, *is* a detective story. Yes, but it was a sensation novel first. And it is to that genre, not just Collins' book, that *The Times* is referring.

If we take it in the *Athenaeum*'s narrower sense, sensation fiction, it seems, is detective fiction. It is the cement that fills the apparent gaps in the development of the detective story, binding the cornerstones to form a continuous wall. Let me risk an unbandaged hand here and say that there are few, if any, plot devices and character-types in the classic detective story of the twentieth century which cannot be found, in some form or other, in the years between Poe and Doyle. 'Dead-but-not-dead' and body substitution were hackneyed when Thorndyke was only a gleam in his father's eye, and sensation fiction also produced that impregnable alibi, the least likely person, tinkering with timepieces, letting-off of nice murderers, not to mention literate butlers, lost wills, lost heirs, blind detectives, dumb detectives, amateur detectives, professional detectives, lady detectives, jealous detectives and so on. Splendid variations and updatings this century has contributed, but the groundwork is here in the nineteenth. Of course there are differences between sensation fiction and detective fiction, which will be looked at in due course; some of these will be revealed as part of a deliberate smokescreen to conceal detective fiction's disreputable origins; none that remains is, I believe, sufficiently basic to alter this proposition of the identity of the two.

Crucial confirmation of this identity comes from the fact that both types of story are plot-based. That the sensational novel consisted of plot and little else was, as we have seen, one of its greatest faults in the eyes of its enemies, and only the unprecedented unanimity of all Victorian critics could make one doubt that a plot, welcome or unwelcome, was an essential feature of these tales. The same applies to detective stories. This common bias does not prove that they are identical. The compelling point is that it is in the criticism of sensation fiction's emphasis on plot that the word 'detective' begins to appear as a critical term. It is not used with reference to the person of the detective, though his activities suggested the use; nor is it used with reference to the supposedly sophisticated intellectual appeal of the detective process, as many in this century have chosen to see it. No, 'detective' was used originally as a useful derogatory description for the type of story which rested on the unravelling of a secret—sensation fiction, in other words—the application coming from the activities of real life detectives who were supposed to unravel the cases they met.

Here, for example, is the *Spectator* on 'The Enigma Novel' in 1861:

> *The Woman in White* was endurable simply because the mystery to be unravelled was of its kind perfect, though we hold silently, nevertheless, that the delineation of Count Fosco was a far higher *artistic* effort than constructing the plot. A good detective might have prepared *that* . . .

The *Saturday Review* makes the same parallel in its review of Miss Braddon's *Sir Jasper's Tenant* (1865): 'A clever detective with a literary knack could not have reported incidents with greater accuracy or more befitting simplicity.' And the same magazine (4 February 1865) sardonically allows that *Uncle Silas* may not be the sensation novel which its author said it was not:

> In one respect it may be admitted that this work differs essentially from those of what is loosely called the sensational school of novelists. It has none of the ingenious dove-tailing and neat workmanship with which those writers have made us familiar. Mr. Le Fanu is too assiduously bent on operating on his reader's nerves, and sending a shiver through his frame, to take much trouble in elaborating details or securing for his narrative strict logical sequence . . . In the present temper of the novel-reading public . . . hints and suggestions are not enough. They like to follow out the track of crime and mystery with the minuteness and particularity of a detective officer.

D. E. Williams, reviewing *Poor Miss Finch* in the *Athenaeum*, not only brings out this equation of the plot with detective-like activity but may also be the originator of the expression 'detective novel' which he here uses eleven years before the *O.E.D.'s* 'detective story': 'He [Collins] has made what may be called the "detective" novel his own,' writes Williams, adding by way of explanation: 'He takes so much and such evident trouble over what he writes, and his workmanship is so good and so conscientious, that the result is always, of its kind, as good as can be got . . . for ingenuity, for cleverness, for power of rousing curiosity and keeping interest alive, Mr. Collins stands altogether alone.'

Is this, then, where our *bête noire* was spawned? Not from the detection, palpable or otherwise; not from the detective, protagonist or otherwise; not from the ratiocination, real or bogus, but from the plot, the puzzle, the secret and its ravelling and unravelling—the things, that is, in which a detective deals and therefore a convenient way of describing them in novels. What a simple yet sensational beginning for detective fiction!

It was this original conception of detective fiction as denoting a style of writing and a quality of authorship which allowed Cecil Chesterton to refer to it as 'the detective or mystery story' without thinking any distinction necessary, and led him to emphasise rather the 'mysterious facts of which the explanation is reserved till the end'. But Mrs. Oliphant was seeing sensation fiction in much the same light more than forty years before Chesterton, though scarcely with his enthusiasm for the end product. She was concerned about the 'confused moral world into which we are admitted by the novelists of the day', and to convey her impression—and dislike—of the keynote and new-ness of this kind of writing, she has to coin an expression: detectivism.[4] This world of the sensation novelist, she believes, is denoted by 'the charm of killing somebody, of bringing an innocent person under suspicion of the deed, and gradually, by elaborate processes of detectivism, hunting out the real crim-inal', and it is a world which 'seems to possess an attraction which scarcely any English novelist can resist'. Mrs. Oliphant, (*Blackwood's* 1863), gives an example of this state of affairs from Mrs. Henry Wood's *The Foggy Night at Offord* (1862), in which the authoress can 'pass over as a thing of no moment, the fact that two consciences have become burdened with the real guilt of swearing falsely in order to deliver her hero from the burden of suspicion, which had no true foundation in it', and Mrs. Oliphant concludes: 'This curious mistake in morals illustrates . . . what we may call the police-court aspect of modern fiction.'

Detectivism, then, and police-court seem the appropriate terms to Mrs. Oliphant; detective or detection would not do. Yet her description of the confused moral world is an amazingly accurate description of detective fiction.[5] And we find this idea of a detective's work as an apt and adequate characterisation of a type of story repeated in 1912 in the *Nation*, in an article entitled 'Detectiveness in Fiction', where the term 'detective-ness' is used to describe in fiction that 'zest for the professional manner of unravelling complicated episodes'. This zest, as Williams made clear about Collins, is the zest exhibited by authors, and to a certain extent by readers, for the intricacies of plotting, not the zest felt by any particular detective to solve the intricacies of a puzzle set for him. Zealousness in the latter sense is admittedly a very real characteristic of many fictional detectives, and it is their infectious enthusiasm that carries many a plot along, but I am suggesting that in its origins 'detective' was applied to an author's concentration on a puzzling plot and to that alone, irrespective of the presence in the plot of a detective or detection. Indeed, as Cecil Chesterton pointed out, a detective, amateur or professional, need not figure in the plot, nor need there be detection as we have come to understand it. Fortuitous revelation, more often than not, was good enough for the Victorians. The Archbishop of York was accurate when in his speech at Huddersfield in 1864 he described sensation novels as being, amongst other things, about a 'will that at some proper moment should tumble out of some broken bureau, and bring about the dénouement which the author wished to achieve'. Later, our intelligent detective would search that bureau and find the will, but this seems a difference of emphasis, not of essence. The important factors are the will and the dénouement. The introduction of a detective to search the bureau is aesthetically more satisfying (and usually more fun) than reliance on accidental disintegration of furniture, but it is simply an improvement in the technique of the author towards that same dénouement. Moreover, it is perhaps in this meaning of 'detective' that we have an explanation why *Mr. Meeson's Will*, *Nicholas Nickleby*, *A Traitor in London* and all those other peripheral and apparently irrelevant books can be called detective stories. Miss Glover ought not to have been looking for detectives but for detectiveness. The detective story may have come a long way from this early use and meaning, but beneath its modern dressing its subject matter has stayed the same: 'death, crime and mystery' and 'secrecy *ad libitum*'—sensationalism.

I suspect that by now I am preaching either to the converted or to the unconvertible, and possibly may have been doing so all along, but it may afford both categories some amusement to play detective and try to decide which item in each of the

following pairs was written over a hundred years ago and
which around forty or less:

1 (a) Hamlet would now apply to a detective instead of a ghost.
   (b) *Hamlet* we treasure as our first . . . detective story and
      Macbeth is even more suggestive of Scotland Yard than of
      Scotland.

2 (a) A new murder is nowadays almost as hard a thing to find
      as a blue dahlia.
   (b) Considering how vast is the output of these stories it is
      natural enough that [authors] should seek to tempt the
      reader's jaded appetite with murders of an extraordinary
      character.

3 (a) . . . nobody dies in an orderly manner.
   (b) . . . the published records contain no mention of a death
      from natural causes since the demise of . . .

4 (a) We should prefer hiring [his works] out as we hire out a
      Chinese conjuror — for the night. As soon as we have
      found out the secret of his tricks, and admired the clever
      way in which he does them, we send him home again.
   (b) It is all like a sleight-of-hand trick, in which the magician
      diverts your attention from the awkward or irrelevant
      moments that conceal the manipulation of the cards, and it
      may mildly entertain or astonish you, as such a sleight-of-
      hand performance may.

5 (a) Their large popularity is an illustration of the wretched
      mental garbage upon which some minds must feed.
   (b) Minds fed on this stuff are like bodies whose drink is the
      froth of the wave and whose meat is the chaff from the
      granary floor.

6 (a) She has acquired [the habit] . . . of stringing together
      . . . names of authors, French, English, German, and
      classic, with references to multitudes of their works, very
      much selected at random, causing a shrewd suspicion to
      take root in the reader's mind, that her knowledge extends
      as far as the names of the authors and the titles of their
      works.
   (b) She displays knowingness about literature without any
      sensitiveness to it or any feeling for quality . . . impressive
      literary excerpts . . . head each chapter.

7 (a) We seem to have read it all before, and to have been introduced under other names . . . to the several personages who meander through its pages, and the various mysteries with which it bristles.

(b) The steady demand of the last decade or so has almost entirely depleted the mother lode. Why write [such] a . . . story when all the good plots have been used, all the changes rung, all the devices made trite.[6]

The nineteenth-century critic would not, it seems, have had any difficulty in coping with detective fiction. These considerations, from the individual points in common through the common 'detectiveness' of approach to this common language, indicate that what started as amusing similarities between sensation fiction and detective fiction have deepened to the point where the two meet, or rather, never really parted. Detective fiction *is* sensation fiction.

To say this, I am well aware, is to go against the traditional view of detective fiction, because it now follows that detective fiction is not new, or only as new as sensation fiction. Yet as *The Times* remarked in 1868, 'It would be unjust to the memory of Edgar Poe . . . to style Mr. Wilkie Collins the founder of the *sensational* school of novels.' (my italics). It also follows that detective fiction is second-rate. Yet it is precisely these two qualities—novelty and superiority—that are singled out by sympathetic commentators as the principal distinguishing features of the detective fiction written during the Golden Age. Due homage having been paid to Poe and a few carefully selected others, the arrival of Holmes is regarded as a genuine innovation, a completely new departure point. 'In 1887 *A Study in Scarlet* was flung like a bombshell into the field of detective fiction,' claims Dorothy Sayers, but a bombshell constructed, if the truth be told, from blueprints on public sale. Similarly, the broad impression given by these commentators is that detective fiction so improved on sensation fiction in style, technique and content, let alone by the replacement of the melodramatic by the intellectual and the institution of the fair-play principle, that it merits consideration separately from and classification above sensation fiction and other lesser breeds such as the thriller and the shocker. All are God's children, but detective fiction, it transpires, is the chosen race while these others constitute the mass of the Gentiles.

Let us look at these claims of the elect.

NOTES TO CHAPTER 4

1 Thomas Hardy, prefatory note to 1889 edition of *Desperate Remedies* (1871).

2 We must, however, tip our caps in passing to the attempts at forward-writing without having backward-plotted — the single-handed efforts, for example, of Victor L. Whitechurch in such books as *The Crime at Diana's Pool* (1926), and the multi-handed experiments of *The Floating Admiral* (1931), *Double Death* (1939) and others, where each of several authors adds a chapter in ignorance of the outcome envisaged by previous contributors.

3 [W. Fraser Rae], 'Sensation Novelists: Miss Braddon', *North British Review*, September 1865.

4 Credit for this neologism may be undue, but the *O.E.D.* has 1894 as its first example.

5 cf. Somerset Maugham: 'The theory of the detective story of deduction is simple. Someone is murdered, there is an investigation, suspicion falls on a number of persons, the culprit is discovered and pays the penalty of his crime.' ('The Decline and Fall of the Detective Story' in *The Vagrant Mood* (1952)); or Auden: 'The vulgar definition, "a Whodunnit", is correct. The basic formula is this: a murder occurs; many are suspected; all but one suspect, who is the murderer, are eliminated; the murderer is arrested or dies.' ('The Guilty Vicarage' in *The Dyer's Hand* (1963) originally *Harper's Magazine*, May 1948).

6 For answers see Appendix 2, p. 331.

5

THE LITTLE AFFAIR THREATENS
TO BECOME THE BIG AFFAIR

'. . . riddles are the short cut to prestige and reputation, and, besides, very intimidating to slow-witted provincials like ourselves.'

A. E. W. Mason, *The Prisoner in the Opal* (1928)

Echoes of discontent about the low esteem in which detective
fiction was held began to appear as the Victorian era gave way
to the Edwardian. Perhaps the new genre title, coinciding with
a new century, imbued enthusiasts with fresh heart. It was
certainly effective in disguising an old song. These stirrings of
mutiny were at first defensive, as when, in his article on 'Art
and the Detective', Cecil Chesterton protested against 'the
modern habit of dismissing whole departments of art as in-
trinsically bad and unworthy'. He goes on:

> We constantly hear people stigmatise a play as 'a mere melo-
> drama' or 'a mere farce' . . . [but] to deny the possibility of a
> good melodrama is to destroy all criticism, including the right to
> condemn a bad one. No form of artistic effort has suffered more
> from this indiscriminate condemnation than the type of narrative
> which we commonly call the Detective Story. That a very large
> number of people write bad detective stories is true; perhaps an
> even larger number write bad sonnets. But this does not prove
> that 'Avenge, O Lord, they slaughtered Saints' is not a great
> poem, neither does it prove that *Le Crime d'Orcival* is not a great
> novel. If the average level of detective-story writing is peculiarly
> low, may not this fact itself be attributed to the refusal of literary
> criticism to take its artistic qualities seriously? Where there is no
> recognition of merit there can be no standard.

That was written in 1906. Cecil's brother, G. K., and their
friend, E. C. Bentley, were shortly to have their merit recog-

nised and to provide a standard, but a standard too high, unfortunately, for most of their followers. Nearly forty years later Raymond Chandler was pointing to the same blind spot on the part of the critics, caused by the same problem to which Chesterton had drawn attention:

> It seems to me that production of detective stories on so large a scale, and by writers whose immediate reward is small and whose need of critical praise is almost nil, would not be possible at all if the job took any talent. In that sense the raised eyebrow of the critic and the shoddy merchandizing of the publisher are perfectly logical. The average detective story is probably no worse than the average novel, but you never see the average novel. It doesn't get published.[1]

Intermittent articles like Cecil Chesterton's and the one book by Carolyn Wells appeared before World War I, but it was in the 1920s that detective fiction's bid for respectability took a more definite shape in the writings of, amongst others, G. K. Chesterton, Dorothy L. Sayers, R. A. Freeman, Ronald Knox and, representing the United States, Willard Huntington Wright, creator, under the name of S. S. Van Dine, of the super-erudite detective, Philo Vance who, according to Ogden Nash, required a kick in the pance. Despite the formation in 1928 of the Detection Club to which many British writers belonged, it would be misleading to see these authors of occasional articles, reviews and forewords as forming a school of thought except in the most informal sense. Knox, for one, was ever less than serious about detective stories whether writing them or about them, while Jacques Barzun, the most discerning of modern protagonists of the genre, has suggested that the arrival of Vance in 1927 in *The Benson Murder Case* signalled the beginning of the end of the classic detective story by subjecting 'the public to a new vice—Pedantry'. Nevertheless, all shared the belief—and it was a genuine belief, however light-heartedly expressed and however marred by an eventually fatal self-consciousness—that detective fiction was essentially different from and consistently superior to other forms of popular fiction, and at least potentially the equal of more critically acceptable forms of the novel.

One of their number—Wright—in an almost mystical passage, goes so far as explicitly to extract detective fiction from 'all other fictional types' and to set it on a mountain where

> it has set its own standards, drawn up its own rules, adhered to its own heritages, advanced along its own narrow-gauge track, and created its own ingredients as well as its own form and tecnic. And all these considerations have had to do with its own isolated purpose, with its own special destiny. In the process of this evolution it has withdrawn farther and farther from its literary fellows, until today it has practically reversed the principles on which the ordinary popular novel is based.[2]

None of the others might have wished to go as far as this, though Knox comes perilously close, as we have seen, in stressing the uniqueness of detective fiction's 'What has happened?' technique. And in an article written in 1948, splendidly entitled 'The Guilty Vicarage', W. H. Auden approaches Wright in mysticism with talk of states of innocence, sin and guilt, and surpasses him in analysis with ease; it should be made clear, however, that Auden is led to this analysis by his belief that 'detective stories have nothing to do with works of art', a belief which he bases on their habit-forming propensities, their formulas and their un-rereadability. R. A. Freeman, whose Dr. Thorndyke ran from early in the century right through the Golden Age, said, in his critic's hat, the opposite of Wright, while in his novels he actually fulfilled and displayed most of Wright's conditions for exclusiveness. Detective fiction, Freeman allows, 'need not be deficient in the . . . qualities appertaining to good fiction . . . [though] they must be, if necessary, sacrificed'. He continues:

> Thus, assuming that good detective fiction must be good fiction in general terms, we may dismiss those qualities which it should possess in common with all other works of imagination and give our attention to those qualities in which it differs from them and which give to it its special character.[3]

This dismissal of those common qualities, for obvious practical reasons in Freeman's context here, is disconcertingly repeated in his stories in the sense that he ignores them or perhaps cannot achieve them in his single-minded pursuit of detection, which as a result makes us feel as if we are, in Symons' phrase, chewing on dry straw when we read a Thorndyke story.

One understandable motive for the assertion of the difference, if not the superiority, of the classic detective story was the pleasant change it offered from the straight novel of the post-war era:

> The detective story has now joined the novel of realism and the tale of passion as fit and proper reading for evenings and holidays . . . . Economy, tidiness, completeness — these are qualities possessed by every good tale of detection, and they are qualities conspicuously lacking in some forms now much cried up, especially in Russian novels and English *vers libre*. Reacting against works of art with little beginning and no end but only a yawning middle . . . we go for solace to the detective of fiction.

So wrote E. M. Wrong in his introduction to the 1926 Oxford University Press anthology *Crime and Detection*. The status of the publishers, an introduction by a don and the quality of that introduction did much for detective fiction's self-esteem. Knox was making the same point as Wrong, only more flippantly, when he denied that a story was a detective story simply because it contained a detective who ran away with somebody's wife 'as is the wont of heroes in modern novels'. Dorothy Sayers, who fluctuated between optimism and doubt in her affair with detective fiction, was full of confidence and fighting talk when she wrote her Introduction to *Great Short Stories of Detection, Mystery and Horror* in 1928:

> At the time of writing the detective story is profiting by a reaction against novels of the static type. Mr. E. M. Forster is indeed left murmuring regretfully, 'Yes, ah! yes — the novel tells a story,' but the majority of the public are rediscovering that fact with cries of triumph. Sexual abnormalities are suffering a slight slump at the moment; the novel of passion still holds the first place, especially among women, but even women seem to be growing out of the simple love-story. Probably the cheerful cynicism of the detective-tale suits better with the spirit of the times than the sentimentality which ends in wedding bells.

Another source of detective fiction's hopes for itself was its claim that it had introduced intelligible, intelligent plots and rational, sensible explanations in place of the irrational, illogical stories which comprised much of sensation fiction. Its improbabilities had long been a favourite criticism of sensation fiction, and neither a change in title nor the advent of Holmes had done much to improve matters. The reviewer of *Victorian Detective Fiction* in *The Times Literary Supplement* for 8 December 1966, cries plaintively: 'We can find no hint, either in Graham Greene's preface or John Carter's introduction, that these early detective stories are worth reading.' As a catalogue pure and simple, and not a *catalogue raisonné* the book does not set out to judge, but in a general way his point is justified, and the brief, broad, belated answer is, 'No, they are not worth bothering about.' That is their fate as literature; there are of course exceptions, and as sources they are mines of constant surprises, but one has only to read a few of these appallingly plotted, abominably written products of the late nineteenth and early twentieth centuries to appreciate the need of a drive for all-round improvement; virtually any book by William Le Queux or Lawrence L. Lynch will do, or, to take a specific example, consider the plot of Richard Marsh's *The Crime and the Criminal* (1897), which hinges on Lady No. 1's being murdered and thrown on a railway embankment a few seconds after Lady No. 2 has accidentally fallen unharmed, down the same bank from a passing train; No. 2's hand is being sought by the father of No. 1, but she prefers No. 1's murderer who has a twin brother employed as private detective by No. 1's father to look for his long-lost daughter; and I should add that an old flame of No. 2 was alone in the carriage with her when she fell out . . .

Potting plots is a dangerous practice, however; a depressing number of Golden Age stories would not survive the process any better than *The Crime and the Criminal*, and as for lax writing what could be worse then Louis Tracy's *The Park Lane Mystery*, written in 1924, in which the hero's name suddenly changes from Richard to Alec and the time of the murder from two o'clock to three o'clock, coupled with a chapter entitled 'How

Simpson Died' when the book contains no Simpson, dead or alive ? Perhaps most amazing of all is the fact that Steinbrunner's *Encyclopedia of Mystery and Detection* (1976) describes this as one of Tracy's best books. Nevertheless, the Golden Age did make a commendable effort to combat the glaring coincidences of plots like Marsh's and the generally poor quality of earlier efforts, even to the extent of producing rules governing the writing of detective stories, which is in itself an indication of the depth of the problem. It is sometimes urged that these rules had a stultifying effect, but as the best stories took a delight in breaking them, I am not convinced of the force of this argument. It seems to me rather that there was, generally, an improvement, but that it was an improvement in the techniques of disguising improbabilities, not their banishment, a point to be taken up later.

Some protagonists of detective fiction wished, however, to press its claims beyond its advantages as a sounder-plotted change from other fiction to its establishment as supreme within popular fiction and deserving of critical consideration within fiction as a whole. This was a tall order, partly because it accorded ill with the open attempts at isolation, and partly because to achieve these objects they would have to overcome a background, and the stigma that went with it, of three-quarters of a century in the second class or below. The priority, therefore, was somehow or other to disguise detective fiction's connections with the sensational, and here they felt they had a trump card in the intellectual appeal of what they were writing —the belief, as Freeman put it, that 'the distinctive quality of a detective story, in which it differs from all other types of fiction, is that the satisfaction that it offers to the reader is primarily an intellectual satisfaction'. 'Intellect' was the magic word that opened all doors for detective fiction and answered or pre-empted all criticism. Detective fiction, we learn, is not a game, but (world of difference) an intellectual game; to read it is not just respectable, but intellectually respectable. The word was used on every unnecessary occasion to such good effect that today we still accept it as a valid though unfashionably snobbish description of an antiquated genre, whereas the facts indicate that this was the last word that should have been applied to the genre.

One justification for the use of the word was that detective fiction appealed principally to 'men of the definitely intellectual class: theologians, scholars, lawyers . . . they are all men of a subtle type of mind.' And Freeman—one could have guessed it was Freeman—goes on, in echo of Poe: 'The disputant enjoys the mental exercise, just as a muscular man enjoys particular kinds of physical exertion.' One wonders what the reaction of these intellectuals was to Freeman's demonstration a little later in this article of how easily he fooled them. Perhaps they enjoyed that more than the supposed mental exercise; it is certainly more substantial. Yet Freeman was far from alone in his belief. So many others made the same point that the contention, whether true or not, has come to be accepted as fact. As recently as 1961, the publishers, Messrs. Collins thought it worthwhile to hold a Dons' Detective Story Competition; and when in 1930 Dorothy Sayers, writing on 'The Present Status of the Mystery Story' in the *London Mercury*, is found regretting that detective fiction is not read in back-kitchens but 'in bishop's palaces and in the libraries of eminent scientists' and as a result 'is in danger of losing touch with the common man, and becoming a caviare banquet for the cultured', we may take it that at least some intellectuals themselves believed in the intellectual qualities of these stories. The argument seems to be that since men devoted to intellectual pursuits enjoy detective stories, these stories must appeal to them on intellectual grounds; they do not read them as escape literature (that has overtones of the sensational at odds with the intellectual), but as a sort of busman's holiday. It is the up-dating of Poe's analyst deriving pleasure from the most trivial occupations—an unfortunate choice of adjective by Poe, but Barzun is not to be deterred as is clear from his formulation of the idea in 1971:

The genre has been the preserve of the intellectual and the cultivated, and not so much for relaxation in the ordinary sense as for the stimulation, in a different setting, of the same critical and imaginative powers that these persons display in their vocations.[4]

In 'The Decline and Fall of the Detective Story', however, W. S. Maugham disagrees on the bare fact of Barzun's claim: '. . . these clever books, which are read by everybody, high-brows, middle-brows and low-brows'. If Maugham is right, then Dorothy Sayers' pessimism was unjustified. Perhaps these books were being read in back-kitchens. But if they were not, one possible reason is that the scullery maid was put off by the propaganda about the genre's intellectual nature which does not exist in the true sense of the word but is a piece of camouflage, partly unfolded by Maugham as an attempt by writers 'to show the supercilious that they can be as learned as any Fellow of the Royal Society of Literature'.

Moving from readership to content we find the intellectual claims of detective fiction repeated. The genre dealt with intellectual topics such as scientific investigation, logical argument, deduction, hypotheses and so on, hence it was believed that reading and writing it were intellectual pursuits. Few might have openly supported Freeman when he wrote that 'the plot of a detective novel is, in effect, an argument conducted under the guise of fiction,' but many acted in accordance with this principle and welcomed its implication that a basis in philosophical-style arguments bestowed superiority on the stories. The argument here seems to be that detection, in fact or in fiction, is a science and what more intellectual and commendable than the scientific method?

And if you come to compare the methods by which the scientist or the philosopher has reached his conclusions, you will find that they are merely those of his favourite detective. Only two methods are open to him, as to them. He may work by the Baconian method of Scotland Yard: he may laboriously and carefully accumulate all possible clues, passing over nothing as too insignificant, filling his little boxes and envelopes with all that comes his way, making no hypotheses, anticipating no conclusions . . . His loot finally collected, he of Scotland Yard will select the 'dominant clue', and that he will follow with grim persistence until the end . . . That is one method. But, if he is of the opposite nature, he will follow the method of 'intuition', upon which the detective bureaus of the country of Descartes have based their work. To him the torn cigarette and the discarded blotter are of little importance . . . Tucked away behind the rose bushes in the garden maze, he devotes himself to thought. Having, like his great predecessor, thought away all else in the universe, nothing remains but the culprit. By strength of logic alone, he has reconstituted the universe, and in his proper place has set the villain of the piece.[5]

The bantering tone of this 1929 explication is typical of the style of many Golden Age apologists, but it should not be taken as indicating underlying disbelief by the writer, as a study of this article by Marjorie Nicolson makes clear.

In all the arguments for the intellectual appeal of detective fiction there seems to be an unwarranted jump in reasoning from, for example, scientific content or elevated readership to a value judgement that fiction with such characteristics is itself necessarily intellectual and, a giant leap here, necessarily good. Beyond this is the more general point that throughout there is confusion between using one's reason both to create and to solve a problem, and using it to wrestle with a problem which may or may not have an answer. The first process has its merits, particularly on the part of the composer, and it may be a mentally stimulating exercise for both author and reader, but it is questionable whether it qualifies for the description 'intellectual' in the way that the second, more productive process does. The appeal of a detective story is more to the reader's curiosity than to his intellect, and if the Golden Age had confined its case to having produced intelligent and intelligible stories, this would have been more easily accepted, but there was this gentle but crucial slip from intelligent to intellectual, which are, despite appearances, two different kettles. But whether the description is appropriate or not, there remains the problem that many of the features on which the intellectual claims are based—the scientific methods of detection, the reasoned arguments, the application of logic, the analysis of problems—resolve themselves on closer inspection into the confused and confusing jargon of pseudo-science, mixed with a liberal dash of tongue-in-cheek sophistry.

86

Or, to put it more bluntly, it's all hokum; very enjoyable when done well, but none the less hokum.

I do not mean by this simply what Routley in *The Puritan Pleasures of the Detective Story* calls the 'harmless humbug' in the Holmes' stories—the erroneous assertions about the tyre marks in 'The Solitary Cyclist', for example, where the true scientist would, one hopes, have conducted some literal ground research. The instantaneous deduction is part of Holmes' appeal and as Routley says, 'it looks pedantic to refer to [the humbug] at all, and most readers hardly notice it.' This is because it is instantaneous. One is in and out of the revolving door of Holmes' reasoning in a flash and crying 'Wonderful!' with Watson, with never a thought for valid arguments. With Freeman on the other hand, one gets stuck in the door and subjected to a dissertation. In *The Red Thumb Mark* (1907), for instance, in a passage deliberately aimed at deflating the Holmesian system, Freeman has Thorndyke claim, 'after the fashion of the inspired detective of the romances', that a passer-by is a stationmaster. This proves correct, as the faithful Polton happens to know the man. (So faithful is Polton that one suspects he would have known the man to be whatever Thorndyke had said, but that is another matter.) But, says Thorndyke, 'I happen to be right . . . but I might as easily have been wrong,' and he launches forth into a lecture on the anatomy and causes of fallen arches and kindred topics on which he based his deduction, concluding, 'All that the observed facts justify us in inferring is that this man is engaged in some mode of life that necessitates a good deal of standing; the rest is mere guess-work.' It is all correct, of course, but is it story-telling? We provincials prefer the humbug, as Freeman himself sorrowfully admits a few lines later: 'a fortunate guess brings more credit than a piece of sound reasoning with a less striking result.'

The distinction—and confusion—between deduction and induction to which Freeman was drawing attention has long caused twinges of conscience in authors and commentators alike, and is an issue where the humbug, while still harmless, tends towards the more accurate Victorian description of it as 'spurious profundity'.

In a rare Teutonic excursion into the genre, *Sherlock Holmes, Raffles und Ihre Vorbilder* (1914), Friedrich Depken brings up the distinction.:

> Incidentally, the term 'deduction', in the case of Poe and Doyle, is intended to mean no more than the inference of a cause from an effect, and not always the deduction of something particular gleaned from the general. If we wished to apply the philosophical *termini technici*, we would be considering, in most cases, inductive conclusions by detectives.

It is unlikely that Depken was the first to notice this and he was far from the last. Barzun adverts to it in *A Catalogue of Crime* under 'Miscellaneous Information':

> DEDUCTION. Conan Doyle popularized the mistake by asking Watson what he *deduced*. Properly speaking, a deduction merely draws out an instance from a generality; if the sum of the angles of any triangle is 180° and this before us is a triangle, we deduce that its angles will equal 180°. Far different is the leap in thought by which Sherlock Holmes *inferred* that Jabez Wilson had been in China from seeing some peculiar tattooing on his arm. As a carping critic could point out, the tattooing might have been done in London by a transplanted Chinese craftsman. Unlike a deduction, an inference is always chancy until buttressed by several other converging inferences; and even then the conclusion only acquires a higher degree of probability, not certainty.

In their closing sentence above the authors are careful to use 'conclusion' and not 'deduction', but the latter term can be applied to Holmes' reasoning in a perfectly legitimate sense. He, too, is drawing out an inference—Wilson has been in China—from a generalisation—tattooing of this kind is done only in China. His trouble is that he established his generalisation by induction which is the preocess of arriving at a general rule or law from the observation of at least one, but preferably several, particular instances, and which, as Barzun says, is a chancy process. The similarity and difference between the examples from geometry and from Holmes can be seen more clearly if they are set out as syllogisms:

The angles of any triangle add up to 180°
This is a triangle
Its angles add up to 180°

All tattooing of this kind is done in China
This is an example of such tattooing
This example was done in China

The syllogism can also be used for particular cases:

The angles of any triangle add up to 180°
This is a triangle, of which one angle is 50° and a second 60°
Therefore the third angle is 70°

All tattooing of this kind is done in China
This on Wilson's arm is an example of such tattooing
Therefore this tattooing was done on Wilson in China, or, as
Holmes put it, Wilson has been in China.

Both arguments follow the same pattern and both are *logically*
valid, but while we accept the triangle one as necessarily true,
almost self-evident, we are entitled to reject the tattooing one
because its premiss that tattooing of this kind is done only in
China is open to question. Barzun and Taylor mention one
alternative explanation and it is not difficult to think of others,
for example, that it is also done in Peru, a fact of which Holmes,
unlikely as it may seem, was unaware. Holmes' argument is
really based on the premiss: 'All instances of this tattooing that
I have encountered have been done in China.' Put thus, the
weakness of his case is clear. But he is still making a deduction.

Deductions which are both valid in logic and true in fact are
largely confined to mathematics where the premiss can be
proved incontestably, and beginning with Aristotle purists have
tended to reserve the word for nice, solid pieces of reasoning
with irrefutable premisses. This has given deduction an almost
emotive connotation; one hesitates to dissent from a conclusion
that is described as a deduction; deductions, we recall from
somewhere, are cast-iron. The value of this in detective fiction
is obvious. Holmes is given to saying that there may be explanations other than his, but never for a moment do we give credence
to such humility, and it is in this loaded sense rather than in
deliberate misuse that the hokum comes in.

Some deductions by detectives are so wide a leap that they are not easily reducible to the pattern of inductive reasoning, let alone the formal pattern of the syllogism. One such might be Dupin's 'legitimate' and 'sole proper' deduction that because one of the voices heard on the stairs of the house in the Rue Morgue could not be ascribed to a major European language, it must have been an animal's voice. Africans and Asiatics, we are told, are scarce in Paris; scarcer than orang-outangs? A better description of Dupin's reasoning here would be intuitive, though Poe would object strongly because for him intuition is no more than 'the conviction arising from those inductions and deductions of which the processes are so shadowy as to escape our consciousness, elude our reason or defy our capacity of expression'. As Depken points out, however, these assertions by Poe in 'The Murders in the Rue Morgue' are only one theory as to how our minds work, and he adds:

> In the main, the proofs contain nothing conclusive or positively convincing; various other arguments would correspond just as well with the observed facts. Thus when the results obtained are always the correct ones, this can only be ascribed to an intuitive comprehension of the true circumstances.

Depken's ideas here about intuitive comprehension may be correct in terms of psychology, but as far as his remarks apply to detective fiction, there is a much more obvious and tempting explanation of the fact that detectives always get it right.

This is simply that they are the correct ones because the author wills it so. As J. C. Masterman says in *The Case of the Four Friends* (1957), 'The story-teller is like God. He knows what has happened, and furthermore he knows the motives and the reasons which caused his characters to act as they did. Nothing is hidden from him, but he releases to his audience only such facts as seem good to him, and at the time which he judges to be appropriate.' The God-like situation of the novelist is a commonplace, but it is particularly relevant to a detective story, the argumentative nature of which demands that everything must be explained and accounted for—or at least ought to be. The difficulty of achieving complete and, for preference, simple dénouements is a major problem for detective story writers, and this difficulty is perhaps one reason for there being so few of those ideal ones postulated by Cecil Chesterton. But it is only fair to point out that the author has on his side a weighty box of tricks, the over-use of which could explain why there are so many less than ideal specimens of the genre. The trick on top of the box is circumstantial evidence and its malleability, coupled with the author's reliance on the type of reader described in John Dickson Carr's *The Eight of Swords* (1934): 'Get to the point,' a character tells Dr. Fell, '. . . Tell us why you thought the girl was guilty. We don't want these characterisations. Not in a detective story, anyhow. The public will only glance at this chapter, to make sure it hasn't been cheated by having evidence with-held . . .' The quality of the evidence, in other words, is not crucial.

An example may help to illustrate this point. In *The Poisoned Chocolates Case* (1929) Anthony Berkeley took his short story 'The Avenging Chance' and extended it into a full-length novel intended as a parody of the Detection Club of which he was the first secretary. In the novel he causes each member of his Crimes Club to investigate, in his or her own style, the murder of a lady by poisoned chocolates. Each comes up with what appears to be a cast-iron case, only to have it demolished, but—and this is the point—any one of these solutions could have been made the final 'correct' one if the author had so wished it; Berkeley even proposes at one stage the solution as given in his short story and promptly invalidates it!

It is the same with almost any 'who did it' type of detective story, if we care to break it down. 'The reader is happy', claims the *Nation* in 1912, as long as 'the chain of causation is kept logically perfect', but this idea of watertight solutions and inevitable dénouements is simply another aspect of the futility of applying science to literature. Berkeley himself gives the game away in a moment of cynical introspection:

> . . . given time [says his detective novelist in *The Poisoned Chocolates Case*] I'm quite prepared to prove to you just as convincingly that the person who really sent [the chocolates] was

the Archbishop of Canterbury, or Sybil Thorndyke, or Mrs. Robinson-Smythe of The Laurels, Acacia Road, Upper Tooting, or the President of the United States, or anybody else in this world you like to name.

So much for proof . . . I told you nothing but the truth. But I didn't tell you the whole truth. Artistic proof is, like artistic anything else, simply a matter of selection. If you know what to put in and what to leave out you can prove anything you like, quite conclusively. I do it in every book I write.

But Poe had given the game away almost as soon as he had unknowingly invented it, in a now famous letter to Philip Cooke in 1846:

You are right about the hair-splitting of my French friend: that is all done for effect. These tales of ratiocination owe most of their popularity to being something in a new key. I do not mean to say that they are not ingenious — but people think them more ingenious than they are — on account of their method and *air* of method. In the 'Murders in the Rue Morgue', for instance, where is the ingenuity of unravelling a web which you yourself (the author) have woven for the express purpose of unravelling. The reader is made to confound the ingenuity of the supposititious Dupin with that of the writer of the story.

It was his own admissions that the *Saturday Review* used against Poe and others in its regular comments on the vicissitudes of circumstantial evidence, for example on 22 February 1868 in an article entitled 'Amateur Detectives' devoted to the mysterious disappearance of a Mr. Speke which caused much speculation at the time:

The excitement produced by Mr. Speke's disappearance has illustrated some odd peculiarities of popular thought. It is only natural that . . . every one, wise and foolish, should have some pet theory to establish . . . Until the mystery is cleared up . . . we cannot determine who has had the merit or the good fortune of having made the best guess. But both the acute and foolish guessers make an assumption which is worth a passing notice, because it is common in inquiries of wider interest than that of poor Mr. Speke's fate. It is an assumption the truth of which is generally accepted in constructing the well-known detective of fiction . . . You allow him a few scraps of clothing, a lost hat, or the marks of a pair of shoes, and he constructs a theory, by a process generally described as an 'inexorable induction', which infallibly identifies the murderer. Given any fragment of the universe, it has been said, and a person of sufficient knowledge and ability might construct all the rest. Let a man of really acute mind have the most trifling foundation to work upon, and he will erect a superstructure of reasoning which may lead him anywhere . . . It is easy enough to show that the doctrine, even in a less exaggerated form, is absurd, and that there must really exist in the ordinary circumstances of life what a mathematician would call indeterminate problems. In fact, it is scarcely possible to find any set of data which, rigidly speaking, are compatible with the truth of one, and only one, hypothesis. As a rule, an indefinite number would fulfil the conditions of the case, although some one may have sufficient probabilities in its favour to justify us in sentencing someone to be hanged.

So much for the *Saturday's* opinion of Holmes' claim-to-be that 'from a drop of water a logician could infer the possibility of an Atlantis or a Niagara without having seen or heard of one or the other'. The *Saturday* obviously preferred to believe in the difficulty of conveying the idea of the ocean to the frog at the bottom of the well. Others have used critiques similar to the *Saturday's* to consign detective fiction to its doom on grounds of logic. The logic is impeccable, but the consignment has never reached its destination. We should be grateful that logic is an influence to which literature is rarely susceptible. Those who enjoy detective fiction, however, should be thankful that one man's wish to confound and another man's willingness to be confounded proved stronger than what Poe and intellect tell us is the true state of affairs, or, to put it less alluringly, that most of us are like Hardy's loungers in *Desperate Remedies*: 'Immediately circumstantial evidence became exchanged for direct, the loungers in court yawned, gave a final survey, and turned away to a subject which would afford more scope for speculation.'

It is in fact a pleasing paradox that detective plots, which could not exist but for the fact that a given set of circumstances is capable of several interpretations, are invalidated the moment an author settles for a particular one, other interpretations having been supposedly shown to be flawed. But there is no such thing as blocking off what Edmund Crispin has called the alternative explanation; there is only varying ability in authors to persuade readers that this has been done. The author himself supplies us with a possible alternative explanation each time he builds a case against a suspect. Any one of these, or another one, could be rendered 'valid' if he so wished.

This is not to carp at the so-called infallible deductions of the Great Detective. As with the more practically demonstrable falsity of Holmes' claim about tyre impressions, these logically unsound deductions are still enjoyable. It would be pointless to campaign about misapplication of the term 'deduction' since it has so embedded itself in the language in its loose sense that, whatever its philosophical usage, it is now correctly used as far as everyday speech is concerned. When one comes across the occasional use of 'induction' in a tale, it tends to grate, though in the aforementioned *Poisoned Chocolates Case* Berkeley makes much ado about deductive and inductive methods of detective reasoning, and anyone who has survived the foregoing treatise and is panting for more is recommended to this book for total but enjoyable confusion. At the same time I should add that the introspection betrayed in those comments by Carr and Berkeley proved, as we shall see later, the greatest obstacle of all to the aspirations of detective fiction.

More hokum at the superficial level can be seen in the fake erudition of the glib formula ('when you have eliminated the impossible, whatever remains, *however improbable*, must be the truth') and the high-sounding phraseology ('Ellery had not yet at that time crystallised his famous analytico-deductive method'). But the hokum goes deeper than this, biting into what were considered, and to a certain extent still are considered, unique and distinctive features of the genre, and revealed usually, not by its enemies, but by its friends. To illustrate this I do not think I can improve on Régis Messac at the end of *Le 'detective novel' et l'influence de la pensée scientifique*. This is an elaborate study, to the tune of nearly 700 pages, of detective fiction in general and an enquiry into its relationship with science in the broad sense of the word to include logic, philosophy, and mathematics as well as the natural sciences. The relevant part of his conclusions from this exhaustive investigation follows. I would, however, first ask the reader to bear in mind that this was written in 1929, the same year as Marjorie Nicolson wrote the passage about Bacon and Descartes quoted a few pages back; the relevance of this injunction will become only too apparent as Messac unfolds. But in fairness to both sides I must also mention Barzun's warning in 'Not "Whodunit?" But "How?" ': 'There is valuable matter in Régis Messac's big book . . . but it will lead you into damnable heresies until you are absolutely sure that you can tell a Holmes from a Hawkshaw.' Now for Messac:

> The detective novel, the real one (and not the penny dreadful with which it is too often confused) is aimed above all at the intelligence; and this could constitute for it a title to nobility. It is in any case perhaps one of the reasons for the favour it enjoys. A good detective story possesses certain qualities of harmony, internal organisation and balance, which respond to certain needs of the spirit, needs which some modern literature, priding itself on being superior, very often neglects in order to indulge in orgies of sentimentality or eroticism. After reading some of them it is almost a relief to follow step by step the pedestrian muse of a Dr. Watson.

> It is in this, and through some other rather loose links, that the detective novel joins with scientific thought. Having already examined this question in detail in connection with Poe, it would be superfluous to go over it again at length. Let us remember only that, like other kinds of scientific literature, the detective novel meets with increasing difficulties in trying to assimilate what there is of specific truth in science . . . The modern detective novel . . . seems a toy by the side of the structures raised by true scientific reasoning. When Rouletabille, in *The Mystery of the Yellow Room*, warns Larsan 'not to set reason on its end', that is to say, not to twist the facts to fit his system, his remarks can be compared with these words of Bacon: 'He (Aristotle) did not consult experience before arriving at correct propositions and axioms, but once he had established his system to his liking, he forcibly twisted experience round his system'. The comparison may seem to flatter Rouletabille, until one remembers that the

comparison straddles several centuries. Rouletabille and his like can only be paralleled with those who represent the infancy of scientific thought.

A large number of authors have tried to ameliorate this fault by increasing the occasions where the applications of science can play a part in the detective story. There are flying detectives, radio-detectives, detectives who are chemists or doctors — a common enough presentation (Sherlock Holmes, himself, for one) — surrounded by retorts and test tubes and evil-smelling liquids. Then there is the other approach whereby a rather puerile comparison is drawn between the researcher and the detective who searches for the criminal in the same way that a philosopher seeks to find the truth in nature. Dare I suggest that these techniques and parallels seem superficial and even disquieting. The mechanical applications of science are not all there is to science. They do not contain even for those who use them more than an infinitesimal portion of the scientific spirit. A man can make daily use of the most perfect of motor cars and yet carry in his head only the most primitive, the most barbarous and even the most anti-scientific ideas imaginable. Moreover, detective novelists, often badly informed, frequently select the most venturesome and least proven results of scientific research; there is almost always a tendency to confuse science with pseudo-science; the most outlandish and debatable theories in medicine, psychology and psychiatry are always the most attractive, and usually when these authors believe they are coming closest to science they are in fact moving further away from it; they are never further from the true spirit of science than when they strive to adapt to the demands of their framework the aphorisms of Bacon.

So much for the intellectual aspirations of detective fiction in the direction of science. In the light of Messac's reluctantly unfavourable conclusions and of Barzun's warning about him, the comment of the dual authors of *A Catalogue of Crime* about the Frenchman's book is equivocal:

> [It] does not miss a trick. If, after reading it, anyone disbelieves in the influence of scientific habits of thought (or *thought clichés*?) on fiction at large and detection in particular, he ought to start reading again on p. 1. But note that the discussion stops with Sherlock Holmes and the nineties: no attention paid to the English renaissance of the twentieth century (my italics).

Notice, too, that when Messac commends detective fiction it is in terms of its appeal to the intelligence, not the intellect, and if that distinction is too fine, note that the specific points which he mentions—harmony, organisation and so on—are points of literary technique and artistry. These may be true indications of intellectual achievement, but they are, as Freeman was aware but chose to ignore, the criteria of fiction in general to which a detective story ought to aspire, but which it does not possess automatically and for which there can be no substitutes.

One moral from Messac's words is that the more technical and science-biassed a plot, the less chance it has of retaining any permanent appeal. This helps to explain the survival, long after she ought theoretically to have gone out of fashion, of Agatha Christie; her great asset was her simplicity of approach. Short of quoting Messac in full it is not possible to give chapter and verse for his conclusions, but examples of what he is getting at spring readily to mind. Messac himself in a note mentions Arthur B. Reeve whose books about the exploits of Craig Kennedy, Scientific Detective, had an enormous vogue in the United States around the time of World War I. The gadgetry deployed in these stories must have been impressive at the time. For example, in *Guy Garrick* (1914), whose eponymous detective is less well-known than Kennedy, Reeve introduces us to rayographs, sphygmographs, liquid bullets, anaesthetic shells, stupefying guns, optophones and detectaphones. Where these devices have become commonplace today—and to give Reeve his due most of them have, though under other names— their presence in the story, usually loudly proclaimed, gives it a *passé* air. Where a device mentioned has remained un-developed it illustrates Messac's point about reliance on unconfirmed research. Dorothy Sayers, in 'The Present State of the Mystery Story' (1930), bears out Messac's argument when she suggests that Freeman has a preference for 'the more recondite mysteries of twentieth century science'. Nor, ap-parently, was she impressed by those writers who 'have fled to the study of morbid mental conditions', giving as an example Van Dine's *The Bishop Murder Case* (1929), which she does not refer to by name but by the discouraging description of it as a novel turning 'upon criminal obsessions produced by the suppressed emotional complexes accompanying the intensive study of relativist mathematics'. The ultimate in the application of psychology to detective stories is perhaps C. Daly King's series with the word 'obelist' in each title—*Obelists At Sea* (1933) and *Obelists En Route* (1934), to name two; an obelist, we are informed, is a person who harbours suspicions, and in the latter book there are four psychologists of different persuasions to whose theories we are treated at length, plus a seminar on Social Credit, plus seven diagrams and a clue finder. Sayers herself was not averse to the odd excursion into the recondite, witness the air-in-the-blood method of murder in *Unnatural Death* (1927), but three years later she was again lining up with Messac and taking a swipe at popular science:

> All these get-clever-quick articles and sixpenny text books [complains a scientist in *The Documents in the Case* (1930)]. Before one has time to verify an experiment, they're all at you, shrieking to have it formulated into a theory . . . If anybody says there are vitamins in tomatoes, they rush out with a tomato theory. If somebody says that gamma-rays are found to have an action on cancer cells in mice, they proclaim gamma-rays as a cure-all for everything from old age to a cold in the head. And if anyone goes quietly away in a corner to experiment with high voltage electric currents, they start a lot of ill-informed rubbish about splitting the atom.

None of which, *mutatis mutandis*, is irrelevant to the present. It does not really matter that Messac stopped at Holmes.

A consideration of one manifestation of detective fiction's alleged superiority not dealt with in detail by Messac may help to dissipate any lingering doubts about the humbug surrounding the genre, namely that much-vaunted aspect, the rule of fair play. This even has a scientific-sounding title: the postulate of deducibility, which ought to make us immediately suspicious. It was in this rule, however, that detective fiction was held to score heavily—and intellectually—over sensation fiction, for the reader was now being presented not just with a mystery which might or might not be satisfactorily explained, but with a problem which, if the author played fair (and woe betide the one who did not), the reader could solve for himself or try to do so, in the same way as a scientist or philosopher.

This concept of it as a game played to rules was for many *the* great contribution of the new detective fiction of the twenties, and was the essential feature which gave the genre its intellectual appeal. Fair play was the first of W. H. Wright's set of twenty rules: 'The reader must have equal opportunity with the detective for solving the mystery. All clues must be plainly stated and described.'[6] It is inherent in all Knox's ten; it was one of the oaths administered to candidates for the Detection Club: 'Do you solemnly swear never to conceal a vital clue from the reader?'[7] (Another of the oaths, that to honour the King's English, might be thought more important, as more often broken.) These formulations of the rule were anticipated by a year or so by T. S. Eliot who propounded a set of 'Do's and Dont's' in the review pages of the *New Criterion* for January 1927, the second of which includes the wish that 'in the ideal detective story we should feel that we have a sporting chance to solve the mystery ourselves'. Even Eliot was pre-empted in a way by G. K. Chesterton in his introduction to W. S. Masterman's *The Wrong Letter* (1926). Chesterton may have regretted this undertaking, for the best he can do by way of eulogy is a list of the ways in which the author does *not* offend etiquette— he does not indulge in master criminals, he does not conjure up the long-lost twin and so on. But conspicuous by its absence is the claim that Masterman has not witheld anything from the reader; on the contrary, we are treated to the following from Chesterton: 'and tortures shall not [make me] reveal the precise point in this story at which a person whom I had really regarded as figuring in one legitimate capacity suddenly began to figure in another, which was far from legitimate.' That last phrase, one suspects, describes less the changed role of the character in question than Chesterton's opinion of the change itself.

But twenty years earlier, in 1906, Cecil Chesterton had mooted the idea of the need for a feature at least akin to the fair-play rule, using *The Moonstone* to illustrate his point, and so perhaps starting the campaign for that novel's admission, willy-nilly, into the select ranks of detective fiction:

> In an ideal detective story all the clues to the true solution ought to be there from the first, but so overlaid as to pass unnoticed. If anyone wishes to see how this can be done, let him read attentively the first two or three chapters of *The Moonstone*, wherein for example, the all-important conversation between Franklyn Blake and the doctor is given at length, but in such a context as to appear a mere incident designed to throw light on a phase of Franklyn's temperament.

Indeed, the rule in broad terms can be traced back well into the nineteenth century. *The Times* was drawing attention to it when it noted, as we saw in the last chapter, how sensation novelists 'present a real clue and a pseudo, and tempt the reader on to follow the pseudo clue'. Again, here is the *Saturday Review* writing on 'Criminal Romance' in 1889:

> . . . in one sense the best criminal romance belongs to the highest order of fiction. It demands infinite care and intense conscientiousness. Robinson Crusoe-like ingenuity and readiness of resource must be brought to the aid of a somewhat perverted and morbid imagination. To win its author celebrity, or even credit, the finished work should be a marvel of constructive skill, with an exquisite adjustment of the details of each part and an all-pervading sense of proportion. Foresight should forestall destructive criticism, and foresight should anticipate all possible objections. The complicated machinery, working smoothly on converging lines, should move steadily and swiftly towards the central point or *dénouement*.

Seen in the *Saturday's* terms of the anticipation of all possible objections, the rule of fair play reveals itself as an over-elaborate extension of a basic principle of plot technique, that if x is going to occur at the end of the story, then the possibility of x's occurrence ought to be mentioned or hinted at earlier in the proceedings; in a word, common sense, difficult to achieve perfectly perhaps, but far from a twentieth-century invention. Within the broad principle of foresight an author is free to manoeuvre as he pleases. That Collins appreciated its value can be seen not only from *The Moonstone*, but from his attempt to persuade Dickens to insert some clues at the beginning of *A Tale of Two Cities*, rather than, as Dickens chose to do, roll 'back bit by bit the terrible story of Dr. Manette without intimating at all clearly its significance or even its nature'.[8]

Common sense it may be, but it was the ignoring of this principle which largely contributed to the proliferation of sensation fiction with too obvious a reliance on coincidence, luck and disguise and overflowing with implausible motives and actions. The remedy took the form of the lists of rules already mentioned, of which the fair-play requirement was the chief.[9] No doubt they seemed a good, even necessary, idea at the time, but by 1941 Howard Haycraft was casting doubt on the value of such specific codifications. Yet when in *Murder for Pleasure* he manages to reduce the rules to two, one is that there should be fair play. (The other is readability—scarcely a unique requirement.) It has been pointed out often enough that, while not worse than the illness, the cure by way of an overdose of formalisation tended to inhibit the development of the detective story of the Golden Age and contributed to its demise by concentrating on the puzzle and, coming to the fair-play rule in particular, by insisting on the possibility of its solution by the reader. The feeling was that it ought to be possible to write detective stories without subscribing to a set of rules, a point to be taken up later.

Nevertheless, for those who enjoy such stories (and I do) there is a very real pleasure to be had from that self-administered kick under the bedclothes which only fair play in talented hands can induce. The improvement brought about by playing fair is not in dispute. What is in question is the description of it at work as intellectual—the belief that the presentation of a puzzle and the information necessary to solve it were elevated and elevating mental activities. That this was in fact the belief can be seen from Anthony Berkeley's introduction to *The Poisoned Chocolates Case*:

All the time one is having a game with the reader-to-be, trying to trick him into thinking evidence is important which has no importance at all, giving him quite fairly the really important evidence but in such a way that he will miss its significance . . . The reason why detective stories are so popular is simple enough. They are, after all, only a glorified puzzle; and everyone enjoys a puzzle. To read a detective story as it should be read is really a test of intelligence; in fact one might say that whereas the ordinary novel appeals only to the emotions, the detective story appeals to the intellect, which surely should be the more important.

Lord Birkenhead, according to Amy Cruse in *After the Victorians* (1938), is said to have described the detective story as a gigantic fraud practised on a credulous public. One hesitates to go as far as that, but it is possible that this particular aspect of detective stories, the postulate of deducibility, is the biggest propaganda trick ever practised on suspecting readers. For that problem is scarcely intellectual the solution of which is rarely attempted except in the most desultory and un-scientific manner. How many people have ever bothered to take the thought and time to try to solve a detective mystery? How many 'read a detective story as it should be read'? If they do solve it, it is by a lucky or inspired guess, based perhaps on the least-likely-person theme or on knowledge of a particular author's methods. I recollect 'solving' Dorothy Sayers' *Whose Body?* for no better reason than that Sir Julian Freke did not like detective stories. And following the guess—and it is amusing how often that word is used by *afficionados* in this connection when the proper term should surely be something like 'successful analytical synthesis'—how many readers can state even the broadest details of how whoever did it did it? So far from taking an active part alongside the detective in the elucidation of the mystery, the reader, I would suggest, reads a detective novel as he would read any popular novel, allowing facts, events and conversations to impinge upon him without thinking long and deeply, if at all, about their meaning, relevance and subtle implications. He is Colonel Carbury in Agatha Christie's *Appointment with Death* (1938) of whom Poirot asks:

'You read the detective stories, yes?'

'Thousands of them', said Colonel Carbury. He added, and his tone was that of a wistful schoolboy. 'I suppose you couldn't do the things the detective does in books? Write a list of significant facts of things that don't seem to mean anything but are really frightfully important — that sort of thing.'

'Ah,' said Poirot kindly. 'You like that kind of detective story? But certainly, I will do it for you with pleasure.' He drew a sheet of paper towards him and wrote quickly and neatly . . . [A list of 'Significant Points' in the case follows.]

The Colonel perused this with great satisfaction.

'Capital!' he said. 'Just the thing! You've made it difficult and seemingly irrelevant — absolutely the authentic touch! . . . I don't get it at all . . .'

The reader may pause for a few seconds, as Colonel Carbury does, and wonder about the possibilities of a specific incident, but this is idle speculation, not deliberate calculation. And just as the reader of a thriller presses on to find out what happens, so the reader of a detective story wants to push on to find out what has happened. Knox's distinction between the two types may be valid enough, but the effect on the reader is the same in both cases: un-put-downable, if the story is a good one; on to the next one after a cheating flip at the last page if the book fails to engage. It does not seem relevant whether the object is to find out what happened or what is going to happen. Given the tediousness, indeed, of some explanations and the far-fetched or disappointing nature of others where the plot as it were blows up in the author's face after perhaps the most engrossing of puzzles (Eden Phillpott's *The Grey Room* (1922) and Lord Ernest Hamilton's *The Four Tragedies of Memworth* (1928) spring to mind here), then there is much to be said for the attitude of the examining magistrate in Gaston Leroux's *The Mystery of the Yellow Room* (1908) who 'was never so pleased as when unable to solve a mystery'. The reader of a detective story may feel the odd twinge of conscience, having been in-doctrinated with the idea of solvability, but he quickly excuses his laziness with the promise to work things out in a minute if

103

the author will just tell him whether . . . but the author will already have told him more than enough.

Statistics will never be available, but I have little doubt that they would show a zero before, and several more after, the decimal point of any percentage figure for readers who have stopped at and seriously tried to take up an Ellery Queen 'Challenge to the Readers' with which he interrupted his early books, claiming, quite truthfully, that the reader now had all the facts needed to solve the case. Queen's first 'challenge' is in his first book, *The Roman Hat Mystery* (1929) and this coincided with Knox's attempt to indicate the 'caesura', as he calls it, in the stories comprising *The Best Detective Stories of the Year 1928*. Baroness Orczy had come close to this every-reader-his-own-sleuth idea in her 'Old Man in the Corner' stories of the first decade of the century. In his *Murder Must Appetize* (1975) H. R. F. Keating mentions that he has come across several detective novels in the London Library annotated by readers, but their comments seem to constitute hole-picking in the plots (a venerable pastime; *The Times* did it to the time schedule in *The Woman in White*), or clue-checking, which indicates activity of a somewhat belated nature, rather than any systematic effort at solution. Keating admits that he himself was not even a clue-checker, and recounts his exhilaration at his sole success in this sport—when he realised that in Dorothy Sayers' *Five Red Herrings* (1931) the colours in an abandoned landscape painting did not correspond with the tubes of oils left with it. Significantly, he does not claim to have solved the whole mystery as a result of this one episode. We readers like to think that we have as much chance as the detective, which makes us all the more susceptible to flattery like Berkeley's and prime for the confidence trick, whereas we are really Dorothy Sayers' terriers—ready to run after what is thrown to us. And while the dog may deserve her epithet 'intelligent', we are really dullards on a par with Watson, as A. A. Milne admits, with more than a grain of truth behind his humour:

> Why I should insist on identifying myself with the detective I do not know. I seem to make no objection to the architect-hero of an

architectural novel knowing more about architecture than I do. Indeed, it seems to me right that he should . . . Indeed, I will admit now that I never was a very good detective; for I know nothing about wines save that I like some of them, and I rarely drive my car at a higher speed than fifty miles per hour. In future I shall identify myself with the Watsons. When I ask questions I ask for information, not because I doubt for a moment that the detective is right.[10]

Discussions abound on the benefits of fair play, on what constitutes fair play, as well as on the problems and disadvantages it brings with it, but few even among detractors of detective fiction query the intellectual nature of the puzzle. The reduction of literature to a puzzle, and the frivolousness of devising and reading such puzzles are the usual bases of criticism, but the reality of the mental exercise for those who indulge as readers is rarely brought up. A noteworthy exception is Harrison Steeves' article 'A Sober Word on the Detective Story' which appeared in *Harper's Magazine* for April 1941. Steeves is far from being a detractor, but his article fully lives up to the promise of its title, not least on this topic:

> . . . the sustained vogue of detective fiction is dependent upon the type of challenge presented in the actual treatment of the unvarying problem. The prevailing view is that it is a challenge to the wits that holds us—patent as the challenge may be. It is a game, a pleasantly and harmlessly agreeable game of solitaire in which human beings take the place of paste-boards or pieces and the problems are problems of human activity. But is that imagined challenge to the intellect any more than imaginary? Does the detective story really rank with the 'intellectual diversions'? For the majority of readers I am inclined to think not. I deeply doubt whether the process of deduction, as it is commonly called (though goodness knows the larger processes of detection are inductive) is followed with the conscience that one brings to chess, or even to contract bridge. We like to imagine the scrupulous 'fan' ticking off point after point of evidence, matching character against character as the most promising suspect, carrying throughout the narrative a complete picture of the interelations of events and characters, always on his caution of course against that final turn of the trick which will both defeat and dazzle the unwary . . . But in stories of this [elaborate] type—

and they are, after all, far the greater part of our modern mystery stories—complication of matter and method go far to defeat themselves. The casual reader tends to accept the fact that the author can, and will, fool him, keeps the events loosely in his mind, and nonchalantly looks back over the path of cause and effect (if it is at all clear) after he has reached the end. The use of the mind hasn't much place in that experience.[11]

Sobering, indeed. Sobering, too, and amusing, the thought that no one would be more disappointed than the reader if he did consistently solve mystery stories; but then there would be no stories.

It should be emphasised that none of the foregoing is directed against the detective story as such. More serious charges can be brought against it which are hinted at in that remark by Steeves that 'the author can, and will, fool' the reader, and which will be considered in due course. For the moment the criticism is only of detective fiction's intellectual aspirations. That there should have been an effort towards respectability was wholly laudable and justifiable as long as the effort confined itself to improvements in technique and style, and campaigned against the atrocious rubbish that was produced in the wake of Holmes; as long as, in other words, it concentrated on itself as literature. But the effort went beyond this and with misplaced enthusiasm based itself on the specious grounds of intellectual appeal, inherent superiority and exclusiveness. In the case of the fair-play rule, for instance, I am not saying of it, as Chandler says of Agatha Christie's *Murder on the Orient Express* (1934), that only a half-wit could guess the solution of these stories, but that, half-witted or otherwise, few try or want to go beyond a guess, and also that the existence of such a rule, however cleverly applied, cannot elevate the genre to an intellectual level. And in the argument from readership, there seems to be another of those leaps of thought from the intellectual callings of some readers to the conclusion that what such people read for pleasure must also be intellectual. As for the scientific-cum-philosophical content and techniques, this is certainly the stuff of which these stories are made, but it is also the source of the liberal ladlings of spoof in them:

The unfinished sentence of which we are tempted to ignore the conclusion; the general principles which are never at hand when wanted; the pseudo-syllogism which invites a false conclusion; the inadequate evidence which is worse than no evidence at all; the statement deliberately confused so that its purport may be missed by the lazy; the false opinion accepted from an incompetent witness: all these are traps for the unwary reader which become, at one remove, clues to the truth when seen for what they are. They exploit those human failings—of ignorance, unreason, carelessness and above all lack of charity—from which the characters, like the rest of us, suffer.

So writes Felix Aylmer in *The Drood Case* (1964). Such morbid seriousness suggests that the classic detective story is best appreciated and left at the level of 'what fun it all was'—and lucky to achieve that. The twenties have been described as the age of the stunt. These stories were literature's contribution to the age. We read them to be fooled, but we must not also be fooled by their pretensions to superiority on grounds of their own making, grounds not applicable to literature in general.

NOTES TO CHAPTER 5

1 Raymond Chandler, 'The Simple Art of Murder' in *The Art of the Mystery Story*, ed. Haycraft (1946), originally *Atlantic Monthly*, December 1944. This was Chandler's response, not wholly unfavourable, to Edmund Wilson's first article in the *New Yorker* (see p. 26).

2 W. H. Wright, 'The Detective Novel', *Scribner's Magazine*, November 1926.

3 R. A. Freeman, 'The Art of the Detective Story' in Haycraft *op. cit.*, originally *Nineteenth Century and After*, May 1924.

4 J. Barzun and W. H. Taylor, *A Catalogue of Crime* (1971). For reason of space, if not accuracy, quotations from this book are attributed to Barzun only.

5 Marjorie Nicolson, 'The Professor and the Detective', originally *Atlantic Monthly*, April 1929 in Haycraft, *op. cit.*

6   S. S. Van Dine (pseudonym of W. H. Wright), 'Twenty Rules for writing Detective Stories' in Haycraft *op. cit.*, originally *American Magazine*, September 1928.

7   'The Detection Club Oath' in Haycraft, *op. cit.*

8   W. C. Phillips, *Dickens, Reade, and Collins: Sensation Novelists* (1919).

9   There was also a spate of books and articles to tell us how to write detective fiction. Carolyn Wells' effort has already been mentioned. Others include Marie F. Rodell's *Mystery Fiction: Theory and Technique* (1954), Nigel Morland's *How to Write Detective Novels* (1936) and there is even one to tell us *How to Enjoy Detective Fiction* (1947) by Gilbert Watson.

10 A. A. Milne, Introduction to *Detection Medley*, ed. Rhode (1939).

11 See also William O. Aydelotte, 'The Detective Story as a Historical Source', in *The Mystery Writer's Art*, ed. Nevins (1970).

6

THE CLOSING OF A DOOR

Such tales . . . have taken, as it would seem, permanent possession of all the lower strata of our light literature . . . [and] all our minor novelists, almost without exception, are of the school called sensational.

Mrs. Oliphant, 'Novels',
Blackwood's Magazine, September 1867

Ironically, there was nothing especially new in the claims of detective fiction. Very similar pretensions were a feature of sensation fiction which Victorian critics were quick to notice and quick to ridicule. The questionable value of building up a puzzle only to knock it down again was one of their recurring complaints about—does one call it sensation fiction or detective fiction? Then there was James' appeal for an index and a note book to help him master the plot of *The Woman in White*, which he pretends to liken to a work of science requiring the same intellectual effort in the reading as Motley or Froude. At this level of gimmickry sensation fiction had its moments. James had obviously not read *The Notting Hill Mystery* (1862) with its tabulations and diagram, and when the thirties produced books like *The Floating Admiral* with a new author for each chapter, it was only elaborating on a suggestion by the *Atlantic Monthly* in 1898 that one writer should start a detective novel and another finish it.[1]

The progress of the classic detective story through this century is in fact a replica or action replay, as television would have it, of the path trodden by sensation in the nineteenth century. The first round in the renewed battle was perhaps

G. K. Chesterton's reproduction of Le Fanu's chestnut about Shakespeare in 'A Defence of Detective Stories': 'It must be confessed that many detective stories are as full of sensational crime as one of Shakespeare's plays.'[2] Then followed what amounts to the same manoeuvres of explanations, justifications, even self-justifications with Freeman's prefaces paralleling Collins', all meeting with condemnation ranging from the nice to the violent, and if ever detective fiction seemed to be getting altogether too big for its boots, the big literary guns could be got out to quash it—Q. D. Leavis on Dorothy Sayers, for example, and Edmund Wilson conducting his personal Pearl Harbour on the whole genre. The overall impression, however, is that the critics' attitude to detective fiction was one of what Dorothy Sayers calls 'lethargic amiability', as if they were willing to extend the truce agreed, if only by implication, with sensation fiction towards the end of the nineteenth century. Discontent within the genre itself provides a telling parallel in the way that Francis Iles (alias Anthony Berkeley, both pseudonyms of A. B. Cox), Raymond Chandler, Dorothy Sayers and after World War II, Julian Symons, amongst many others, queried the route of the classic detective story, albeit each in a different way, and set sensation fiction on other paths, including the path back to the original nineteenth century concept of sensationalism, just as the two Chestertons and Freeman and other enthusiasts for the classic style sought to divert the sensation fiction which they inherited. For these writers were fully aware of the origins of their detective fiction in the Victorian novel of sensation; the change in name did not deceive anyone who did not want to be deceived. It was this unwelcome knowledge that led them into a diverting variety of measures to disencumber themselves of disreputable sensation.

In all the intellectual claims of detective fiction there is ever present the comparison, usually quite explicit, with sensation and melodrama, a comparison in which sensation is always the odious partner. In 'The Art of the Detective Story', Freeman even commits the sin of which he and Cecil Chesterton accused other critics, the sin of indiscriminately applying the depreciatory 'mere' to a whole genre, except that now it is sensation fiction, not detective fiction, on the receiving end: 'A widely prevailing error is that a detective story needs to be highly sensational. It tends to be confused with the mere crime story . . . Now no serious author will complain of the critic's antipathy to mere sensationalism.' It was realised, however, that the purely intellectual detective story, if it existed at all (examples tend to run out after 'The Mystery of Marie Roget'), was less than practicable, if only for bread and butter reasons. Emotion and thrills and drama had to figure, though naturally on intellect's terms. By admitting some sensation H. D. Thomson, in *Masters of Mystery*, manages to make its disparagement all the more telling:

> The main ingredient must be logic. If there is to be sensation . . . it should *seem* rather incidental . . . there is quite enough excitement in a problem without calling in the aid of death, crape and flying squad. The logical detective story is the finer form because it recognises a technique. The highbrow form wins.

In *Murder for Pleasure* we find Haycraft tabulating the genre into the physical or sensational on the one hand and the mental or intellectual on the other, and then playing apothecary to produce the ideal formula which he calls 'the balanced type—the detective story at its best'. This is an elaboration of a division made by Dorothy Sayers in her introduction to *Great Short Stories of Detection* (1928) towards the end of which she enters another of her pessimistic phases, forecasting the eventual demise of the intellectual detective story or its amalgamation into the novel of manners thus 'separating it more widely from the novel of adventure. The latter', she continues 'will, no doubt, last as long as humanity, and while crime exists, the crime thriller will hold its place'. But she cannot resist a Parthian shot: 'It is, as always, the higher type that is threatened with extinction.'

The most subtle method of combining the sensational with the intellectual, while emphasising only the latter, is to talk of mental thrills. An early example of this technique is in the *Nation* in 1912:

Whatever thrills of horror are excited come by way of the intellect, never starting directly in the emotions . . . It is only when one's reason is baffled, leaving the murder unexplained . . . that one feels privileged to shudder. And such a shudder is remarkably different from a start that is unthinking.[3]

In so far as I have suggested that we do not do much thinking when reading a detective story, this argument makes little impression, but it was presented, modified and refurbished at regular intervals in the following years. Here is Barzun's 1944 version from 'Not "Whodunit?" But "How?" '

. . . the shocking contrast between the order of a private life and its untoward interruption is one of the two great feelings generated by detective fiction . . . [it] reaches its acme in the grotesque: the nude corpse of a vagrant is pushed through the window into an irrelevant bathtub ('Whose Body?'). The other emotion grows out of the first and is its resolution: by what process does the bathtub become relevant? . . . It is not the thrill of the chase, nor trembling suspense, nor mere bepuzzlement. It is the thrill of the *Aufklärung*, the passion for demonstration. Just as a good ghost story . . . makes a cold shiver run down the spine, so does a soundly dramatic moment of detection.

That opening sentence, it may be noted in passing, is an excellent description of sensation fiction, but the whole passage is a splendid example of the arbitrary deployment of words at its majestic best, with the reckless sowing of expressions associated with sensation—shocking, feelings, emotion, thrill, passion, shiver, dramatic—which we know are going to bear fruit in any way except Barzun's admission that detective fiction is sensational in the Victorian sense. He is honest enough to deny this outright, and astute enough to work the denial into the middle of the passage quoted above:

. . . the same [shocking] contrast can exist without sudden death and is actually lessened by a surfeit of corpses. Strangeness is sufficient. 'The Red Headed League' is the great example of what I mean, infinitely above 'The Speckled Band', which yields only the vulgar horrors of snakebite. That the sensation of contrast differs from the sensational can be seen, again, in Dermot Morrah's 'Mummy Case Mystery'—a poor title for an enchanting tale of detection without murder.

Barzun's point is well made here, but strangeness and restraint
in the production of bodies, even total abstinence therefrom, if
adequate criteria for the best classic detective stories are also
peculiarly apt criteria for the best Victorian novels-with-a-
secret—Le Fanu's *Uncle Silas* and *Wylder's Hand*, for example,
and Miss Braddon's *Lady Audley's Secret*, not to mention Collins'
The Woman in White and *The Moonstone*, all of which, besides
fulfilling Barzun's criteria, also arouse our 'passion for demonstration'. And to read Mrs. Oliphant writing in *Blackwood's*,
1862, on *The Woman in White* is almost to re-read Barzun:

> The distinguishing feature of Mr. Wilkie Collins' success is, that
> he ignores all these arbitrary sensations, and has boldly under-
> taken to produce effects as startling by the simplest expedients
> of life. It is this which gives to his book the qualities of a new
> beginning in fiction. There is neither murder, nor seduction,
> nor despair—neither startling eccentrics nor fantastic monsters in
> this remarkable story. A much more delicate and subtle power
> inspires its action. We cannot object to the means by which he
> startles and thrills his readers; all the exaggerations of excitement
> are carefully eschewed . . .

The efforts of detective fiction towards respectability and
exclusiveness had repercussions and a degree of success, the
effects of which are with us today. Indeed the effort was so
successful that for a time the term threatened to supplant
'thriller' and 'mystery' and 'crime story' as the global description for what the Victorians called sensation fiction, an achievement in the direction opposite to the one intended. Dorothy
Sayers' opinion of 1936 that 'careful writers now reserve
['Detective Story'] for those stories of crime and detection in
which the interest lies in the setting of a problem and its solution
by logical means' was, as we have seen, replaced in 1944 by a
complaint that 'Even today, few readers and few reviewers
attempt to distinguish accurately between the 'detective story',
which acknowledges the rule [of fair play] and the 'thriller',
which does not.' A few years ago *The Times* held a detective
story competition, the best stories being published in a volume
entitled *The Times Anthology of Detective Stories* (1972). The only

explanation for the use of 'detective' in this context can be the prestige still attaching to it, for many of the stories are remote from detectives, detection, crime and thrills. Similarly, Susan Hill, writing in the *Daily Telegraph* in February 1978 about her discovery of a trunkful of Golden Age detective stories, admits that 'this was a branch of literature I knew next to nothing about' but she has been sufficiently well indoctrinated to add: 'The reading of detective novels has long been *intellectually* respectable' (my italics).

Even those who deny the pre-eminence of detective fiction may admit its segregation. *The Times Literary Supplement* of 23 June 1961 was devoted to 'Crime, Detection and Society', and one of the contributors, Norman Shrapnel, writing on 'The Literature of Violence and Pursuit', advocates the removal of the barrier between crime novels and novels in general, but sees this as 'a formidable demolition job'. He then goes on:

> To add to the complication, before knocking down one wall it would be necessary to build another, between what is usually known as the detective novel, and what is usually known as the thriller. It is curious how indiscriminately these two sorts of writing are lumped together and how the distinction, when it is made, usually dignifies the first at the expense of the second.

The supposed contaminating influence of the sensational is the cause of Murch's pains in *The Development of the Detective Novel* to disassociate detective fiction from the infectious species—unrealistically, as I have suggested, even in the case of Dickens and Collins; and she has this to say of Mrs. Gaskell's 'The Squire's Story' (1853): 'It is a neat little tale of crime and detection, though presented as a social commentary, thus escaping the stigma of "sensationalism" '—as if the two categories of detection and sensation were mutually exclusive. On this approach, Murch is not surprisingly obliged to play down the detective elements in *Lady Audley's Secret*, the sensation novel to end all sensation novels—and, perhaps, to begin all detective novels. Murch's opinion, however, is that 'it contains nothing comparable to the detective theme in Collins's novel [*The Woman in White*] . . . Eventually [Lady Audley] meets retribution through the efforts of a former victim, whose success is due to coincidence and good luck, rather than to any detective skill.' By 'victim' Murch presumably means Robert Audley, who is arguably as much, or as little, or more a detective than Walter Hartright—the reader will shortly be able to decide for himself—but suffice it to say here that Murch is going against the opinions of hard-core Golden Age addicts, including Barzun and Anthony Boucher. In interesting confirmation of my general argument, the latter is on record as saying of Miss Braddon's book, 'Imagine my astonishment to realize that I was reading precisely the same plot and motivation as were contained in a mystery tale I'd read (in a slick magazine) the day before!'[4]

It is only when confronted by the reluctance of the past fifty years, as instanced by Thomson and Murch, to call a spade a spade and sometimes the refusal even to recognise the existence of that excavatory implement, that one can appreciate the courage of Maurice Richardson in asserting in 1945 in his Introduction to *Novels of Mystery from the Victorian Age*:

> In our own over-specialised, disintegrated times, there are the rigid categories of detective story, thriller, and ghost story with several sub-divisions to each: 'who done it', or mystery; spy-story or gangster; sadist or masochist; spook or spirit; but in the last century they could all be lumped together as Tales of Mystery and Imagination.

To test the ice on which any knife-edged boundary between detective fiction and sensation fiction is skating, let us consider one of these 'intellectual' detective stories. Is Dorothy Sayers' *Murder Must Advertise* (1933) a fair choice? I pick it partly because it contains a snide warning to purists against all that was regarded as bad in 'sensational' stories. Wimsey is with his sister, Mary; she speaks first and he replies:

> '...if the telephone rings, take care it isn't the mysterious summons to the lonely warehouse by the river, or the bogus call to Scotland Yard.'
> 'All right. And if the door-bell rings, beware of the disguised gas inspector. I need scarcely warn you against the golden-haired girl in distress, the slit-eyed chink or the distinguished grey-haired man wearing the ribbon of some foreign order.'

But I pick it mainly because at the above point in the story we have already been regaled with dope-smuggling, murder by catapult, murder on the underground, murder by lorry, two assaults, a car race, the attempted seduction of Wimsey and Wimsey himself traipsing around the countryside disguised in a harlequin suit. Perhaps Edgar Wallace would have been a fairer choice, and small wonder that a purist like Barzun specifically excludes *Murder Must Advertise* from his category of *detective* fiction. It is, he says, a *mystery* story. Quite.

Of course Dorothy Sayers goes about it all less 'volcanically', more—isn't the word 'cosily'?—showing her ability, shared oddly enough with Miss Braddon, to 'sufficiently excite the sensations of her readers without the aid of vulgar and nauseous appeals to the purient or the sensuous feelings'.[5] The sensational, in other words, does not have to be violent or sex-orientated; it can, and does, make very pleasurable reading, but it is nonetheless sensational. Granting that chinks and lonely warehouses and so on were overdone in popular fiction of Wimsey's time, granting that the rules effected an improvement and granting even that despite the impression of physical excitement in the plot of this book, Sayers primarily achieves her excitement 'in the problem', there is nothing inherent in this or any other book based on a problem or puzzle which automatically elevates it above the sensational. Excitement, it must be admitted, was the prime mover of sensation writers, as Mansel points out in the *Quarterly* in 1863: 'Excitement, and excitement alone, seems to be the great end at which they aim— an end which must be accomplished at any cost by some means or other, *"si possis, recte; si non, quocunque modo"* '. And if the *modus* is a problem, does this necessarily make the resulting *opus* any the less sensational? There is nothing in Dorothy Sayers' treatment of the subject-matter of *Murder Must Advertise*, despite its presentation wrapping, which warrants its promotion from the 'good-of-its-kind' class of sensation fiction.

The improvements in technique and style achieved by many Golden Age writers, when reduced to essentials, appear as differences of emphasis only within the common ground of the sensational, not differences on fundamentals, as if the two were disparate theologies. But I am now in danger of remounting that roundabout with which we began—the confused situation which Symons is tilting at when, in *Bloody Murder*, he advocates the use of a general term to cover all sensational works. My debt to him is obvious from his statement that 'The truth is that the detective story, along with the police story, the spy story and the thriller, makes up part of the hybrid creature we call sensational literature.' My doubts about Symons' views stem from the suspicion, voiced once by Edmund Crispin,[6] that he is glad the Golden Age has tarnished; I am prevented from sharing his pleasure partly by doubts about the supposed improvements in sensation fiction since the Second World War, but mostly by deliberate blindness caused by a severe dose of nostalgia, also known as Barzun's syndrome. But to shake myself free from the malady—and indulge in one last circuit, it seems that while detective fiction changed the manner in which the common subject matter was handled, it was scarcely in the direction of Dostoievsky; away from the solution by accident, confession or luck, perhaps, but not out of the context of locked rooms, spurious alibis and bodies in bath-tubs, which are and remain sensational however rationally explained. The only tangible and far from consistent advances effected by the twentieth century were more sensible demonstrations, more moments of detection and more interesting detectives, though even here *Murder Must Advertise* contains a disturbing hint at the true state of affairs: ' "Detectives never 'think' anything", replied Mr. Braden [Wimsey undercover], reprovingly. "They collect facts and make deductions—God forgive me!" The last three words were a whispered lip-service to the truth.' But back in 1861, at the outset of the saga of sensation fiction, the *Sixpenny Magazine* seems to have seen through the veneer of respectability and domesticity which marks the more accepted works of both sensation and detective fiction. The following passage is from its review, in 'Literature of the Month', of a forgotten novel, *The Silver Cord* (1861), by Shirley Brooks, who was a better editor of *Punch* than he was a novelist. The review refers to various contemporary writings, but it is not difficult to think of twentieth-century substitutes:

> [This] is eminently a melodramatic novel, and one of the best of its class, that is to say, a superior Adelphi piece . . . where every scene is elaborately put on the stage to produce a thrilling effect, where human nature is systematically brought under the glare of the footlights, and where every dialogue is wrought into a powerful appeal to the shilling gallery.
>
> The composition is, we readily admit, infinitely superior to such productions as *Alone in the World* . . . as superior in every way as 'The Colleen Bawn' . . . is to 'The Midnight Murder', as represented at a penny *gaff* in 'the New Cut'; but we cannot help affirming, though with great reluctance, that this is one of the same manufacture. Unfortunately for the English novel there has long been a demand growing for fictitious excitement, and many of our popular writers, to gratify this, have found it necessary so to exaggerate their characters and incidents, as to invest them more and more with those theatrical characteristics that have been found most to the taste of the popular mind . . . [and] not a few have brought forward villainy and crime about the domestic hearth.

I began by indicating some terminological difficulties in the ideology of the classic detective story, which was diverting, Humpty-Dumpty stuff. More seriously, I suggested that it was not realistic to see detective fiction as leap-frogging across the history of nineteenth-century literature, because on closer scrutiny well-nigh impossible gaps were left in the history of the genre, evident even in a work like *The Development of the Detective Novel*, which purportedly sets out to fill the gaps. It does fill many, but, it seems to me, it cannot do the job properly because of its reluctance, indeed refusal, to use sensation fiction as the starting point and basic ingredient. We saw also how Poe's stories about Dupin and *The Moonstone* are often, and almost to the exclusion of other works of the period, dissected to bring out similarities with later detective fiction. The fair-play motif in *The Moonstone* and the undeniable detective features in Poe have led the twentieth century to see these stories as detective stories in twentieth-century terms; that is, critics have taken the features they see as distinguishing modern detective fiction and looked for these features in earlier works, usually by 'good' or recognised authors, in order to give their detective fiction a pedigree, or, to put it more bluntly, to give their second-rate genre an aura of respectability. *The Moonstone*, backed by Collins' reputation as an author of at least minor classics, is the obvious example. *Bleak House* is manna in the apparent desert. But Miss Braddon's *Lady Audley's Secret* contains as much detection as *The Moonstone* and more similarities with later detective fiction, yet there are no erudite discussions of it. Of course *it* is a second-rate sensation novel . . .

Now that the histories and commentaries have been written against the background and from the viewpoint of the euphoria of the Golden Age, the time may have come for a less anthropomorphic approach. The judging of earlier works in terms of later ones is a perfectly legitimate, sensible and common literary practice, but in the case of detective fiction it seems to have caused the mirror-image, detective fiction, to be treated as the image-giver, and the danger is that we may lose the prey by grasping at the reflection. The histories may have been written forwards in time, but they have worked backwards in precepts. The process ought now to be worked the other way. Instead of taking preconceived ideas about detective fiction as produced in the 1920s and 30s and seeing how earlier works conform to them, we should be taking sensation fiction of Victorian times and comparing detective fiction of the later period with it. I have suggested that there is a preponderance of conformity, but the only way of demonstrating this is to work forward objectively from the past. We might then be able the better to distinguish what is new and what is worthwhile in recent detective fiction. The definitive history of the mystery-mad period between the wars has yet to be written, let alone the history of detective fiction as a whole.

It was implied earlier that this book was about the detective, and it is now time to turn to him, principally in his Victorian incarnation. This will lead, I believe, to an answer to that question about the appearance of the term 'detective fiction' in the 1880s. Moreover, the detective's progress across the pages of sensation fiction will confirm and reinforce my suggestion of the continuity between that kind of fiction and later detective fiction. It should also help to substantiate some at least of what may appear as unsupported assertions in the foregoing chapters. His progress will also show him to have been the life and soul—and death—of the classic detective story.

In considering the literature of the detective, however, let us have no illusion that we are dealing with anything but secondary literature. When Tillotson remarks of *Bleak House* that 'lurking in that great novel are the beginnings of the sensation novel as well as the detective novel', her participle is apposite. With this cautionary reminder, let us go in search of the detective in the murk of Victorian England.

NOTES TO CHAPTER 6

1 'Detective Fiction', *Atlantic Monthly*, April 1898.

2 G. K. Chesterton, *The Defendant* (1901), a series of essays in defence of various things, orginally appearing in the *Speaker*.

3 'Detectiveness in Fiction', *Nation*, 15 August 1912. (Also *verbatim* in Wells, *The Technique of the Mystery Story*, but without acknowledgement or even quotation marks!).

4 Quoted in Norman Donaldson, Introduction to *Lady Audley's Secret* (1974).

5 Review of *Henry Dunbar* (1864), *Saturday Review*, 9 July 1864.

6 See 'Is the Detective Story Dead?' a dialogue between Julian Symons and Edmund Crispin, *The Times Literary Supplement*, 23 June 1961.

Part II

THE DETECTIVE

7
FINE BODY OF MEN

'Hallett, what d'ye think of the detective business?'
'Good enough for them that likes it,' says I . . .
'All right, my ole feller,' says he; 'but how would you like it by way of variety, supposin' it was yourself that took it up for a livin'?'
'Make yourself clear,' says I, a openin' my eyes a little.
'Well,' replied the young man, 'the long and the short of it is this. They've come to the conclusion at Scotland Yard that there ain't quite enough system about the way they're on now for the nabbin' of rascals, and they've concluded to agonise a special force for that intention.'

Charles Martel, The Detective's Note-Book (1861)

The inspiration for the detective of sensation fiction came, not from Poe's imaginary projections of an investigation conducted by an analytic amateur or dilettante, but from the actual police of the time, English and French, those same pedestrian gentlemen so easily outshone at their own trade by Dupin's superior intellect. The paradox of Poe is that he was so prophetic as to write his stories without recourse to the word 'detective', so premature that his version of the incarnation had to incubate for a seemingly inordinate period. It would be an exaggeration to say that no one in the decades following Poe dared postulate, even amid the liberty and licence of sensation fiction, anything so outrageously contrary to the mid-Victorian concept of the order of things as an amateur reasoning machine not only superior to the model supposedly trained for detective work, but actually derisory of the professionals' efforts. An exaggeration, but not a complete untruth, for the Victorians, despite their jokes and jibes at the police's expense and despite their frequent and often justifiable dissatisfaction with the force, were attached to the 'Buckets of the Detective' in their own perverse, contrary fashion. There are various reasons and theories for the acceptance of the Poe-Doyle genus of fictional super-detective, where the genus Poe on its own had been unacceptable, but one factor was the change, between the middle of the century and its end, in the public's attitude towards the detective from one of suspicion and even rejection to one of tolerance and even expectation, tempered always by a realisation of his limitations. This change helped to create the situation in which Holmes could be welcomed, perhaps as the embodiment of the expectation, where previously Dupin had stood no chance.

There are amateurs in fiction before Holmes, occasionally in his private or 'consulting' capacity—Gaboriau's Père Tabaret, for example—but more often genuine amateurs, forced to act on their own because their suspicions are so vague that the police could not help them even if approached or the matter so delicate that they do not wish to approach the police —Robert Audley in *Lady Audley's Secret*, for instance, or David Arden in Le Fanu's *Checkmate* (1871), who 'can't dismiss the suspicion. I can't get it out of my head . . . and yet I can't account for it'. But I do not know of any story in English between Poe and Doyle (though no doubt there is one) in which an amateur is deliberately set by the author to score off the police, Dupin-fashion, though there are cases of official detectives scoring off their kin, as with Cuff and Seegrave in *The Moonstone* and Gorby versus Kilsip in Fergus Hume's *The Mystery of a Hansom Cab* (1886). Indeed, in Collins' short story, 'The Biter Bit', we have the reverse of what was to become the norm for many years after Holmes, with Scotland Yard besting the amateur or, rather, would-be professional, Matthew Sharpin. The only amateur who begins to shape like Dupin is Tabaret in Gaboriau's *L'Affaire Lerouge* (1866) with his demolition by deduction of the celebrated Gevrol, chief of the French detective police, but even then Gaboriau made quick amends to authority by creating in his subsequent tales a successful police detective in Lecoq.

Sensation fiction thus has a preponderance of professional detectives, based with varying degrees of firmness on fact, and an outline of the real-life detective of Victorian Britain is an almost indispensable background to the development of his fictional counterpart. I say Victorian Britain, but Victorian London would be more accurate as the history of detection in this country hinges on the history of the detectives of the Metropolitan Police, beginning with the occupation in the summer of 1842 of three modest rooms at Old Scotland Yard by a squad totalling an equally modest eight.

No trumpet blast heralded the setting up of this separate detective office. Its size scarcely warranted one—two inspectors and six sergeants out of a total of some 4,000 in the Metropolitan Police as a whole. Moreover its creators probably did not want one. The formation of the New Police thirteen years before at the instigation of Peel had been and still was attended by sufficient and sometimes violent accusations about 'private armies' and 'spies' for the authorities to be quite content to allow this new department, with its even more obvious overtones of espionage, to slide into existence via the back door rather than see it enter with fanfare at the front. How far the Home secretary, Sir James Graham, and the two Commissioners, Charles Rowan and Richard Mayne, were guilty of a deliberate conspiracy of silence is open to doubt, but if they were, the reserve of the sizeable press normally hostile to the police at the least excuse indicates the extent of their success. The reticence in both camps may also be partly accounted for by the fact that the Commissioners were simply formalising a situation already in existence for a number of years, namely, the presence in the Divisions of men who acted as detectives when necessary, the period, as George Dilnot calls it in *The Story of Scotland Yard* (1926), of 'detection without detectives'. Another reason for the apparently painless birth of the detective office was that the immediate cause of its creation was a series of events highlighting the need for an improvement of the detective qualities of the police. The first of these was the Good case of April 1842 which cast serious doubt on the ability of the police to trace even a known criminal; a month later came the Cooper case in which Cooper, known to the police as violent, was tackled separately in heroic but perhaps needless self-sacrifice by two policemen and a civilian, Cooper killing one policeman and seriously injuring the other two. Finally, there was the attempt on the life of the Queen by John Francis on 30 May, an attempt of which the police had been forewarned, but an occasion on which a certain P.C. Trounce, having watched the suspicious behaviour of Francis was, even so, taken by surprise when the latter fired at the royal carriage. When papers such as the *Weekly Dispatch*, a regular police critic, and *The Times*, a staunch defender, joined in condemnation of this run of ineptitude and in demands for a detective department, it is not surprising that a move was made in this direction and unopposed when it materialised—for a time.

The institution of this centralised detective force—if 0.2 per cent of police strength can be called a force—seems to have been nothing more than a cautious experiment. These eight men could not be expected to handle more than the major crimes. Graham's query to the Commissioners as to 'what regulations are suggested to ensure the proper employment of the detective officers when not immediately occupied in the pursuit of offenders'[1] betokens an ostrich-like attitude to the crime rate, and the Divisions obviously had to continue using their own men in a detective capacity.

A half-hearted atmosphere hangs over the whole affair. Belton Cobb in *The First Detectives* (1957) argues eloquently for Mayne's deep conviction of the need for a detective department, suggesting that over the years prior to 1842 Mayne deliberately manoeuvred towards this end against the opposition of Rowan; eloquently, but scarcely cogently, as the relevant records are sparse. Even the 'Memorandum relative to detective powers of Police' which the Commissioners submitted to the Home Secretary on 14 June 1842 and which led directly to the formation of a detective office, is primarily devoted first to a justification of the police over the Good affair and then to assertions of the Commissioners' belief in the sufficiency and efficiency of their current arrangements for the detection of crime. The case for a separate detective force, when eventually broached, is not based on any positive advantages that might thereby accrue in the fight against crime, but on the administrative inconvenience of taking men away from their routine duties to act as detectives:

> This employment of the men [as detectives], however useful and necessary for the purpose, interferes with the regular routine of duty assigned to each individual in the Police, and where the enquiry is prolonged and requires the whole of his time to be devoted to it, considerable inconvenience arises in supplying the place and carrying on the other duties of the individual so employed, and in the cases of Inspectors and Serjeants, the interference with the other duties is still more convenient.
>
> The Commissioners submit that it would facilitate the carrying on this branch of the Police operations, if they had a certain number of men specially applicable to the duty of following up cases, whenever it became desirable that steps should be taken which cannot be so effectively performed by those of the Police who have other duties to attend to.[2]

Cobb's case is interesting, but it rests largely on the spaces between the few available lines. An article on 'The Detective System' in the *Saturday Review* in 1877 reckoned that, given six detectives in the department, Mayne 'thought these were five too many'. Without going as far as that, there is against Cobb's conjectures the unalterable fact that in the twenty-six years following the establishment of the office, for eighteen of which 'King' Mayne ruled alone, the staff of that office rose to a mere fifteen—a percentage decrease on the original 0.2 per cent of the force, which by the time of Mayne's death in 1868 numbered around 8,000.

It is from this negligible expansion, as Sir John Moylan points out in his history of Scotland Yard (1929), that 'the strength of the old prejudice against detectives can be gauged'. The prejudice took two forms. First, there was the reluctance within Scotland Yard itself to recognise the need for a separate detective force. Any such recognition must have seemed to the Commissioners a contradiction, almost a betrayal, of the basic function of the police as a *preventive* force, a principle enshrined in their *General Instructions for the Police*:

> It should be understood, at the outset, that the principal object to be attained is 'the prevention of crime'. To this great end every effort of the police is to be directed. The security of person and property, the preservation of public tranquillity and all the other objects of a Police Establishment will thus be better effected than by the detection and punishment of the offender after he has succeeded in committing the crime.

In the light of this *diktat* the creation of a central detective office was tantamount to an admission of the failure of the preventive approach; the size of that office reflects the extent of the admission.

The protagonists of detection over prevention included the London magistrates who controlled the Bow Street Runners and who, up to the dissolution of the Runners in 1839, formed a second, anomalous police authority in the city. There was concern at the threat to disband the Runners since the New Police seemed ill-qualified to fill the Runners' primarily detective role, and this view was urged before a Commons Select Committee of 1838. The following is from Dilnot's account of the evidence given to that Committee:

> Sir Peter Laurie, a City magnate, was positive that the Metropolitan Police could not supersede the Runners. They had not the training, nor did he believe that they could acquire it. 'These men have been thief catchers all their lives, and know almost every thief in London, and of what he is capable' . . . Mr. John Clark, the Clerk of Arraigns at the Old Bailey, also insisted: 'The prevention of crime merely depends on a man's activity, and upon his keeping his eyes open to see what is going on; but the detection of crime is only to be learnt by considerable experience, and by enquiry in places which nothing but long experience will enable a man to find out . . .'

The Commissioners' answer was, generally, that they had men competent to deal with anything that might require detective work, and, specifically, that in their route-paper system, whereby details of a crime and the officer responsible for its investigation were quickly circulated to all Divisions, they did have a detective system. Dilnot puts his finger on the nub of this problem:

> There appear to have been some cross-purposes in this discussion on the art of detection. The Commissioners of Police were speaking of a machine; the others of individual training. No individual thief-taker, however brilliant, could compare with organisation in the detection of crime. The Metropolitan Police had a sort of detective system without detectives. It was a combination of the two that was really wanted.

Many years were to elapse before there was a true marriage of these two concepts and only in this century can it be said to have become a productive union.

If officialdom's hesitations and doubts about the practical value of a detective system were eventually overcome, the second source of prejudice is still with us today. It is founded broadly on the traditional belief that detective is synonymous with spy and hence reprehensible—unless, of course, he is on your side—and it can be seen, at one extreme, in the positive antipathy of the cry of state interference with the liberty of the subject, heard most often in the wake of some uncovered undercover activity; and at the other extreme in the vague but more continual middle-class misgivings about the power, methods and venality of the police in general and of detectives in particular. And, to be sure, one reads, if not daily, then certainly weekly reports of alleged corruption, brutality and false arrest, of planted evidence and of *agents provocateurs*. Even when the allegations are not proven, they still leave a nasty taste in the mouth. Similarly, one reads the legendary phrase 'acting on information received' and one cannot be blamed for wondering just from whom it was received and why and how; again, bugging devices of increasing sophistication and decreasing size are developed and it occurs to us that *someone* must be using them. But when the allegations are proven, as they sometimes are, the prejudice has become a fact, unavoidably attracting more than the share of publicity rightly due to such misdemeanours, for the detective is in the unenviable position of Caesar's wife. Midshipman Easy had no monopoly on zeal, and Milton none on exasperation, nor for that matter do detectives, but an error on their part in these or any other directions will always seem the greater sin, meriting a more severe punishment. Otherwise one has to ask the unanswerable question about the police force of any democracy: *quis custodiet ipsos custodes*?

Today, 'realistic' police dramas on television bring literally home to people the frustrations and temptations facing a policeman in a way not possible a generation ago, but while the details and background may be new, the same problems and doubts have always surrounded those entrusted with enforcing the law and detecting crime. Concern about these matters a hundred years ago was no less deep for the want of visual enaction. The nineteenth-century novelist may not have been interested in police work, as Symons asserts, but the nineteenth century was, and its interest usually worked to the detriment of the 'invisible blues'.

The way in which the police and the 'defectives' were considered fair game throughout the last century for the humorists, cartoonists and satirists was one of the many growth industries of the age. *Punch*, *Fun* and *Judy* are full of jibes and jokes at their expense: 'his face shines not with intelligence, but soap'; 'the police are more popular . . . for their services as street guides and traffic regulators than for their services as regulators of crime.'[3] Protests of varying degrees of sanity filled the correspondence columns of the newspapers and the Commissioners' desks; corruption, apathy, interference, brutality, stupidity, let alone plain inefficiency—the police were accused of all these and more. The inevitable lack of a policeman when wanted is a long-standing joke still with us, perhaps with greater appropriateness today since the withdrawal of beat policemen in many areas; when it is remembered that another favourite complaint concerned policemen patrolling 'respectable' districts, thus lowering their tone, instead of being busy thief-taking, it will be seen that the poor policeman was never going to win in this respect.

The predecessors of the New Police, the watchmen or 'Charleys', had also been a standing topic for witticisms and worse, for Charley-thrashing was a regular pastime of the young bloods of the day. The *Quarterly Review* of 1856, in an article called 'The Police and the Thieves' contributed by one Andrew Wynter, tells how the notorious capacity of these watchmen for sleep had its beneficial aspect:

> A friend of mine was suffering from a continual wakefulness, and various methods were taken to send him to sleep, but in vain. At last his physicians resorted to an experiment which succeeded perfectly. They dressed him in a watchman's coat, put a lantern in his hand, and placed him in a sentrybox, and— he was asleep in ten minutes.

For any journalist so inclined, and most were, the coming of the New Police and a detective office were a bumper gift, simply widening the scope of the original game of Charley-baiting. Even the normally staid and often sympathetic *Saturday Review*, writing on 'Literary Policemen' in 1874, could not resist the temptation of a jest—elevated, of course—at police expense. Referring to the effort by the police to close fried fish, pie and oyster shops early, it comments that some inspectors 'seem to think it enough that "loose characters" frequent a shop in order to condemn it, but we venture to remark that even a prostitute may be lawfully supplied with eel-pie'.

The humorous criticism, however, was the surface expression of much deeper-set and serious prejudices, based mainly, in the case of the detective, on his association with 'spyin', pryin' and lyin'', as a Wallace villain was later to put it, but also on grounds of inefficiency, corruption and excessive cost. None of these accusations was without foundation. Thus opponents could point to the definitely dubious activities of the French political police, the *mouchards*, who did act as spies and *agents provocateurs*. The possibility of an honest policeman was for some people a contradiction in terms; their motto was Sartine's reply to those who reproached him, as head of the French espionage system, for employing repentant thieves and reformed criminals as police spies. 'Tell me,' he said, 'of one honest man who will be a police spy.' Hence the outcry in the 1830s against policemen in plain clothes, allegations that the police were 'a corps of spies' and the condemnation of their activities as 'unconstitutional, despotic, and, above all, unEnglish'. Very English, on the other hand, were the protests against the supposed vast expense of the New Police, the prospect of a return in the form of security weighing little with the rate-payer. The staunchly pro-Peel *New Monthly* replied on this score by hinting darkly that parishes were charging to the police account sums that did not properly belong to it in order to throw odium on the new organisation.[4] Accusations of corruption had a concrete basis in the well-known susceptibilities of the Bow Street Runners, those 'private speculators in the detection of crime', as Moylan calls them. The favourite ploy of the Runners was to allow a criminal to commit a number of small crimes with impunity, having paid them his bribes, and then to arrest him in the performance of a major one, bringing a worthwhile reward as well as the bribe. The massive turnover in police numbers in the 1830s—Dilnot puts it at 5,000 dismissals and 6,000 resignations, not all voluntary, in the first eight years—is an indication of the dishonesty and incompetence in the force. Some, it seems, were incompetently dishonest. The *Guardian*, writing on 'Law and Police' in 1855, reports the imprisonment of one William Henry Wilson of P Division for one year for 'stealing a grey goose at night from the premises of a lady on his beat at Camberwell . . . The policeman was in the closet picking the grey goose, some of the feathers of which were afterwards found sticking to his clothes'. The same issue refers to another policeman's arrest for running a gang of pickpockets. One wonders whether the wording here was deliberately calculated to disparage detectives, or whether the reporter still felt the need, as late as 1855, to explain about these mysterious individuals:

A startling discovery, if it prove true, has been brought out at Bow-street, where Charles King, a police constable, generally doing duty in private clothes—in other words, a detective—was brought up in custody charged with having been the habitual accomplice of thieves.

When Mayne's successor, Sir Edmund Henderson, expanded the detective department to 200 immediately on taking office in 1869, the pressure of these prejudices must still have been very strong, for he felt obliged to comment in his report on his first year that the detective system was 'viewed with the greatest suspicion and jealousy by the majority of Englishmen and is, in fact, entirely foreign to the habits and feelings of the nation'.[5]

Alongside the opposition, it should be made clear, there were defenders of the police and the detectives, as well as constructive critics, who went less noticed perhaps because they were usually less vociferous. The *New Monthly*, however, devoted two articles in quick succession to the defence of the police soon after Peel's bill became law, and the opening words of the first did not lack fire: 'The reformation of the existing system of police in the metropolis has occasioned much discussion, and like all beneficial innovations in our prejudice-ridden community, has been violently attacked.' It goes on daringly—this is 1829—to suggest that what is needed is a detective force in plain clothes: 'We have some doubts whether it would not be useful to have some portion of the new police, at times, dressed as other individuals; a pick-pocket will be on his guard when a policeman is near . . . It is true this would not be consonant exactly to the preventive plan, but it would aid materially in the apprehension of such offenders.' And the *New Monthly* wanted *more* money: 'We think, too, that the pay of the men is too low. A guinea a week is too little to keep men above temptation to wrong—it should be thirty shillings at least; the money would be well bestowed.'[6]

The *Saturday Review* took up some of these points almost as soon as it was launched in 1855, and throughout the century it never tired of pointing out that the deficiencies in quantity and quality of both uniformed and plain clothes men precluded from the outset any hopes of efficiency. Here it is in 1868 in

its article on 'The Police and Mr. Speke'; note that the pay
has gone down:

> There are too few men to do the work, and the pay is too low to
> attract good men into the service. The impossibility of finding a
> policeman when one is wanted has long been a current joke. When
> the area which each member of the force has under his charge is
> taken into account, we see at once that the joke has a foundation
> in reality. No man not endowed with the faculty of being in two
> places at once can properly keep watch over 72 acres of streets
> and houses, inhabited by 600 people . . . Nineteen officers can
> hardly be sufficient to undertake the detection of all the crimes
> in London . . . The detective service requires very keen intelli-
> gence, and this quality is not so common that we can afford to
> pay it badly. If we do, one of three things will certainly follow—
> either thoroughly competent men will be deterred from entering
> the service at all, or they will soon find opportunities of trans-
> ferring themselves to some more lucrative employment, or, if
> they remain, they will do their work carelessly . . . It is to be feared
> that . . . a salary of 19s. a week affords but very poor security
> against . . . these defects.

As people grew more used to detectives the grounds of
complaint shifted from their alleged illegality and association
with spying to their incompetence, easily proved, it seemed, by
the large number of unsolved crimes. Justified or not, this
feature provided more grist to the vituperative mill that was
Victorian journalism. The *Saturday Review* was no exception:
'We are not believers in the miraculous tact of our officials, and,
certainly, if the newspaper accounts are to be believed, they
either hold no clue, or take strange pains to make their proceedings ineffectual.' But in this 1857 article 'The Murders of
the Day' and in many others the *Saturday* goes beyond the
run-of-the-mill pulverisation of detectives to a deeper problem
which has worried law-abiding citizens since police forces
began: just what can the detective *really* do to defeat the skilful
organised criminal and what can he do—this was a special
concern of Victorian times—about the apparent profusion of
unsolved murders and the even more appalling corollary of this,
the probability of many unsuspected ones. This was the other
great cry of the *Saturday* alongside its intermittent campaign

for more and better-paid police. 'The number of crimes which no human eye detects and no human punishment avenges, is fearfully large', bewails the writer of an 1856 article actually entitled 'Undetected Crime', and through the ensuing years the *Saturday* keeps returning, rather forlornly, to this point. Thus in 1864 the situation is as bleak as ever: 'Anyone who took the trouble to do so might soon make out a fearfully long list of undiscovered [unsolved?] crimes . . . Even in regard to murders, there is every reason to believe that a majority are undiscovered [unsolved?], to say nothing of those which are unsuspected; and of persons actually brought to trial somewhere about 25 per cent are acquitted.' But none of this is really the fault of the detectives. If no clues are left after a crime, what can anyone do? And in other cases the hands of the police are often tied by the strict laws of evidence; they 'know' the guilty party but lack the depth of proof required by law. Inspector Whicher's unprovable conviction that Constance Kent was guilty of the Road Murder in 1860 comes to mind here,[7] and the *Saturday* concludes this article pessimistically: 'There is little scope for ingenuity in the detection of crime, because, if there is evidence, it is almost always easy to produce it; and if there is none, it is altogether impossible to get it.'[8]

This disturbing idea of the existence of many perfect crimes —perfect in the sense that we cannot know about them otherwise they would not be perfect—is also brought up by Wilkie Collins in *The Woman in White* where Count Fosco expounds it:

'The machinery [society] has set up for the detection of crime is miserably ineffective—and yet only invent a moral epigram, saying that it works well, and you blind everybody to its blunders, from that moment. Crimes cause their own detection, do they? And murder will out (another moral epigram), will it? . . . Read your own public journals. In the few cases that get into the newspapers, are there not instances of slain bodies found, and no murderers ever discovered? Multiply the cases that are reported by the cases that are *not* reported, and the bodies that are found by the bodies that are not found; and what conclusion do you come to? This. That there are foolish criminals who are discovered, and wise criminals who escape.'

135

The impression is that even those sympathetic towards the efforts of the detectives were being forced to agree with the detractors, albeit for more valid reasons, that the force was making little progress and meeting with little success. Annoyance, frustration and despair are all combined in the *Saturday Review's* cry:

> We are police-ridden somewhat in the same way that the Italian is priest-ridden. There is little love lost between us and our policemen, any more than there is between a Neapolitan and his priest; but we feel that we cannot do without him. We fear him, and we occasionally malign him, but we call him in on the next emergency all the same.[9]

All the accusations and criticisms must have seemed justified when in 1877 the aftermath of the De Goncourt case revealed that several senior Scotland Yard detectives had been receiving bribes over a period of years from a gang specialising in turf frauds. And outcry there was, but the opportunity was also taken to remind people that they get what they pay for. Even the *Graphic*, no friend of the police, made this clear:

> The conviction is being forced upon us that we have not the right sort of men for the work in their several grades. What then is to be done? The answer which at once suggests itself is that we should get a different class, a higher type and tone of men. But this is a matter of money—and what will the ratepayers say to this aspect of the question? They must, however, face it, if they demand a higher moral standard in the Force.[10]

This scandal had its benefits, however. It led to a thorough overhaul of the detective system and the establishment of the Criminal Investigation Department at the hands of Howard Vincent who based the new organisation, ironically enough, on the highly centralised and previously much-despised French system, Vincent's own title of Director of Criminal Investigations, for example, being a direct translation of his Parisian opposite's *Directeur des Recherches Criminelles*. The fact that the C.I.D. could be modelled on the French system speaks volumes in itself, and it is from this time, if one can date trends, that the full-blooded acrimony towards detectives begins to give way to their acceptance, however qualified. Not that the troubles of the detective service were solved overnight by this reorganisation. In 1880, two years after the C.I.D. was set up, the *Graphic* was claiming that it was all a mistake and advocating disbandment of this separate detective department. Or could John Citizen really not care less? Perhaps *Punch* provided a more accurate reflection of public opinion about detectives in its playlet of 1888 entitled *The Detective's Rescue*. This opens with a 'dismayed detective' pursued by an assortment of sensation seekers who chant at him in chorus:

> Thou must feed the morbid hunger
> Of the grim Sensation-monger.
> Tell us then what thou art doing,
> What and whom art thou pursuing? . . .

To which the detective replies:

> . . . how can I my object gain
> If I my methods must explain?
> It certainly would not be wise
> To tell my plans,—drop my disguise.

Representatives of various interested parties—criminals journalists, editors—make their case for knowing exactly what the detective is up to, and they are not appeased even when the Commissioner, Sir Charles Warren, tries to explain:

> . . . Do you think the detective's so green
> As to let you know all that he's traced?
> Surely, goodness alone knows what next you'll expect!
> You forget a Detective is meant to *detect*.

In the end Sir Charles has to summon 'a powere [*sic*], beneath whose gaze a crew like you will cower'. This is none other than the Goddess of Luke-warm Public Opinion, who has no trouble in dispersing the crowd with her wand. With Sherlock Holmes already beginning to breathe down his neck, it will be seen that the life of the late nineteenth-century detective was no bed of roses, but the establishment of the C.I.D. in 1878 does mark the start of the long haul to the present position of tenuous respectability held by the detective police in Britain today. It also brings us, oddly enough, to the 1880s.

Looking at the half-century of the detective from the foundation of the Metropolitan Police to this point, one is greeted by a depressing picture. The overall impression is, as T. A. Critchley says in his *history* of the police, that 'detective work, during much of the nineteenth century, was the Cinderella of the police service'. Apart from prejudices against detectives on grounds of character, behaviour and the type of job they seemed to be doing, let alone their lack of success at the job, other factors of a more technical nature also operated to keep their effectiveness at a minimum. Co-operation amongst themselves and with other forces barely existed, training schemes were non-existent, and scientific aids were limited to the telegraph, occasional photography and plaster of Paris for what has always struck me as the overrated pastime of taking footprints.

These shortcomings can be explained, but the explanations reinforce the findings. The detectives' shady reputation and poor course record followed in some measure from the poor quality of recruit, which was in turn attributable to the low pay which has dogged the police throughout its history. Yet when promotion examinations were introduced in the 1870s they were met with opposition from within and without the force. Quoting from various divisional inspectors' reports, the *Saturday Review*, in its article on 'Literary Policemen', had this to say:

> This test, [the Paddington inspector] says, though it gives to the public intelligent, well-spoken, and well-informed men, shuts out many who would make the best officers . . . I have, says the writer, divisional detectives who are clever, experienced men, and but for the one drawback of the want of education, would make the best detective sergeants, 'for they are most energetic in the pursuit of offenders, will stand or lie in a mews, in a ditch, in a stable, a cab, or in a box, and will watch for hours without stirring . . . which I am afraid the educated detective would not do' . . . It is doubtful [the *Saturday* concludes] whether an examiner could be found to set a paper on 'Crime and its Perpetrators'; and the capacity for standing up to the neck in a dungheap seems scarcely to admit of being measured by marks.

The Victorian distate for what it saw as an essentially ungentle-manly profession is revealed here. The possibility that the educated copper might be willing to make acquaintance with a dungheap or use his wits to cast around for a more salubrious vantage point did not occur to the writer of the above. One is struck by the apparent incompatibility in the Victorian mind of brains with dirty work, and even of brains with hard-headed-ness to judge from the case recounted in the same article of the constable who 'seized a suspected burglar and held him till assistance came, in spite of a violent blow with a "jemmy", under which perhaps a more scholarly head might have yielded'.

Teamwork, too, was an idea foreign to the times and its slow development was probably fostered by the reward system which operated for most of the nineteenth century; co-operation in catching criminals implied division of the spoils and, given his low wage, one can sympathise with the detective who did not consider it wise to tell his plans or who concen-trated on the recovery of stolen goods, which meant money, rather than the arrest of the thief, which might, at most, mean only fame. Finally, the idea of detection as a science or re-quiring or benefiting from scientific aids, let alone of men being trained in it beyond certain routine procedures, was risible. As if, scoffs the *Saturday Review*, 'detection were a subject on which public lectures were read at Scotland Yard by a well-paid professor'.[11] Thus the novelists of the time who wrote of 'the science of detection' were ahead of the facts, even if they meant by it something rather different from the modern approach.

This unprepossessing picture of the early detective helps to explain the ease with which Holmes outshone him. Yet as we shall see in the following chapters Victorian writers were by no means averse to depicting these apparently broken reeds. The *Saturday Review* was right when it said that 'nineteen-shillings . . . a week is not a glittering prize to dangle before the eyes of men who are expected to be at once hardy, active, bold, educated, and astute.'[12] But the expectation cost nothing at all and there is another side to the coin of the real-life detective.

If the side so far inspected has revealed a man with, so to speak, his tail between his legs, the reverse shows him with a mystic halo round his head.

Whence this mystique? At the risk of over-simplification I would suggest that it consists, in variable proportions, of brains in the person and secrecy in the work. The mystique is an obvious, indeed hackneyed, feature of the fictional detective, but it also enshrouds the real one, albeit to a lesser extent. Do we have here a case of nature following art? Fed on a rich diet of the dazzling mental and physical feats of these story-book creations, we tend perhaps to include some of the fictional glamour in our mental recipe for the real thing. That is probably true, but how far have we strayed from the facts in doing so? Certainly, efforts to bring the star-struck public back to earth are endemic to the opening pages of most memoirs of real detectives, with their emphasis on the essentially routine and often sordid nature of their work. Here, for example is Sir Basil Thomson in *Queer People* (1922):

> Mr. Sherlock Holmes, to whom I take off my hat with the silent prayer that he may never appear in the flesh, worked by induction, but not, so far as I am able to judge, by the only method that gets home, namely organisation and hard work . . . The detection of crime consists in good organisation, hard work, and luck, in about equal proportions.

George Hatherill says much the same in his *A Detective's Story* (1971), altering only the proportions:

> [An] enormous amount of tedious routine . . . is . . . involved in detective work . . . There are, of course, periods of absorbing interest and occasionally of some excitement, but to concentrate on these would falsify the picture . . . It is far from being an easy life and I should say that most cases depend for their solution on a mixture of 98 per cent of hard work and 2 per cent of luck.

These efforts, however, are almost immediately set at naught by the ensuing pages which show how clever the writer and his colleagues have been—on occasion. This is not said to deride these gentlemen, but to draw attention to the very fact that these men *are* clever, that they do perform feats similar to those ascribed to the detectives of fiction—on occasion. One can therefore legitimately ask how much the real detective is to 'blame' for the supposedly misleading picture conveyed by the fictional variety. Admittedly, the feats recounted in these biographies of real detectives are invariably surrounded and often outweighed by the record of the long, slow grind of routine, the revelation of the stupidity of most criminals who are caught, complete with supporting photographs of people really dead. None of this would do for detective fiction. It is not what the reader wants, and so even Freeman Wills Crofts cuts corners off Inspector French's investigations, and 'when [Parker] worked with Wimsey on a case, it was an understood thing that anything lengthy, intricate, tedious and soul-destroying was done by Parker.'[13] And clever rogues are *de rigueur*, for there is no glory in revealing a stupid one. Similarly, a neat, if architecturally-improbable, diagram with X marking the spot replaces the squalor of violent death.

Yet, although the idealisations and simplifications of detective fiction have no equivalents in the life of the real detective, astonishing performances of skill, intuition or sheer native wit do. Luck may play its part, but no more so than in detective fiction. It is in the use made of the luck that intelligence comes into play, and here the real detective has an even chance with the fictional. The opportunities for such performances are, as I have suggested and as the detective would be the first to admit, rare, but they do occur and they are seized, and it is on such coloraturas that the public's imagination fixes and attributes as permanent and daily features of a detective's life. This is as true of London's New Police before even the formal creation of a detective office, as it is of all detective forces today. Each has its fund of true myths.

To take the New Police alone, however, Belton Cobb in *The First Detectives* (1957) cites two instances of 'brilliant . . . imaginative reasoning' by Superintendent Thomas of F Division in the early 1830s.

First was the case of Bishop, Williams and May, known body snatchers, who were arrested in November 1831 while trying to sell a boy's body to King's College. The suspicions of the demonstrator in anatomy had been aroused by the freshness and rigidity of the body and by a cut from which blood had flowed, indicating to all readers of detective fiction that the wound must have been inflicted before death. Accordingly the demonstrator had fetched the police and the three men were arrested. The post-mortem was of little help to the investigators—the doctors agreed that death had not been natural, but could not give the actual cause. Carlo Ferrari, then, as the boy was now known to be, had been murdered, and the murderers were almost certainly in custody. But there was no proof against them, and no hope of proof, it seemed, for Bishop's house had been searched twice, revealing nothing but a pair of blood-soaked boy's breeches, the significance of which was not immediately seen. Superintendent Thomas persevered in his searches, however, eventually turning up Ferrari's cap, implying the boy had been in Bishop's house. Thomas then had the garden dug up and found more clothes, evidence that three more boys had earlier suffered the same fate as Ferrari. Passing to Williams' house next door, the searchers found more buried clothes, a woman's this time, which were identified as belonging to a Mrs. Pigburn who had disappeared some weeks earlier. Her shawl was found at the bottom of a well in Bishop's garden.

On this evidence the trial of the three accused now went ahead, but Thomas was still concerned about the method of murder—remember the doctors could not say how Ferrari had died except that it was not naturally. Thomas then advanced the theory that the various victims had been inveigled into the house and then thrust head-foremost into the well, where they drowned, the water subsequently running out of their bodies because they were suspended head-downwards. He deduced this entirely from the fact that, while Mrs. Pigburn's clothes had been found in the garden, her shawl was at the bottom of the well; it must have slipped from her shoulders when she was hanging head-down. Thomas felt that this was a method of killing which would account for Ferrari's death without signs of the cause, and his theory was confirmed by Bishop's death-cell confession.

Superintendent Thomas's second case concerned the robbery of a watch and purse from the hotel room of a Major Lewis. The latter was awakened by the thief and gave chase, but after a struggle the culprit escaped. Thomas's enquiries eventually revealed that some small pieces of material found in the corridor had been torn from the thief's shirt and braces by the major in their tussle. Cobb goes on:

> Probably, in those early days, the majority of the superintendents and inspectors . . . would have let the major's explanation of those pieces of cloth pass as a satisfactory and sufficient one, throwing them away because they were not going to be of any use . . . [Cobb has a note at this point suggesting that 'readers who fancy their own detective powers may care to pause here and see if they are as clever at deduction' as Thomas was] . . . But Joseph Sadler Thomas had . . . his wits about him. He was not satisfied with the explanation because there was one very definite flaw in it. He therefore asked the Major: 'How were you enabled to tear his shirt and braces under his coat?' Then [the major] gave him the one vital piece of information—that he had not thought worth mentioning before: that the thief had been in his shirt sleeves. Probably that too might have been allowed to pass unquestioned—but not by Superintendent Thomas. Whoever heard of a thief coming through the streets of London at night *in his shirt sleeves*, in order to break into a house? . . . the thief must have come from one of the other bedrooms in the hotel and have returned there when he 'got away'. Mr. Thomas therefore went through the sleeping quarters in the hotel, room by room. In some he found evidence that the thief had robbed other people that night . . . But in one room he found a man in bed with his clothes on. His shirt and braces were torn at the back. And beneath his mattress were a number of stolen articles, including the major's gold watch and purse.

From the start, then, Peel's policemen were doing what we have come to expect of detectives. The unfortunate thing is that these two cases were exceptions, sadly outnumbered by the failures. Moylan gives a misleading assessment of the abilities of the New Police over the Bow Street Runners during the ten years of their co-existence between 1829 and 1839 when he claims that 'the runners took the jewel robberies and left the murders to the metropolitan police. All the murderers were traced but only a sixth of the jewel thieves were brought to justice.' Significantly, perhaps, Moylan does not say anything about jewels recovered for their owners, but taking his claim about the murders, we may set against it Cobb's consideration of a selection of eight murders between these years, of which three were solved (one a possible miscarriage of justice), four were unsolved, and one resulted in acquittal. The facts, it seems, supported the critics. This does not affect the point at issue, however, which is that the real-life professional was showing acumen, and attracting attention because of it, and this before his first fictional appearance.

Turning now to the second element in the mystique, Watson-and-reader-baiting secretiveness has been a hallmark of the detective of fiction since his birth in Dupin. It is sometimes invoked, one suspects, to prevent a tale from ending halfway to the word target. Displaying that 'cheerful cynicism' already noted in Carr and Berkeley, Agatha Christie says as much in the following argument between Poirot and Hastings in *Dumb Witness* (1937):

> We passed a very pleasant evening, though I made the slight mistake of taking Poirot to a crook play . . . Poirot never ceased to complain of faulty psychology, and the hero detective's lack of order and method nearly drove him demented. We parted that night with Poirot still explaining how the whole business might have been laid bare in the first half of the first act.
> 'But in that case, Poirot, there would have been no play', I pointed out.
> Poirot was forced to admit that perhaps that was so.

As we ought by now to expect, the same point was made about sensation fiction. 'Sensation detectives always *are* late', admits Gripper, W. S. Gilbert's version thereof, otherwise 'the novel would come to an end long before its time'.[14]

It would be unfair to accuse the real detective of making a habit of indulging in fiction's deliberately provocative variety of secretiveness, but this characteristic, in the different but overlapping sense of secrecy or justifiable reticence does seem to be a necessity for detection at a common sense level, in that if a detective advertises his findings and suspicions before they constitute a complete case, he may find his bird has flown. This was the argument of both the detective and Sir Charles Warren in the verses quoted earlier from *Punch*, and this approach or technique, with its implications of undercover activities, disguises and spying, is a godsend to the novelist and anathema to the libertarian—or sensation-monger. It can lead to accusations on the one hand of prying, if no good reason or a false one is given for an investigation, or on the other hand of incompetence, if the lack of disclosures seems to be a veil to conceal lack of progress in a case. An element of double-bluff, invaluable to the writer, now enters the proceedings, since one cannot help wondering if behind the apparent failure a magnificent detectival *coup* is but awaiting its final touches. Here the real detective's secrecy comes very close to the fictional detective's 'I-know-but-I'm-not-telling', and the attraction of the unknown, the mysteriousness of it all, acts in favour of the detective in that we who do not know the answer like to think that someone does and so we attribute to the detective an ability and secret know-how which in most cases he unfortunately does not possess and which, if we are honest with ourselves, we know he does not possess. In an article on 'The French Police System', the *Saturday Review* provides a good illustration of this when it amusingly pretends to doubts about the reasons for the slowness of the detectives—French, this time—over the Dumollard case of 1862, in which M. and Mme. Dumollard, taken for one murder, were eventually discovered to be guilty of some fifteen others committed over the previous seven years.:

> One would have thought that the same detective force which has at last brought to light Dumollard's seven or eight years of crime, and which now, in 1862, tells us what he was doing in February 1855, and, with the utmost minuteness, traces his career and his victims . . . might have done something in the way

145

of prevention . . . It almost looks as if there was something in what Mr. Sala and the novelists tell us—that the first rate detectives all along knew everything; but that in crime, as in horticulture, they prefer that the pear should be perfectly ripe . . . before it is fit for the hand of justice.

The *Saturday* of course has no doubts about the true state of affairs:

In this, as in many other things, the French police system takes credit for an excellence and completeness which it does not possess. The police agents, at least if we are to judge from the *procès Dumollard*, are admirable when, like greyhounds, they have their game in view; but it seems that they are really very deficient in scent and true hunting powers.

Just how far a detective should reveal his reasons for asking questions and how justified he is in practising duplicity to achieve his ends have been talking points since his first appearance. Suspicion and fear that these traits signalled the end of civil liberties were a main source of opposition to the Metropolitan Police in its early years. The *New Monthly* could argue that such attitudes stemmed from 'perverseness and blindness' and that 'the very nature of an Englishman's character would render a spy-police system inert and ridiculous here,'[15] but the same doubts and prejudices are still with us today. It is nevertheless interesting to follow the modification in opinion—articulate middle-class opinion, that is—towards the acceptance of the need for some degree of secrecy in the detective's work as the century wore on. This is seen in the use of the French detective organisation as a model for the C.I.D., despite the former's associations with espionage. It is also reflected in the realisation that the police and the detectives were social necessities, though not social assets and far from epitomes of efficiency. The feeling seems to have been that if the detective were to stand any chance of improving on his record and making any headway against crime, he must be allowed more leeway, not less, in his undercover activities.

To take one example of this: in the early 1880s a certain Mr Laing Meason published a series of articles in the *Nineteenth*

Century and in *Macmillan's Magazine* purporting to show the superiority of the French *agents secrets* over their Scotland Yard counterparts; for example:

> A French detective who cannot assume and 'act up to' any character, and who cannot disguise himself in any manner so effectually as not to be recognised even by those who know him best, is not considered fit to hold his appointment. Their ability in this way is marvellous. One of them some years ago made me a bet that he would, in the course of the next few days, address me four times, for at least ten minutes each time, and that I should not know him on any occasion until he discovered himself. As a matter of course I was on my guard, and mistrusted everyone who came near me. But the man won his bet. It is needless to enter into particulars. Let it suffice to say that in the course of the next four days he presented himself in the character of a boot-maker's assistant, a *fiacre* driver, a venerable old gentleman with a great interest in the *Bourse*, and, finally, as a waiter in the hotel in which I was stopping. Assuredly, the man deserved to win his bet, for in no single case had I the faintest suspicion of his identity.

> 'Detective Police', *Nineteenth Century*, May 1883

This and many other examples of French flair Meason adduces in support of his basic contention which is the establishment of a 'secret or really detective' system in Britain. His articles drew qualified support from the *Saturday Review* in its article on 'Detectives' in 1883:

> . . . though there would be very great difficulties in the way, something might possibly be done to improve the present organisation by copying to a certain extent that of the French detective police . . . That, as a rule, detectives cannot work with sufficient secrecy . . . seems hardly to admit of doubt; . . . It can hardly be contended that a system which . . . allows carefully-executed portraits of the leading detectives to appear in a newspaper does not stand in need of improvement.

Perhaps people were beginning to appreciate that the one class with really sound reasons for opposition to the dreaded man in private clothes had long had its problem solved. Meason certainly thought so:

I was having my shoes cleaned outside the Charing Cross Station,
when I noticed two well-built, well-set-up, active-looking men
standing near me. They were in plain clothes, and yet their dress
was so much alike that they might almost be said to be in uniform.
I remarked to a friend who was with me that they looked like
soldiers of the guards in *mufti*. Upon this the youngster . . . who
was brushing away at my feet, looked up at me, winked, and
said—'No, sir, them beant soldiers; they's detectives, they is.'
'How do you know?' says I. 'Oh, sir,' was the answer, 'we knows
all them plain-clothes officers. They try to look like other folks;
but it's no good. We can tell them as well as if they wore helmets
and blue coats.'

'The French Detective Police', *Macmillan's Magazine*,
February 1882

Accordingly, the law-abiding class, Meason argued, should be
willing to consider measures to improve the detective service
before the increasing tide of crime engulfed it.

Astuteness and secrecy were thus part and parcel of the
Scotland Yard detective from the beginning, affording a marked contrast to the other, also real, picture of him as ill-trained,
ill-equipped, ill-mannered and inefficient. His fostering in the
public mind as a man of ability and mystery by Dickens is too
well-known to require emphasis here, but other writers outside
fiction also felt the attraction of the detective's mystique. Even
the sober *Quarterly Review* in the person of Andrew Wynter
indulged itself:

In a fourth [room at Scotland Yard] we see the secret chamber
of the Detective Police—those human moles who work without
casting up the earth lest their course should be discovered . . .
Bow-street, great as was its fame, did not turn out more intelligent
detectives than we now possess.

And the *Leisure Hour* article on 'Police Detectives' (29 October
1857) rivalled the *Quarterly* in naïveté:

The modern police force . . . can bring any amount of activity
and energy to bear upon the pursuit of a criminal, and on the
search after evidence of his guilt. The thief of the last generation
. . . pursued his nefarious trade with comparative impunity.
The thief of today has the eyes of the police on him at every turn;

if he takes to flight, there is the electric telegraph to overtake him in the race . . . The wretch who aims at the life of his fellow-creatures fights with fate at still greater odds . . . the chemist detects the poisonous drug in the body of his dead victim; the microscope declares that the blood on his garment is human blood . . . and while all nature refuses a refuge to the manslayer, the detective is on his track and will drag him to the bar of avenging justice.

The press in fact must carry a major share of the responsibility for the propagation of faith in detectives, for while some papers were cursing detectives for incompetence, others were automatically adding 'intelligent' and 'skilful' to each and every mention of their name. Even 'London' linked with 'detective' took on a glamorous connotation; perhaps the noun on its own was felt to be too dubious a description to give much inspiration to public confidence.

The double vision in which the Victorians saw their detectives is nowhere better exemplified than in an item by W. L. Woodruffe in the *Graphic* in 1880. This starts by promising to disabuse us, once and for all, about the mystique of detection:

> The London Detective Police are a fair illustration of the truth of a familiar proverb. Whatever is unknown, we are willing to assume is magnificent. It is the necessity of their existence that they should be kept secret. We speak of Scotland Yard with bated breath . . . We endow the detectives with a kind of omniscience, and believe they shield us from all sorts of mishaps. Such faith is often blindly entertained in the face of very strong evidence to the contrary. Mr. Agnew has never regained his Gainsborough and Lady Dudley is still without her jewels . . . The omniscience of the London detective is a popular delusion, and Charles Dickens has done more than anyone else to foster it. Mr. Bucket moves through the pages of *Bleak House* like a magician in an Eastern tale, and is sketched with so much skill and realism that we accept him as a reality. It is only when the Londoner finds his house broken into, or his property purloined that he realises that Scotland Yard can do very little to help him.

Having argued that the aura of secrecy conveys a false impression of competence, Woodruffe then seems to contrdict himself by saying that the secrecy does not in fact exist, complaining that 'publicity paralyses the detective. It is impossible to keep things from the newspapers, and the criminal is as well informed as the authorities.' But the basic ambivalence comes out when, having urged that 'the whole tendency of modern life and of English feeling is against the detective . . . [and] that the Detective department was never a favourite institution in England', Woodruffe himself then falls under the spell of the omniscient magicians by going on to recount a series of anecdotes illustrating the cleverness of detectives!

With this splendidly inconsistent approach Woodruffe typifies the paradox of the nineteenth-century's love-hate relationship with its detectives. Considered dispassionately, the Victorians kept telling each other, detectives are failures. By and large, they were correct in their estimate. The causes lay partly in the men themselves, their character, quality and approach, and partly in the philosophy of the times which afforded little support to the Cinderella department, neglecting its training and ignoring its potential. Against this there was a fund of sympathy and goodwill; a willingness to believe. Add to this the fact that—apart from doing away with it altogether—there seemed to be no other course but to continue with a detective force, however imperfect, and it is easy to see how, by turning a blind eye to the facts and concentrating on the mystique, a little wishful thinking could soon persuade one that things might not be as bad as they seemed and that the detectives must surely do better next time. I have tried to show that there were grounds for both points of view, that the mystique had its basis in fact just as much as the antipathy.

Whether or not this is correct, there is no denying that the detective offered an irresistible temptation to many writers of fiction.

NOTES TO CHAPTER 7

1   S. M. Phillipps (Under-Secretary of State for the Home Office), on behalf of Sir James Graham (Home Secretary), to the Commissioners, 16 June 1842, in the Public Record Office Home Office 65/14.

2   'Memorandum relative to detective powers of Police' from the Commissioners to Sir James Graham, 14 June 1842, in the Public Record Office, Home Office 45/292.

3   See also Douglas G. Browne, *The Rise of Scotland Yard* (1956), pp. 145-151. I am indebted to this work for many other details of police history.

4   'The New Police', *New Monthly*, November 1829.

5   Quoted in J. F. Moylan, *Scotland Yard* (1929).

6   'The New Police', *op. cit.*

7   See Chapter 9, p. 189.

8   'Detectives in Fiction and in Real Life', *Saturday Review*, 11 June 1864.

9   'The Metropolitan Police', *Saturday Review*, 20 April 1867.

10 'The Police' (in 'Topics of the Week'), *Graphic*, 11 August 1877.

11 'Detectives in Fiction and in Real Life', *op. cit.*

12 'The Efficiency and Defects of the Police', *Saturday Review*, 15 February 1868.

13 Dorothy L. Sayers, *Unnatural Death* (1927).

14 W. S. Gilbert, *A Sensation Novel in Three Volumes* (1871) in *Gilbert before Sullivan*, ed. Jane W. Stedman (1969).

15 'The New Police', *op. cit.*

8
HIDDEN RELICS

The intelligent detective is a drug in the market.

Leslie Stephen, 'The Decay of Murder',
Cornhill Magazine, December 1869

The drug came in two strengths. There was, first, the hundred per cent solution in the form of stories, usually short stories, dealing exclusively with the activities of a police detective and purporting to be true memoirs, as many of the titles reveal: *Experiences of a Real Detective*, *Diary of an Ex-Detective*, *Autobiography of an English Detective*. Like the Player Queen, however, the titles protest too much, and along with the authors' various attempts to convey authenticity in the stories themselves, they are no more than a veneer over what is in almost all cases unalloyed fiction. In a discursive article of May 1861 inspired by five of these efforts[1] the *Dublin University Magazine* notes that 'just now books of narratives of detectives and ex-detectives are all the fashion. Diaries, note-books and confessions issue from the press in shoals', but it concludes that 'they are plainly fictions, and not the real-life experiences of men, who moved and acted in the scenes described'. Of the five under review, the article allows that Curtis is an Inspector of the Irish Constabulary and accepts his statement that the tales contained in *The Irish Police Officer* 'have been compiled from memoranda made by the author in the course of his professional career', but the *Dublin's* critic— one Thomas Donnelly—is still sceptical: 'We trust we offer no offence to the author when we suggest the possibility of a little colouring having been super-added to the original pictures.'

Often these memoir type of publications first appeared as magazine serials before production in volume form, usually as lurid-covered yellowbacks, the name given to the cheap but eye-catching editions devised primarily to fill the new railway bookstalls. They were the Victorian equivalent of the modern paperback, with only a slightly longer life-expectancy so that good, let alone pristine, copies are very scarce. Of the authors little is known; few are even remembered outside the world of collectors. Least forgotten, perhaps, is William Russell who, presumably in the interests of authenticity, often wrote under the name of his detective creation, Waters. His claim to fame is twofold: he seems to have been the first to write this kind of story with the appearance in *Chambers's Edinburgh Journal* of 28 July 1849 of the opening instalment of his *Recollections of a Police Officer*. (This is the title as printed in *Chambers's;* the first English edition of 1856 (see Note 1, p. 175) has 'detective' added to it, perhaps indicating the sales value of the word, especially when it is remembered that both Dickens' articles on detectives in *Household Words* and *Bleak House* appeared between 1850 and 1853.) Russell's second claim to fame is that he seems to have written more than anyone else, though prolific is a word to be avoided in this context as it might imply an output on the scale of Agatha Christie or John Creasey, whereas Russell's known works total less than thirty, of which under half are about detectives.

A typical Waters' story is 'Legal Metamorphoses' which figured in *Chambers's* in September 1850. M. le Breton, the London representative of a French firm reports to Scotland Yard that certain notes and bills of exchange have disappeared from his office while he has been on a visit to the head office in Paris. M. Bellebon, a junior partner, comes to London and explains that the missing property must be recovered, otherwise his firm will be bankrupt and his own forthcoming marriage imperilled. A reward is offered and this brings a proposal from the thieves for the sale back to the firm of the stolen goods. The thieves stipulate that le Breton is to be the go-between, but these arrangements fall through when the thieves tell the police that they are aware of efforts to trap them. The superintendent now passes the case to his most trusted officer, Waters, who visits the scene of the crime and finds small scraps of letters on scented notepaper. Le Breton has no known female relatives or acquaintances and the clue seems valueless until Waters, pursuing another enquiry, notices an advertisement in a shop window offering a reward for the return of a missing greyhound called Fidèle. He then recalls a few words in one of the letters: '*ma pauvre Fidèle est per*——'. Learning from the shopkeeper that the advertiser is one Mme. Levasseur of Edmonton, Waters provides himself with a disguise and a greyhound and presents himself at the house in question as a Cockney dogstealer. There he manages to see a portrait of M. le Breton before being summarily ejected by Madame's spouse. Redisguising himself as a swell, Waters now follows M. Levasseur to a house of ill-repute, where the latter meets le Breton. In order to recover the goods Waters now plays a waiting game; he becomes friendly with Levasseur and eventually wins his confidence by allowing the Frenchman to see him robbing a gentleman who is of course another metamorphosed policeman. Levasseur is interested to learn that Waters (now Williams) has a market for the proceeds of his 'robbery' and 'blackmails' Waters into arranging a meeting with this 'fence' so that he can sell M. Bellebon's notes and bills. The fence is yet another metamorphosed detective and as soon as Levasseur produces the stolen items, he and le Breton and a third accomplice are 'pinioned and secured'. M. Bellebon is delighted, his business and his marriage saved, and Levasseur is packed off to Australia swearing revenge.

All of which is a far cry from Holmes and his magnifying glass or Poirot and his little grey cells. Any resemblance more or less starts and stops with the presence of a detective. The angled approach and all-revealing punch-line of the later detective short story are missing. Any reader bred on the Golden Age who turns to these nineteenth-century efforts must first be struck by the naïveté of the telling and then disappointed by the overall effect which provides neither puzzle nor surprise.

'Legal Metamorphoses', however, is representative not only of Waters' other cases, but also of those of his contemporaries and later imitators, such as Charles Martel, arraigned alongside Waters by the *Dublin University Magazine*, Andrew Forrester and James McGovan. The last-named is of interest, however, in leading us to the possibly genuine memoirs of a real detective of the time.

Like Waters, McGovan is presented as detective turned author in a series of memoirs beginning in 1878 with *Brought to Bay; or, Experiences of a City Detective*. As a pleasant change from London, the city in question is Edinburgh, where McGovan watches anxiously over his 'bairns'—anxiously though scarcely with affection, for he speedily conducts those who misbehave to the Central Police Office in the High Street as the first stage towards almost inevitable deportation or imprisonment. Honest citizens, of course, see McGovan in a different light from the bairns, especially when they fall victim to these rogues:

> Before explaining what had happened, she threw her arms round me rapturously at the word 'police' and exclaimed:
> 'Oh, but you are a blessed man to me this nicht! There's a robber in the cellar threatening to shoot me, and a mad servant above that should 'a' been in a straitjacket afore she cam' here.'
> 'A Feeble Old Lady' in *The Invisible Pickpocket*

At the same time, there is an uneasy rapport and a grudging respect between the detective and his prey. McGovan is known to them as 'a man that won't be beat' and he in turn is aware that they are not to be intimidated into confessions by his mere presence. A crime is committed and McGovan, like most policemen in similar situations, has his suspicions as to the culprits, but proof is another matter:

> To 'Fifty-two Tom', therefore, I turned, not very sanguine of success, nor at all hopeful that this very wary old bird would be easily caught with chaff.
> I met him in the Canongate one afternoon, strolling easily along with a pipe between his teeth, and he gave me a cool and patronising nod as was his wont. This nod always seemed to me to say, 'Ah, you think yourself smart because you took me once, but try me now.' I was continually trying but not with great success.
> 'A Cracksman's Ruse', in *Strange Clues*

Fifty-two Tom is so called from his persistent attempts to break into a particular shop of that street number, and he is a good example of McGovan's Runyonesque prodigality with nicknames. Rather more lethal than Tom is Snapping Andy who 'had earned his name fron a playful habit he had, when in difficulties with the police, of dropping on the ground and snapping at their calves with his teeth'. Positively deadly, however, is Slotty, with his 'comic habit . . . of slotting people with a knife when he was hard pressed'. McGovan himself is no exception. He tells us how in his youth he was known as 'Wee Jimmy, the Fief-catcher's Doug', from his association with a detective called McDermott.

Light relief is provided by McGovan's henchman, McSweeny:

> 'I want to see the best detective you have on the staff,' said a gentleman who appeared at the Central one day in December, when I was away in Ireland . . .
> 'The best detective? — that's me!' said McSweeny with great alacrity, while everyone else in the room hastened to hide his mouth with his hand.
> 'Your name is McGovan, I suppose?' said the gentleman with a pleased smile, and frankly offering his hand.
> 'No — not exactly,' answered McSweeny, with an ill-concealed writhe. 'McGovan is a kind of chum or assistant of mine; but most people prefers me, because if he blunders he loses the case, while if I blunder, begorra! I'm sure to win it;' and McSweeny posed grandly, as if waiting for an admiring world to crown him with laurel.
>
> 'The Blood-Stone Ring' in *Strange Clues*

From which it will be seen that McGovan himself was not one for false modesty. Needless to say, it is McSweeny who falls victim to Snapping Andy's teeth—' "I'm murdered—I'm kilt!" groaned McSweeny. "Begorra, if that's not Snapping Andy ye've got, I'll let him nibble off the calf of me other leg free gratis." ' And generally if there is a wrong method of conducting an investigation McSweeny can be relied on to adopt it, often with success as he himself points out.

The tales themselves are set firmly in the Waters' mould. McGovan's second book, *Hunted Down or Recollections of a City Detective* (1878), is perhaps noteworthy for the attempt to thread the stories together on the theme of a reformed thief's effort to avenge the death of his wife and child at the hands of The Ruffian, who is also interesting as an early example of the master criminal whose identity is unknown both to the police and to his own gang. McGovan's other books are: *Strange Clues; or Chronicles of a City Detective* (1881), *Traced and Tracked; or, Memoirs of a City Detective* (1884), *Solved Mysteries; or, Revelations of a City Detective* (1887?), plus two others, *Criminals Caught* and *The Invisible Pickpocket*, which were first published in volume form in 1921 and 1922 respectively, and may comprise stories culled from the *People's Friend* in which many McGovan stories made their first appearance.[2]

In 1861, however, seventeen years before McGovan's *Brought to Bay*, there had appeared two books, *Curiosities of Crime in Edinburgh* and *The Sliding Scale of Life*, by James McLevy, who claimed that these were his memoirs of thirty years—1830 to 1860—as a detective with the Edinburgh police. McLevy, we learn from these books, superintends those same bairns, aided by the 'faithful Mulholland'. In perseverance he is second to none: 'I would have waited a hundred years to get possession of this man; but, probably, my good angel, Chance, thought I had waited long enough when the period came to fifteen years . . . I certainly thought so, and some other detectives among the gods must have been of the same opinion . . .' and in 'Long Looked-For, Come At Last' McLevy goes on to tell how by pure luck he eventually caught the elusive McDonald red-handed as he plied his trade on Edinburgh High Street.

McLevy, too, is highly thought of by law-abiding citizens and by his superiors, as he is not slow to tell us:

'It is not the value of the coats,' [the lieutenant of police] said, 'that makes me anxious about this case, but the certainty I feel that if we don't get hold of the thieves, our books will be filled with cases of the same kind. Now let us see who shall be the first to bring in the gentlemen and the coats. I need not say,' looking at me, 'who I expect to be the man.'

'The Hay Seeds', in *Curiosities of Crime*

McGovan, in other words, had in McLevy a ready-made memory bank for his 'recollections'. Plagiarism would be too strong a charge, for to give McGovan his due, he did not, as far as I have been able to check, ever use an episode drawn directly from McLevy. There are similarities in some of their cases, as when McLevy solves one through a man's peculiar laugh and McGovan achieves success because of a suspect's peculiar pronunciation, but this overlapping of ideas is inevitable and was certainly to happen again. The overall impression when comparing the two is of a borrowing in principle by McGovan, not a theft in detail.

There is little doubt that McGovan was never a policeman, but another hack writing under the name of his detective. He has been identified by Ellery Queen, in *Queen's Quorum* (1953), as one William Crawford Honeyman, for Queen can boast possession of a copy of *Brought to Bay* inscribed 'To David L. Cromb this collection of GOOD LIES is given by the author, Wm. C. Honeyman'. Queen goes on to give a few more details about Honeyman from a description by Cromb whom Queen identifies as a literary agent, well-known at the time:

> 'McGovan' was a little, bandy-legged man, with a black spade beard; he invariably wore a velvet jacket; his chief interest in life was playing the violin and he was rarely seen without his violin case; his house in Newport-on-Tay was actually named Cremona.

So much for McGovan. With his good lies and open signature, we can accept that Honeyman had no ill-intentioned deception in mind when he presented his detective tales under the trappings of authenticity.

McLevy is another matter, more complex and more interesting, if only because he was a real person, though it was as recently as 1975 that George Scott-Moncrieff reaffirmed the existence of McLevy as an actual policeman in the Introduction to *The Casebook of a Victorian Detective*,[3] an anthology culled from McLevy's two books. Most detective fiction commentators treat these nineteenth-century police-memoirs as fiction without exception; these 'Pseudo Real-Life books', Queen calls them, and Quayle refers to the writers *en masse* as 'these minor novelists'. Perhaps the identification of some of these author-detectives as hacks—Waters and McGovan, for example—has led to the assumption that none were genuine policemen, and it may now be too late to disentangle fact from fiction or the effort might not be worth the trouble, for there is some truth in John Carter's contention, in his essay 'Collecting Detective Fiction', that we are here dealing with a 'school of writers, whose . . . early date promote[s] them to a position of importance usually . . . disproportionate to the actual quality of their work'. Moreover, any concerted assault on these writings faces the dual problem of establishing not only a writer's existence as a policeman but also the genuineness of what was written. The latter was Donnelly's problem over Curtis and will always be the more difficult to solve.

Of McLevy's membership of the Edinburgh police there is no doubt, and little that he at least gave his name willingly to the two books which bear it. The introduction to *Curiosities of Crime* by an anonymous editor tells us that McLevy was an Irish immigrant who came to Edinburgh first as a labourer, then turned to night watchman, finally graduating to detective, in which capacity he seems to have been a kenspeckle figure in the capital. The following is a description of him from the *Edinburgh Evening News* in 1922:

> Such as met 'Jamie' for the first time might have taken him for a well-to-do farmer from the Emerald Isle on a visit to Scotland intent on a 'deal'. He was of medium height, square-faced, and clean-shaven, and always wore a tall silk hat, from beneath the broad brim of which a pair of quick black eyes scrutinised the crowd as he sauntered along the streets accompanied by his faithful companion Mulholland.[4]

First-hand proof of McLevy's existence, however, can be found in the minutes of the Watching Committee of Edinburgh Town Council:

> Read report by the Lord Provost's Committee to whom was remitted Petition of James McLevie,[5] Principal Criminal Officer, praying to be relieved from ordinary duty on account of indis-

position and advancing years. The Report is of the following tenor: '21 May 1860. The Lord Provost's Committee having considered this Petition, and the Petitioner's long and valuable services recommend that Mr. Linton should be authorised to make his duties as light as possible, and keep him on his pay list at the wage of One Guinea a week.' (signed) 'F. Brown Douglas, Lord Provost.' The Magistrates and Council approved of the foregoing Report and ordered accordingly.

Edinburgh Town Council Records, Vol 280, 29 May 1860

The date of McLevy's retirement—1860—is thus confirmed, and with it his freedom to turn writer. Earlier Edinburgh records are much less detailed or non-existent—the only other reference to McLevy seems to be an application of his for leave of absence in 1857—but it is doubtful if even fuller records would provide substantiation of the earlier career of a mere policeman, and so we must take his editor's version of McLevy's earlier career on trust.

As for McLevy's writings, the *Athenaeum* and the *Saturday Review*, neither of which was fooled by Waters, accepted them and their author as fact. The former's review of *Curiosities of Crime*, on 23 February 1861, opens with a frank statement of belief:

Neither the portrait of the police-officer which figures as a frontispiece to this volume, nor the signature placed beneath it, was needed to give an air of authenticity to the sketches of Mr. McLevy's experiences. Apart from defective literary style, there is abundant internal evidence of the genuineness of the book.

The *Athenaeum's* only complaint is that McLevy is too truthful:

We have nothing to object against Mr. McLevy, except that he tells the truth when it is much better that the truth should remain untold. His revelations are nothing less than a confession that he, the acute detective of Edinburgh, can cope only with vulgar rascals who bear the brand of crime on their brows . . . He owns that his success as a detective is due to *luck* and to the *stupidity* of criminals; and there is every reason for accepting his avowal as a just and truthful statement of the case.

Revealing once more that Victorian contrariness about detectives, the *Athenaeum* would prefer the detective of fiction whose mythical success rate has advantages:

Pernicious and in almost every respect bad as are the fictitious accounts of imaginary detectives, which publishers every now and then put forth for the gratification of those who have a morbid taste for anatomising moral enormities, still they usually possess the one good quality of scaring tamperers with evil from the confines of crime.

Both periodicals, however, do have reservations about the single-handedness of McLevy's literary efforts. The *Athenaeum* finds no fault with his first book, but the *Saturday*, in its review, remarks that 'if the work before us be really the genuine, unadulterated composition of an Edinburgh detective, we must ascribe to its author very great and varied talent'. In *The Sliding Scale of Life: or, Thirty Years' Observations of Falling Men and Women in Edinburgh*, to give McLevy's second book its full title, the *Athenaeum* in its review, 24 August 1861, claims to detect the presence of three hands: 'the writer of the confused and scarcely intelligible preface . . . Mr. McLevy, who, besides supplying the raw material of the "Observations", philosophizes with triumphant self-consciousness on things in general; and the melo-dramatic hack, who has worked up the parts of the narrative which appeared to demand more pathos and delicacy of touch than it would be fair to look for in a policeman.' These hints at ghosting do not of course entail the falsity of McLevy's experiences, and the remarks of both papers are perhaps more interesting as showing the implausibility to the Victorian mind of a literate detective.

So did McLevy actually write these books and are his stories true? Given the fact of his existence and the generally favour-able contemporary opinion, there must be a strong presump-tion for the truth of at least some of his tales or some part of each. Beyond this lies conjecture. Thus little store can be placed on McLevy's justification of his apparent romancings by way of condemnation of others' failings in these respects:

No kind of literature can be more detrimental to morals than that of which we have had some melancholy examples from the London press, where the colours that belong to romance are thrown over pictures of crime otherwise revolting. Nor is much required for this kind of writing, — a touch of fate calling for sympathy, or a dash of cleverness extorting admiration, will suffice . . . And yet I have been a little weak sometimes in this way myself, when I have found boldness joined to dexterity.

'The Pleasure Party' in *The Sliding Scale of Life*

Little store, because Russell in the guise of Inspector F was making much the same plea at the same time:

'Detective' literature, if it may be so called, appears to have acquired a wide popularity, chiefly, I suppose, because the stories are believed to be, in the main, faithfully-told, truthful narratives. I have read them all and need hardly say have discovered mistakes which proved to me that the best, most popular of them were the handiwork of a literary man, not the records of an actual experience.

Inspector F *Experiences of a Real Detective* (1862)

Yet McLevy makes his point more modestly and hence more convincingly, and it is in understatements like this, when compared with the style of known hacks, that he scores heavily in the authenticity stakes. Scott-Moncrieff says of McGovan that 'his raw material is derived directly—if made slightly less raw— from McLevy' and that he 'dolls up his stories with deathbed confessions and the like'. McGovan *is* given to greater ornamentation and euphemism than McLevy, but the essential difference between the two lies less in McLevy's indelicacy than in McGovan's exaggeration. For example, McLevy also has nicknames for his bairns, but they are much less flowery concoctions than McGovan's—the Bolter, the Watcher and so on. McGovan generally emerges from his stories as larger than life (comparatively speaking: he is no Holmes), whereas McLevy, with his brevity and continuous use of the first person, which McGovan forsakes as it suits him, can still persuade the reader of today to agree with the *Saturday Review* that here is a real detective telling 'what he did and how and why he did it in simple and clear language, scarcely using a word too much'.

McLevy's indelicate moments bear this out. His stories are raw, it should be stressed, not in any prurient sense but, as the *Athenaeum* recognised, in their revelation of the harsh realities of crime and its detection. In 'The Club Newspaper', a tale which the *Athenaeum* saw as 'the best, and at the same time most unpleasant, sketch' in *The Sliding Scale of Life*, McLevy so plays up to a credulous wife the seriousness of her husband's petty pilfering of newspapers from the club where he works that she is persuaded first to search for and then to hand over £180 he has stolen, in the belief that the theft of the money is the lesser crime and that the theft of the newspapers will be 'scored aff'. This is too close to the alleged police belief in 'anything for a conviction' to be anything but factual, and however justified—McLevy's sophistry here is proof to the *Athenaeum* of the presence of a hack—this flaunting of immoral and illegal tactics is not risked by the pseudo-police writers of the time. Perhaps Russell's nearest descent to this immoral level is in 'The Revenge' (*Chamber's*, 9 November 1850); captured by a gang and threatened with death, Waters persuades a female member of the gang to free him on the promise that he will produce her missing child—a promise he knows he cannot keep. Note, however, that Russell is careful to tell us that this lady eventually recovers from the shock of the truth, while there is no happy ending for McLevy's victims. Waters and his like certainly resort to trickery, but of obvious criminals, not gullible wives. That is not the stuff of which myths are made, though it may be nearer reality. And that is perhaps the nearest we can come to a conclusion about the genuineness of McLevy's books: that if they are not genuine autobiography, they are the most persuasively authentic of all these nineteenth-century detective 'memoirs'.

Whatever the truth about McLevy, the stories in his books, although a cut above Waters' in style, breadth and social interest, do, as detective stories, share with Waters' a basic, elementary approach to detection in that the tales both tell are usually straightforward accounts of a criminal investigation. When Holmes said it was 'elementary', he conveyed the opposite; here the word means what it says. Waters and his imitators may have been writing fiction, but they were either too clever or too ignorant to try to overstep the bounds of possibility.

These writers nevertheless appreciated the value of a break in the pattern and their efforts at variety are often more enjoyable than the descriptions of routine investigations, although in these variations they inevitably drift away from even their crude detective theme. One method was the inclusion in a series of an instance where the detective fails, often humorous and in the context of a none too serious crime. In 'The Pursuit' in Waters' *Recollections*, the detective is rowed across Plymouth harbour to arrest an escaping swindler who he suspects is on board a vessel about to sail to America. His search of the barque is fruitless, and it is only on his way back that he notices his boat is a hand short, by which time of course the barque has sailed. Sometimes the theme of a story is more medical than criminal—'The Monomaniac' in *Recollections*, for example, and 'The Tragedy in Judd Street' in *Experiences of a Real Detective*, in the latter of which a doctor seeks fame and fortune by producing in himself faked symptoms of hydrophobia, hoping to claim the discovery of a cure when he miraculously recovers. He falls victim to the real disease, however, and Inspector F is involved simply because he lives in the same boarding house.

The Detective's Note-Book, which Charles Martel (pseudonym of Thomas Delf) modestly claims only to have edited and which he dedicates to Dickens' hero, the then recently retired Chief Inspector Field, provides what seems an accidental, perhaps careless, variation. The book starts off in typical fashion with a first-person description of how the hero-to-be, Sergeant Bolter, 'was born for the thing; cut out for it; one of Nature's policeman—it came quite natural. Why, sir, I was a policeman long before the new police was thought of . . .' The first story is an account of jealousy and love in his native village in which he does not figure, but the next nine are indeed episodes in his career as a detective. In the last four, however, there is no Sergeant Bolter. Two of these have no detective at all, while the other two go so far as to introduce new detectives; first, Officer Tinman, a German detective of Inspector Field's force, who is invaluable in finding out what the Bavarian Esther of the title has to say, but who needs to be reminded by the author of the up-to-date aids to detection: 'Officer Tinman! why have you been sitting so long within sounds of the Electric Telegraph, ticking, clicking in the next room, and haven't thought of asking the stations all over town to look out for an Esther . . .'; and second, Hallett, who tells the 'Ex-Policeman's Story'. This is perhaps the best tale in the book, but it is more the ex-policeman's love story than anything else. And why Martel dispensed with Bolter we shall probably never know.

In general, however, these stories follow the set pattern of a crime, an investigation often bringing with it the excitement of a chase, and finally a solution, not in the modern sense of the explanation of a puzzle but simply in the form of an arrest based, it sometimes seems, more on hope than on proof. In 'Robbery at Osborne's Hotel', for instance, Inspector F pinpoints the guilty party—a lady thief—to his own satisfaction because she registered at an hotel immediately after the victim. Again, the interest in Martel's story of 'The Absconding Debtor' does not lie in a problem but in a chase on skates down a frozen river which is well put over and need concede nothing to modern thrillers.

Even when the story revolves round accusations against an innocent party, there is no circle of alternative culprits with suspicion cast around and a surprise ending; instead, there is usually only one other very obvious person who could have done it and he can be relied on to play into the hands of the pursuing detective without the latter's straining himself with analytical reasoning and debatable deductions from cigar ash. Shrewd, Waters and his like may be, but at a practical, work-a-day level; armchairs for them are strictly for relaxation after a hard day's chase.

The influence of Poe on these writers is non-existent, a fact regretted by the *Dublin University Magazine* in its article of 1861 on 'Crime and its Detection' which bewails the ordinariness and 'commonplace incidents' of these volumes of memoirs, and claims that 'were the brilliant but unfortunate Edgar Allan Poe now living and disposed to take advantage of the hunger for such productions, what a series of thrilling and exciting inventions would he not produce!' The 'spirit of logical and philosophical enquiry' which Donnelly, the author of the *Dublin's* article, supposed to be the necessary basis of criminal investigation is certainly lacking in these stories. Their source, like many of today's police procedural stories, is exclusively routine police work to the extent that just as much of that work is boring, so too are the stories, not only to Donnelly but even more so to us, accustomed as we are to the sophisticated fare of the Golden Age and after.

To some contemporary readers, however, this was the *New* Police, and as we saw in the last chapter the hope inspired by this fresh attempt to defeat crime could at times outweigh the antipathy and distrust engendered by earlier examples of law enforcement bodies. In *Bloodhounds of Heaven* (1976), a study of the Victorian detective, the author, Ian Ousby, bears out this idea of contemporary favour towards detectives:

> They [police detectives] tackle crime and mystery with a native shrewdness and an armory of police techniques rudimentary in modern eyes but then sufficiently novel to be regarded by contemporaries with an almost superstititous awe. For example, they can trace a missing man through the banknotes he was known to be carrying at the time of his disappearance, or use the telegraph system to transmit information about a wanted suspect.

Except that Officer Tinman had to be reminded that the telegraph existed, and Miss Braddon's detective in *Henry Dunbar*, Mr. Carter, 'did not employ the telegraph, by which means he might perhaps have expedited the arrest of Henry Dunbar's murderer . . . because in doing so he must have taken the local police into his confidence, and he wished to do his work quietly . . .' and not share the reward? Tinman and Mr. Carter are of course fictional detectives but their behaviour is closer to the picture of the ill-trained, unco-operative, hard-up souls of the preceding chapter. And not everyone was impressed by the latest gadgetry, Donnelly in the *Dublin University Magazine* for one:

We have now, as alleged, an improved police, electric wires, rapid communication, bright street lamps, and other aids to discovery which were wanting some years ago; and yet not the faintest gleam even of suspicion has been fixed on any one in connexion with this event [the Waterloo Bridge murder of 1860 in which parts of a body were found in a carpet bag floating near the bridge].

And the *Saturday Review* for another. Throwing in a sly dig at Dickens for good measure, it preaches a little parable to show that detectives are no more clever or efficient than we ordinary mortals, taking as its text, oddly enough, banknotes, though as a means of tracing their thief, not their owner:

Detectives, no doubt, have their triumphs, which they relate to gentlemen in search of articles for popular magazines; but, in fact, they are very ordinary people who are worth nothing when they are taken beyond their routine. Not long ago a gentleman's pocket was picked of a bank-note. Knowing the number, he went to the Bank of England and found that the note had been paid in by a private bank. The private bankers had received it from a customer, who had got it from a shop, where it had been taken across the counter. Here the owner of the note stopped, and put the matter in the hands of a detective, simply telling him that he had lost such a note on such a day. A few days afterwards the dective returned in triumph, saying that he had a clue. He had discovered the shop at which the note had been changed, by the very same process which had been already adopted by its owner, whom he expected to be delighted and astonished at his clever-ness. It is needless to say that his "clue" never led him any further.

In this article—'The Detection of Crime'—the *Saturday* is again on its hobby-horse of 'what can the police really do about crime?' Three years later it has remounted, and in a sympathetic review of Waters' *Autobiography of an English Detective* (1863) comes out with the question in so many words:

It is a curious question to ask what detectives really do, and how they do it — how much crime is found out through their agency and what are the means they employ? . . . We believe that the experience of all lawyers who have had much to do with the working of the criminal law is that the detectives do exceedingly little. The crimes which are found out, in ninety-nine cases out of a hundred, reveal themselves. The police merely conduct an inquiry which is perfectly obvious. A dead body is found, and the law sets a particular set of persons to make inquiry about it. The police ask simple questions of the people most likely to know, and get answers which show who was the murderer . . . They have unbounded time before them; if they succeed, they are complimented and paid extra; if they fail, they are still paid as much as their labour is worth in the market.

This analysis of police work is, I think, one on which policemen of both today and yesterday would agree. They might quibble at such expressions as 'unbounded time' and doing 'exceedingly little', and the modern police could point to more sophisticated techniques and a more scientific approach, as well as the absence of rewards, but in broad terms the *Saturday's* description accords with the down-to-earth, routine idea of detective work conveyed by real detectives when speaking and writing about their job. Moreover, the *Saturday* believes that its contentions about the real police are borne out by the book under review, which is perhaps why it is commended:

Then what can detectives really do? These volumes . . . supply an answer that is, we think, tolerably correct. They can do two things if they are masters of their business. They can catch, better than most men, a person supposed to have committed a crime; and, secondly, when they have caught him, they can deal with him better than most persons can. Both these things are distinct from unravelling the secret of a crime.

Yet these stories are fiction. While they may offer, as far as they go, a factual picture of the mid-Victorian detective at work, they are at the same time simplified, selective and sentimentalised, and in these respects, quite apart from authorship, their fictive quality is revealed. With this foot in each camp the stories seem to occupy a literary limbo. They do not offer any of the twists and turnings which could lead us to see them, except in the most indirect way, as a link with later detective fiction, but equally they are as far removed from factual crime writing, whether in the form of real detectives' memoirs or of the *Famous Crimes of Recent Times* type of book.

It is nevertheless tempting to try to fit these tales into our preconceived notions of the development of detective fiction in particular or of crime writing in general. One obvious and attractive similarity between them and later detective fiction is that both have the detective as hero. Scott-Moncrieff speculates interestingly that since McGovan's books were appearing in Edinburgh at the time when Conan Doyle was a medical student there, the creator of Holmes may owe something to our good liar or even to his source, McLevy. I suspect, however, that if Doyle did read McGovan and if he was influenced by him, then he was influenced *away* from McGovan's style and type of detective. One reads Doyle for Holmes; one sometimes does not notice the detective in these earlier stories. If nothing else, a social gap separates these detective creations: ' "Confide in me, ma'am, [Inspector F has to say] it is true I am but a police-officer—a detective police-officer . . ." ', while Holmes, so far from having to make an apologetic confession of his trade can make a bold profession of it: '[I am] the only unofficial consulting detective . . . I am the last and highest court of appeal in detection.' The proof of this particular pudding is in the reading; try a story by Waters or Martel or Forrester or McGovan or, for that matter, McLevy, and then compare their detective with Holmes or Father Brown or Poirot or whom you will of that breed; try one, that is, if you can find one, but perhaps the difficulty in finding them is my best argument.

In *Bloodhounds of Heaven* Ousby suggests a link between Waters and Co. and subsequent detective fiction by way of content:

> The later work of Russell and his successors shows a number of changes, keeping pace with developments in the more serious detective literature of the age. With advances in police method, the detective's investigations become more scientific and orderly; his adventures thus approach closer to the detailed and ratiocinative structure of the detective short story of modern times.

Unfortunately, Ousby does not give an example of this development, and Russell's stories of 1862 in his *Experiences of a Real*

Detective, such as 'Robbery at Osborne's Hotel', already mentioned, convey exactly the same approach by the detective as his earliest efforts in 1849. As the *Saturday Review* says of what seems to be Russell's last detective volume, his *Autobiography of an English Detective* of 1863, 'almost all the stories in these volumes fall in with this account [quoted above] of a detective's business. We are supposed to know the criminal at the outset, and the detective is set to catch him'. If these stories are susceptible to a one sentence summary, the *Saturday* has here framed it. The later approach to the detective story, to state the obvious, is the reverse of this: we are *not* supposed to know the criminal, and the detective is set to *reveal* him. The *Saturday's* verdict applies not only to Russell in the 1860s, but to Honeyman in the 1870s and 1880s and, in the 1890s, to J. E. Preston Muddock, better known as Dick Donovan and perhaps the last notable writer of this kind.

If, then, these stories do not link up in any meaningful way with the detective short stories of Doyle and the Golden Age, it it tempting to place them (if pigeon-holed they must be) in the real crime class. Their apparent faithfulness to police procedure of the time argues for this, but they are at base much too genteel and middle-class in both content and the telling to be put on a par with reality. The fact that they are factual does not make them any the less fictional, designed to be read for amusement by upright people in good homes, albeit perhaps not left lying openly about—which of course added zest to the whole affair, for we are in an era of only surface decorum and propriety. So innocuous are these books really that the *Saturday* felt it necessary to reassure its readers about Russell's *Autobiography of an English Detective*: 'It ought to be added, that although they treat of all sorts of crimes committed by persons of both sexes, there is nothing in them that the most sensitive mind could consider as rendering them unfit for general reading.' John Carter in 'Collecting Detective Fiction' has a rather lower opinion of these books, calling them the ' "below stairs" school of detective fiction' which, he claims, 'gradually split into two branches . . . On the one side it turned to fact; on the other it joined up with that huge stream of "bloods" which had run so strongly all through the Victorian period.' These links may exist but I suspect they resemble less a fork than a spaghetti junction. Even more doubtful is the suggestion that these books were read solely below stairs—below the bedclothes, perhaps, but publication in the *Sixpenny Magazine*, while not reaching the top rank in periodicals, is five pennyworth above the penny press, and reviews in the *Athenaeum*, the *Saturday Review* and the *Dublin University Magazine*, whatever their verdicts, argue a rather more elevated readership for these writers than Carter allows.

This is borne out by the relative gentility of the stories themselves. If they had adopted a style and conveyed an atmosphere anything short of conventional, they would never have seen the light of day. Michael Sadleir, in *Things Past*, remarks of this period that 'while editors, publishers and public wanted stories of high life and crime, they would not stomach highlivers and criminals as they really were.' To highlivers and criminals we can add detectives. It is interesting that in borrowing from McLevy, McGovan may have felt it necessary to bowdlerise him, but he was probably wise to do so, given that he was writing fiction, otherwise the *Athenaeum* might have said of him what it said of McLevy in its review of *The Sliding Scale of Life*: 'Some of his stories are very painful, and some so coarse that they are unfit for the drawing-room table.' Which probably did McLevy's sales no harm. In any case, as we have seen, McLevy's painfulness and coarseness were less immoral than the *Athenaeum's* words imply, and looked at from a century later there is little essential difference between his approach and that of Russell and McGovan.[6] Lacking McLevy's excuse of authenticity, for what it was worth, Russell and his imitators had to keep within the limits of acceptability applicable to their age. They seem to have succeeded in this and consequently in making and retaining their appeal to the class which could afford to buy their books.

'In his life style, as well as his attitudes, Waters offered his middle class public a reflection of themselves', remarks Ousby, though this reflection of middle-class values can also be seen as a deliberate manoeuvre by Russell to overcome the distrust and suspicion of detectives which I have tried to show was a continuing shadow on them throughout this period, rather than proof positive of the general acceptance and even popularity of detectives both real and imaginary. Russell takes great pains to show how his detectives are gentlemen fallen on hard times: '. . . adverse circumstances . . . compelled me to enter the ranks of the metropolitan police, as the sole means left me of procuring food and raiment', confesses Waters in his first story in 1849. Ousby actually quotes this passage, but concentrates on showing how Waters manages to reconcile himself to his lower status, yet Waters' words are a glaring indictment of the police as the bottom of the barrel in career terms. If detectives had been truly popular, one feels that Russell would have started off with a hero who had joined the police as one of several equally honourable options, a scheme which would have better served his middle-class pretentions. Instead we have Waters signing on almost as a last resort, and as late as 1862, the post-Bucket heyday of the detective according to Ousby, Russell again forsakes facts in order to separate his Inspector F from the *hoi polloi* of Scotland Yard:

> Several months previous to the organisation, in 1829, by the then Mr. Peel, Secretary for the Home Dept., I had made myself conspicuous to a certain degree in the neighbourhood of Covent Garden as an amateur, supplementary sort of constable, and in several instances wherein the Charleys were completely nonplussed, succeeded in bringing criminals to justice. This seemed to be my natural vocation; and when, the new police force being in process of definitive formation, I received a communication from Colonel Rowan, proposing to appoint me inspector, if such a post were worth my acceptance, I instantly closed with the offer, disposing of my business — not a very profitable one (I had attended more to the affairs of the public than to my own) — and entered with alacrity upon the duties of my new profession.
>
> Inspector F, *Experiences of a Real Detective*

A superlative liar. The point surely is that Russell, wishing to capitalise on interest in detectives but realising that this interest by no means entailed the acceptance, let alone the popularity, of this new breed, solved his problem by a compromise: a detective in the Metropolitan Police, who is, if only in origins, a cut above his brethren socially. (What might we be writing now if Russell had left his detective an amateur?) Simple common sense, and a device to be adopted more than once as the years went by—Emile Gaboriau's Lecoq, Fergus Hume's Octavius Fanks, Henry Wade's Inspector Poole, Michael Innes' Appleby and Ngaio Marsh's Alleyn, to name but a few, but all of whom have a background superior to that normally associated with detectives, with all the supposed advantages that brings to the author. However snobbish this may be, and whatever other motives they may have had for adopting this technique, these authors must have felt the device necessary as a means of avoiding the perennial distaste among their readers for the job of the detective and often for the detective himself.

As we shall see, Waters' avowedly fictional contemporaries are not blessed by their authors with gentle birth, but are truly portrayed as low on the social ladder, and in other respects, too, they will show that there was by no means the universally sympathetic presentation that Ousby alleges. The old doubts of the 1830s lingered on and have never been quite dissipated, either in fact or in fiction. Hence in the 1970s Sir Robert Mark's purges at the Yard and the institution of the Police Complaints Board, composed of laymen, to supervise the conduct of inquiries into complaints against the police and so break the tradition that the police are competent to guard themselves. And in fiction, apart from the occasional qualms felt by amateurs such as Wimsey and Philip MacDonald's Anthony Gethryn (' "Oh, I know I'm a filthy spy" '), one has the 'tough' school of detective stories which emerged in the late 1920s to counterbalance the too-nice post-Holmes depiction of detectives. In so far as the tales of Waters and his like were accepted, one suspects that there is about the acceptance an aspect of that ambivalence towards detectives which here takes the form of a desire to read about them but a dread of having anything to do with them. When Inspector F says ' "Confide in me, ma'am; it is true I am but a police officer—a detective police-officer" ', the reiteration of his employment qualified by that ominous word is the playing of the last psychological card in his hand; it is as if he were saying, 'There! I have bared my soul to you by telling you the awful truth about what I am. Now you can bare your soul to me, as your secret cannot be more horrible than mine!'

The problems of writing stories with a detective hero in the mid-nineteenth century are thus revealed in these books at least as clearly as middle class values of the time, and the fact that these stories died out leaving no obvious progeny comes as no surprise. Equally, the fact that they were written is logical enough. Their approach—here is a detective and this is what he does—is the straightforward, natural reaction of hacks motivated by little more than the 'desire to make a quick penny out of a new taste', as Ousby says; which brings us full circle to the earlier point about the novelty of a body of men dedicated, however erratically, to the side of law and order and punished if caught running with the hares. Small wonder that people wanted to read about them in their most fascinating (from a distance) incarnation as detectives, and that writers, in satisfying this demand, did not think it necessary to exaggerate the men and their powers beyond reality or at least probability. Care not to offend current moral standards was all that was needed. The detective and the chase alone were sufficiently exciting unto the day. The idea of a totally fictionalised story such as 'The Purloined Letter', complete with amateur detective, did not occur to these writers as possible or necessary.

One can of course pick out similarities between these workaday detectives and later variations. Social superiority and the reflection of middle class values have been mentioned. Ousby also points to domestic interludes, disguise, the detective's sympathy for the weak and 'the metropolitan officer's contempt for his rural equivalents'. These are far from outstanding and frequent features, however, and similarities are not to be confused with influences. We must beware of crediting this relatively small and short-lived brand of book with a strong impact on detective fiction, especially in the light of the strong dissimilarities outlined above. In their limbo, Waters and his companions form a curiosity within the genre, coherent but isolated, rather than a vital stage in its development. They are the product we would expect of the times, semi-documentaries, and their aim and air of authenticity were all too successful. As the novelty of the detective wore off and his lack of success became apparent, these tales of 'demi-detection', as Haycraft calls them, died away before the end of the century, and sensation fiction, to survive, had to jettison this kind of detective. E. M. Wrong remarks of the pre-Holmes period, '*vixere fortes ante Agamemnona*'—there were heroes before Agamemnon, but if he had Waters and his like in mind he might well have added Horace's next lines: 'but they are all unmourned and consigned to long oblivion.'

NOTES TO CHAPTER 8

1 Namely:
Recollections of a Detective Police Officer, 'Waters', 1856
Same, Second Series, 1859
Diary of an Ex-Detective, ed. Charles Martel, 1859
The Detective's Note-Book, ed. Martel, 1860
The Irish Police Officer, Robert Curtis, 1861.

2 There are at least two other McGovan titles published only in the U.S.A.: *The Edinburgh Detective* (1883) and *Secret Confessions* (no date). I have not seen these but it is likely that they are the same stories as published in Edinburgh under new titles.

3 Scott-Moncrieff died in 1974 before this book was published. From internal evidence, such as quotations from Edinburgh newspapers which accept McLevy unquestioningly, 'reaffirmed' is correct.

4 Quoted on dustjacket of *The Casebook of a Victorian Detective*, ed. George Scott-Moncrieff (1975).

5 Spelled 'McLevy' in the index to these minutes.

6 The stories in *Clues: or Leaves from a Chief Constable's Note-Book* (1889) by William Henderson, which can bid for truthfulness in that the author ended a police career as Chief Constable of Edinburgh, are also indistinguishable from pseudo-memoirs.

9

THE GUEST DETECTIVE

The detective looked at the boy's sharp thin features with a
scrutinising glance common to men of his profession.

'Then you'll serve me faithful, if I want you, Slosh? I thought
perhaps you might let family interests interefere with business,
you know.'

'Not a bit of it,' said the youthful enthusiast. 'I'd hang my
grandmother for a sovering, and the pride of catching her, if she
were a downy one.'

Miss Braddon, *The Trail of the Serpent* (1861)

The hundred per cent solution of stories centring on a detective
was, like Poe's, too strong too soon, and lacking anything like
Poe's quality it failed to survive and procreate. Alongside these
detective-memoirs, however, a diluted preparation of the drug
—what can one call it but the seven per cent solution?—was
being marketed, and it was in this version that the detective of
fiction was nursed to maturity.

This seven per cent solution consisted in the inclusion in a
novel of a detective, not as the hero or even as the protagonist,
but as one ingredient in the recipe for a sensation novel. The
recipe, it will be remembered, ran

> Paint, as more effective,
> Villain, knave and fool,
> And always a detective.

The 'always' cannot be taken literally as there are sensation
novels without detectives, either official or amateur, even taking

sensation fiction in that narrow sense of novels concerned primarily with the unravelling of a secret, unless Providence is reckoned to be on the pay-roll of Scotland Yard. More importantly, the 'always' can be misleading since it implies a wealth of novels about detectives, which just does not seem to be the case. Now the translation of the detective (we are still concerned only with the official variety) from the streets of London to the pages of the novel comes as no surprise. The factors which motivated—and restricted—Waters and his fellow short-story writers operated again in the field of the novel. No sensation novelist, however pedestrian, should have failed to see that the detective was grist to a genre largely concerned with murder and mystery. No sensation novelist really worth his salt was going to pass up a character combining, *ex officio*, the twin attractions of astuteness and secretiveness. Here for the likes of Dickens and Collins was ready-made flour. But used, be it noted, once only by each in a major way.

Which brings us to Mr Bucket and Sergeant Cuff who are the obvious examples of this relatively intermittent and minor role of the detective in sensation fiction and, Dupin apart, certainly the two most widely discussed before Holmes. It is almost true to say the only two discussed, and even if we adjust the recipe to read 'and sometimes a detective', obligingly forgetting that, written in 1864, it pre-dates Cuff by four years, we must still wonder whether two swallows make a summer. Yet a summer of no little remark there surely was, to judge from some critics' response to the *début* of the detective in the novel.

The list of fictional detectives of this time can of course be extended beyond Bucket and Cuff. Some of them appear below and their paucity must be due in part to my failure to locate more, but a complete list of detectives of the 1850s and 60s, granting one could be assembled, would not, I believe, affect the present contention of their minor role; any such list would certainly not approach the multiplicity of the first two decades of this century, let alone the detective industry, cottage and factory, of the 1920s and 30s.

An indication of relative output within the nineteenth century itself is given by Carter in his Introduction to *Victorian Detective Fiction*:

> The years 1846-1870 (Poe to *Edwin Drood*) provide about forty entries; 1871-1890, the period ending with the Sherlock Holmes revolution, more than twice as many; and the last decade of Queen Victoria nearly twice as many again.

This total over the twenty-five year period from 1846 to 1870—less than two a year on average—is alarmingly meagre. Moreover, the recipes in *Blackwood's* of 1864 and 1875 refer specifically to sensation *novels*, so that if we deduct the twenty or so books in *Victorian Detective Fiction* which are of the short story, detective-memoir type, the figure for novels pales to an insignificant twenty.

Nevertheless the volume of novels before 1870 which could be called detective fiction, or, grinding my axe, sensation fiction with a detective, obviously impressed contemporary commentators, including the usually unimpressionable *Times*, in its review of *The Moonstone*:

> Cuff is the inevitable detective, a character apparently so regularly retained on the establishment of sensation novelists that it would be convenient for a due appreciation of their new works to find appended to advertisements of them, along with extracts from critical journals, such remarks as 'Very true to life' and the like, dated from Scotland Yard.

As early as December 1861, under the heading 'Literature of the Month', the *Sixpenny Magazine* was making the same point: '. . . what a complete *Deus ex machina* a detective now is in a sensation novel!' and by 1869 the *Cornhill*, as we have seen, considered him 'a drug in the market'[1] On evidence of this sort we would seem justified in accepting the prevalence of the detective in mid-Victorian fiction; but we are still left with the gnawing question of where they all are.

The beginning of some answers to this dual problem of quantity and whereabouts may lie in the following. To start with, the total output of stories with detectives must be larger than the twenty in the Glover/Greene collection, which its compilers would be the first to admit is incomplete. It would also seem reasonable to assume that under sensation novels the reviewers quoted above included the short-story detective which would help swell the quantity. Thus in *XIX Century Fiction* (1951) Michael Sadleir lists just under forty different detective yellowbacks, mostly of the short-story variety, twenty of which are not named in *Victorian Detective Fiction*. Still with yellow-backs, Quayle has pointed out that 'many titles, known through the medium of advertisements in other volumes, seem to have completely disappeared', and while this may not apply to the same extent to the more durably-bound three-decker, doubtless a number of these relevant to detective fiction have also been lost without trace. More optimistically, others are perhaps lying forgotten and unread in libraries, bookshops and houses throughout the country. A deal of detective work remains to be done on the detectives of Victorian fiction.

Short of reading every work of fiction published in at least one year during the 1860s, a herculean and soul-destroying, not to say impracticable task, it is impossible to produce accurate figures for the actual proportion of books with detectives around this time. The following arithmetic is therefore confessed guesswork, 'a mental exercise', as Holmes has it in *The Valley of Fear*. If we combine the works, long and short, listed by Sadleir and Glover/Greene, the total comes to around sixty; suppose, for the sake of argument, that we double this on grounds of incompleteness caused by the points mentioned above, not forgetting the detectives of peripheral penny fiction; this would give an average of five books a year between 1845 and 1870, the later years of course producing well above the average, perhaps as high as twenty. The *Saturday Review*, commenting on 'Literary Activity in England' tells us that in 1866 the total number of novels, by which it seems to mean fiction in general, was 390, of which it reckons at most seventy were reprints. Hence fiction with detectives might in 1866 have formed up to six per cent of new output. This may still seem a paltry figure to us, but two points are worth bearing in mind.

First, the claim by the recipes for the omnipresence of the detective was patently exaggerated, so the same may be true of the remarks by *The Times* and the *Sixpenny* and others about even the frequency of his appearances. Not all commentators on sensation fiction thought it necessary to single out the detective from all the other obliquities of the genre. Mansel, for example, takes twenty-four specimens as the text of his article in the *Quarterly Review* of 1863 but does not once mention detectives. The *North British Review* in 1865 and the *Eclectic* in 1868 devoted full length articles to Miss Braddon, who even by the first date had several detective characters to her discredit, but neither article saw fit, in its detailed condemnation of her and her works, to include detectives save for a couple of passing remarks in the former. This reticence may stem from the contempt bred by familiarity, but it may also be due to the fact that the detective was something less than the inevitable character some made him out to be. Second, while twenty or forty or even two hundred books with detectives is insignificant today, it must be remembered that in the period under discussion the growth of fiction generally was in itself remarkable, and the advent within fiction of a number of books, whatever their total, featuring members of a none too salubrious profession, was a noteworthy development, if only as an aspect of the lamentable tendency of many novels to answer 'all the purposes of lengthened Police reports'.

It is in this climate of exaggeration and expansion that comments like those in *The Times* and the *Sixpenny* must be seen. Yet when all is said and done, Wrong seems to have been well-advised in omitting the adjective from that line by Horace: '*Vixere fortes ante Agamemnona* multi'.

But however many detectives were produced in the heyday of sensation fiction, the original contention stands: none of them was the hero of the book in which he figured. One has to go to France and Gaboriau to find the nearest thing to a police hero in a full-length novel. Of English literature's two prime detectives of the time, Bucket is introduced about a third of the way through *Bleak House*, to disappear quickly and appear again only at intervals; and Cuff, after a longish *début* early on, is in the wings for the second half of *The Moonstone* until the finale. The pattern is repeated in the novels of Miss Braddon, with whom detectives were favourite but far from essential characters, and certainly never heroes. Sometimes she cast them in strong supporting roles, as with Mr Carter in *Henry Dunbar*, who is rather too obviously moulded on Bucket, and, in *The Trail of the Serpent*, Joseph Peters, who must have a claim to fame as the first dumb detective. At other times Miss Braddon grants detectives only walking-on parts, like the un-named 'intelligent detective' of *One Life, One Love* (1890) who gives up on page thirty, muttering, 'It's hard lines for a man to let such a chance slip through his fingers, but I don't believe any man will ever grow rich out of the Denmark Street murder. This job was too neatly done, and the people in it were too clever.' Her *Wyllard's Weird* (1885) is a pageant of bit-part detectives— Distin, Drubarde, Trottier, all of them unsuccessful. (I realise I seem to have cheated in mentioning books written as late as 1890, but in defence it can be said that Miss Braddon spanned nearly three-quarters of a century from the 1850s to World War I without any appreciable change in style or technique.) Other now long or largely forgotten detectives of the 1860s are Inspector Wily and Detective Meadows of Mrs Yorick Smythies' *Alone in the World* (1861), 'M', the chief of the Paris secret police in Shirley Brooks' *The Silver Cord* (1861), which occasioned the *Sixpenny's* remark about the detective as *deus ex machina*, Sergeant Delves of Mrs. Henry Wood's *Mrs. Halliburton's Troubles* (1862), Joseph Grimstone of Miss Braddon's *Aurora Floyd* (1863) and Mr. Carter of the same author's *Henry Dunbar* (1864), Detective Somerton of Mortimer Collins' *Who is the Heir?* (1865), and M. Durbec and Sergeant Skinner of John Berwick Harwood's *Lady Flavia* (1865).[2] This list must be far from complete, and as the statistics from *Victorian Detective Fiction* indicate, the number begins to increase after 1870 and especially after 1878, which marks the publication of *The Leavenworth Case*, the first book by the prolific and underestimated Anna Katherine Green, creator of the New York police detective, Ebenezer Gryce. All these earlier detectives, however, are subsidiary characters.

The one possible exception that I know of occurs in *The Notting Hill Mystery* (1863) by Charles Felix, which first appeared between 1862 and 1863 as a serial in *Once a Week* and which owes more than a little to *The Woman in White*, with its Fosco-like villain, Baron R., its mesmerism and its documentary construction. The book consists of reports and letters written or procured as potential evidence against Baron R. by an insurance investigator, Ralph Henderson, and it is his commendable, continuous detective work which makes the story not only exceptional for its period (it even has a diagram), but still very readable in ours. Maurice Richardson included it in his 1945 anthology, *Novels of Mystery from the Victorian Age*, in the Introduction to which he describes it as 'the work of an educated, literate and highly imaginative writer', and in *Bloody Murder* Symons, too, is laudatory, going so far as to claim for this book the distinction of being the first English detective story, but I refuse to be drawn on this point.

In its concentration on the efforts of the 'hero', Henderson, to find out what the Baron is up to, *The Notting Hill Mystery* differs radically from the pattern of contemporary sensation literature and the minor role played therein by the detective, but I put hero in inverted commas, not because Henderson is an insurance investigator rather than a policeman—that would be quibbling; he is, after all, a professional—but because he does not come across, and probably was not intended to come across, as a figure in permanent limelight like Holmes, or even intermittent limelight like Bucket. The emphasis is on the unravelling of the secret to the virtual exclusion of the unraveller. Henderson remains in shadow throughout. We learn nothing about him—his very name is known to us only through his signature on the reports to his employers; he has no aura of secretiveness—clues, indeed, being refreshingly interpreted as soon as they are discovered; he has no gimmicks, no tantalising mastery of innuendo and the obscure question; he has no Watson, no wife, no witticisms to alleviate the grind of his gumshoe existence. This all helps to keep the plot moving and is an inevitable result of the epistolary style in hands less gifted than Collins. But is Henderson then the hero? The issue is not crucial, since one exception, if such it be, is proverbially necessary to prove the rule.

Occupying this minor role, the police detective is not a key figure in the plottings of sensation fiction. Many of the books in which he appears would be the poorer without him, but it is not too difficult to envisage the problems of *Bleak House* being resolved without Bucket, and while today we cannot mention *The Moonstone* without thinking of Cuff, it must be remembered that he fails to solve the mystery of the missing gem. Despite the recipes, authors do not seem to have felt themselves under any obligation to include a detective to throw light on their secrets, and there are instances in reading their stories when, fed on the twentieth-century pattern, we anticipate the timely arrival of the expert only to be disappointed. For example, in *The Woman in White*, when Mr Gilmore is anxious to trace Anne Catherick and Mrs. Clements following their sudden departure from Todd's farm, Collins has created for himself the perfect situation for the introduction of a detective, but a perfunctory investigation is made by a servant and Collins chooses to take his plot in a quite different direction. Similarly, one can easily imagine work for a detective in *Uncle Silas* or *East Lynne*, but nothing materialises. Julian Hawthorne makes this point: 'Many narratives involving a puzzle of some sort . . . are handled by the writer without expert detective aid.' And he goes on, '. . . the detective was an afterthought, or, more accurately, a deus ex machina to make the story go. The riddle had to be unriddled; and who could do it so naturally and readily as a detective?'[3] This was the obvious, pedestrian approach to the detective by many sensation authors—if you have a fire, send for the fire brigade; if you have a crime, send for a detective. Having put in this token appearance, the detective often disappears just as quickly, as happens to Sergeant Bulmer in Collins' *No Name* (1862). To say this is not to take these authors to task for not concentrating on detectives; far from it, for this take-him-or-leave-him approach confirms the earlier point that these writers, including the begetters of Bucket and Cuff, were in no conscious way writing detective stories as we understand the term today. They were rather building houses of secrets, off which the roofs had to be lifted to reveal the solution, but for which process a detective was strictly optional. The attitude is epitomised by Miss Braddon's treatment of detective Grimstone in *Aurora Floyd:* 'It is scarcely necessary to this story to tell how the detective went to work.' As long as the secret could be withheld for three volumes, it did not matter too much how it was revealed. Secrets, not detectives, are the lowest common denominator of sensation fiction— and of detective fiction.

The part played by the detective was in some cases even less honourable than that granted by Hawthorne, whose words above imply that when he does appear, he is successful. Yet with depressing frequency the detective does not manage to unriddle the riddle. The defeat of Cuff, the early retirement of the detective in *One Life, One Love* and the multiple failures of *Wyllards's Weird* have been mentioned, but many of those other detectives are also failures in one way or another. They may promise much, but little comes of their efforts in the end. Miss Braddon whets our appetites by telling, in the manner of Watson's name-dropping of Holmes' unpublishable cases, that Mr Carter has been wrapped up in 'the great Scotch-plaid robberies', and by giving us the linguistic basis of his method: 'learn the alphabet of the case, and work up into the syntax and prosody'. But after a misdirected chase, Bucket-fashion, across half England, Carter has to admit defeat: ' . . . it's humiliating to an officer of my standing in the force; but I'd better confess it freely. I've been sold, sir—sold by a young woman, too, which makes it three times as mortifying.' Cuff is forced to a similar confession at the end of *The Moonstone.* Drubarde in *Wyllard's Weird* is a curious mixture. His hobby—a roof flower-garden—is reminiscent of Cuff and his roses; his vanity in recounting how Distin is a great detective but how he would have failed but for Drubarde bridges Lecoq and Holmes, and his philosophy of

detection reads like Doyle, or, to be precise and fair, Doyle
reads like Braddon:

> Professional acumen like Mr. Distin's is apt to run in grooves —
> to be too intent on following the practical and the possible, to
> shut out the romantic element, to strangle the imagination, and
> to forget that it is very often by following the apparently impos-
> sible that we arrive at the truth.

In the event, however, he proves a broken reed, and it is left
to an amateur, who has kept a clue to himself, to solve the
problem of this particular book. In *The Notting Hill Mystery*,
Henderson makes a good case against Baron R. but cannot
bring it home:

> Link by link you have now been put in possession of the entire
> chain. Is that chain one of purely accidental coincidences, or
> does it point with terrible certainty to a series of crimes . . .?
> Supposing the latter to be the case, are crimes thus committed
> susceptible of proof, or even if proved, are they of a kind for which
> the criminal can be brought to punishment?

Delves, in *Mrs. Halliburton's Troubles*, manages to arrest the wrong
man, and even Bucket is not omnipotent, as Ousby points out:

> The fact that Bucket's powers are limited is emphasized at
> several points during the final part of the book. He blusters
> impressively in the face of the attempt to blackmail Sir Leicester
> about the secret of his wife's past, but he finally advises the peer
> to pay up. His production of the missing will promises a happy
> solution to Jarndyce versus Jarndyce, but is in fact proved
> irrelevant by the course of events . . . although he may at times
> appear superhuman to the other characters, Bucket is ultimately
> neither magician nor demigod but merely an intelligent human . . .
> He cannot undo the past by bringing Tulkinghorn back to life . . .
> he cannot alter the outcome of Lady Deadlock's tragic destiny.

Noting this unexpected tendency towards failure in other
contemporary detectives, though on a more mundane level,
Ousby suggests two explanations:

> These instances of failure are to some extent explained by these
> author's desire to retain a structural balance in their work.
> These detectives are not, after all, protagonists but are merely

among the more interesting secondary characters, and their complete success might make them predominate unduly over the book's closing pages. As it is, their ultimate failure usually functions as a convenient device for removing them discreetly from the action, leaving the hero and heroine to occupy the center of interest at the end. There is also a deeper reason for this insistence on the detective's failure, a reason that partly explains the novelist's reluctance to make him more than an interesting supernumary. It derives from the writers' almost obsessive reliance on the abstractions of Providence and Destiny to dictate the progress of their plots and to bring the action to neat and satisfactory conclusions in which the mystery is dispelled, the good rewarded, and the bad punished.

This preference for Fate as the final, vital instrument that resolves the plot is undoubtedly a feature, not only of many a sensation novel, but of nineteenth-century fiction in general and it usually does a better job than the detective. The frequent use of the technique struck critics even at the time as a cover for poor plotting, a too handy sword for authors to sever those self-made Gordian knots. Here, for example, is W. Fraser Rae in the *North British Review* in 1865:

> *John Marchmont's Legacy* may be summarily characterised as a tale of destiny. 'The awful hand of Destiny' menaces us in the first chapter, and in the sixth the authoress asks — 'Has the solemn hand of Destiny set that shadowy brand upon the face of this child?' Indeed, Miss Braddon reiterates shallow phrases about 'Fate' or 'Destiny', as if she thought that, by so doing, her readers would be reconciled to the improbabilities with which she surfeits them.

Nevertheless, one can appreciate what the detective was up against if the *Dublin University Magazine's* opinion is anything to judge from:

> While we are fully impressed with the sense of the duty which is cast upon those charged with the administration of justice to strain every nerve, and adopt every legitimate means for the detection of the criminal, we cannot but feel the conviction . . . that in this peculiarly, human investigation is powerless until the decree of the Almighty, for the exposure and apprehension of the offender, has passed the great seal of heaven.[4]

It is also amusing—and instructive—to note that often both critics and authors equate the activities of the detective with the operations of the Almighty. 'The policeman', says Mrs. Oliphant, 'is the Fate who stalks relentless . . . after our favourite villain.' Given some of the far-fetched achievements of later detectives of fiction, one wonders sometimes whether the supposed replacement of Fate by the humanistic super-sleuth was not purely nominal.

A predilection for Providence coupled with a need to clear the stage goes some way towards explaining the secondary role and the failures of the detectives in sensation fiction. But there are, perhaps, other simpler reasons. Simplest of all is the possibility that the detective in fiction was a failure because the detective in fact was a failure. Another is that authors sometimes started and finished with clear stages by dispensing with police detectives altogether and using the hero or other lay character in a detective capacity, amongst his other functions in the plot. These part-time amateurs are really a variation on the seven per cent solution and form an important strand in the detective's progress which is yet to be considered.

Given an awareness of this technique, it may be asked why the process was not reversed, that is, why no novelist cleared the stage by making the police detective the hero, who can then capture, providentially or otherwise, both criminal and heroine. The answer is best given by asking another equally naive question: can you imagine a Bucket or a Cuff wooing, let alone winning, an Esther Summerson or a Rachel Verrinder? The idea verges on the comic. We have to go well into the twentieth century before we can find a policeman being allowed to approach the heroine as lover. Parker in Dorothy Sayers' books is probably the first notable example, and even then there is something less than complimentary in his being placed somewhere between a 'Socialist Conchy . . . , a card-sharping dark horse . . . [and] a decent, God-fearing plumber' in the Lady Mary Wimsey marriage stakes.[5] It can also be argued that Parker, a self-confessed 'common police official', is not a hero in a romantic sense, and this is certainly true of his contemporaries

such as Inspectors French and Wilson, who are at most avun-
cular in their relationships with heroines. A landlady, at best,
was all a policeman might hope to be caught by before this, the
genteel damsels in distress being reserved for the Watsons, like
Thorndyke's medical or legal coadjutors.

Going back into the nineteenth century, 'cop-gets-crook-
gets-girl' was just not the kind of book the Victorian sensationalist was writing, and to be able to say that sums up the situation
in life and novels of the Victorian detective. All things but a
police hero could, it seems, come within the scope of sensation
fiction. There could be horrifying crimes, beautiful fiends, evil
uncles, illegitimacy, fraud and that sin which, in Mrs Oliphant's
delicate phraseology, 'we . . . make . . . bigamy but which might
bear a plainer title.' The girls could run off with men too old for
them, men too young for them, with ne'er-do-wells, with
grooms, even, God forbid, with actors—but never a detective.
The gap in the social scale between a heroine, however giddy,
and a detective, however astute, was measurable only in light
years. Even with Waters' device of down-graded gentility
before him, no author was willing to risk a detective hero over
three volumes, granted the unthinkable thought occurred to
him; and even if it did, he was faced with the almost insurmountable technical difficulty of keeping up a detective theme
for upwards of 150,000 words.

This aversion to many aspects of the detective, already noted
in the short stories of Waters and others, comes out much more
clearly in his presentation in novels, more clearly even than his
supposed infallibility.

Bucket is probably the least obnoxiously portrayed of all,
yet he is variously described as a 'common person' and a 'rum
customer'. Dickens' portrait of him is in fact far from uni-
formly favourable, as his relationships with Jo, Gridley and
Tulkinghorn reveal, and his 'beautiful case' is not held up by
Dickens as a ratiocinative miracle to be admired in a vacuum;
its unpalatable implications—that revelations damaging to the
good and the bad must be made—is put into the mouth of its
constructor: 'When I depict it as a beautiful case . . . I mean

from my point of view. As considered from other points of view, such cases will always involve more or less unpleasantness. Very strange things comes to our knowledge in families.' But accepting Bucket as 'a jewel among detectives',[6] he is an exception amongst his fellows.

In Cuff, Collins gives us perhaps the most memorable detective of fiction, probably because he was not trying to write a detective story. Yet *The Moonstone* leaves us in no doubt about the status of detectives in general. Before Cuff appears, Betteredge, the prototype of the educated butler, remarks of Rachel's refusal to be questioned by Seegrave, the detective initially in charge of the case: 'Being anxious for the honour of the family, it distressed me to see my young lady forget herself—even with a police officer.' When Cuff implies to Lady Verrinder that Betteredge has acted as his Watson, the servant explodes: 'To be held up before my mistress, in my old age, as a sort of deputy-policeman, was, once again, more than my Christianity was strong enough to bear. "I beg to inform your ladyship," I said, "that I never, to my knowledge, helped this abominable detective business, in any way, from first to last".' Betteredge is here forgetting that a little earlier he was confessing to 'detective fever', and these disparate reactions of his reflect once more the contradiction in the public's attitude to detectives—fascinating, at a distance.

Most significantly, however, when Cuff insists on telling Lady Verrinder what she must do to recover the Moonstone, for 'I shall then have done what I undertook to do', Betteredge's comment is: 'In those words Sergeant Cuff reminded us that, even in the Detective Police, a man may have a reputation to lose.' It is with these words that Collins lifts Cuff out of the ruck of detectives. Attention has been drawn often enough to the fact that in writing *The Moonstone* Collins drew on the case of Constance Kent or the Road Murder, as it was known at the time. In 1860 the murder of a four-year-old boy in the Wiltshire village of Road was investigated by, amongst others, Inspector Whicher from Scotland Yard. Whicher fastened on the boy's sixteen-year-old step-sister, Constance, as the guilty party.

Public opinion picked on everyone but Constance, principally on the boy's father, Mr Kent, and on the family's nurse, Elizabeth Gough, who was twice arrested and released. Whicher could point to opportunity in that Constance was in the house when the murder occurred, but so too were the rest of the family and the servants; he tried to establish motive by showing the girl's dislike of her father's children by his second marriage, but this was discounted as mere childish jealousy. Whicher's case would have been greatly improved if he could have found a missing nightdress belonging to Constance; she claimed to have given it to the washerwoman; the washer-woman denied this; but it was not to be found. The magistrates regarded the detective's case as weak, which it was, and released Constance, a decision which the country at large applauded as much as it reviled her accuser. Whicher seems to have had the courage of his convictions, however. Over three months after Constance's release we find him writing to the chief superin-tendent of the Bristol police as follows: 'I have little doubt but that that confession would have been made if Miss Constance had been remanded for another week. Miss Constance possesses an extraordinary mind: the two medical men in the present case believe her to be a monomaniac.'[7] Whicher was neverthe-less taken off the case and retired soon after, a disillusioned and perhaps a broken man. In 1865, in confirmation of the century's faith in Fate, Constance Kent confessed.

That Collins was aware of the Road Murder is obvious from his use of some of the trimmings, such as the nightdress. That he was much more deeply impressed by its aftermath is revealed by his sympathetic, even pathetic, picture of Cuff. The irony of Whicher's situation must have appealed to the novelist, but Collins does not make use of this aspect of the case. Cuff is left a failure. Prompted perhaps by a personal knowledge of Whicher through Dickens,[8] Collins goes beyond the irony itself to the individual affected by it; beyond the rueful 'so Whicher was right after all' to what Whicher must feel. Vindication cannot cure the harm already done—even to a detective, for that detective is also a human being. Much lip-service is paid today to the need to present fictional detectives as human beings, and too many authors think that this is satisfied by an exhibition of the detective's sexual prowess. Collins achieves it simply by letting his detective fail. He is concerned to bring out, through Cuff, the dreariness and squalor of the detective's round. Geraldine Jewsbury, reviewing the book for the *Athenaeum*, found the detective element 'somewhat sordid'. She was a better critic than she realised. But most of all it is the thankless-ness of the task that Collins brings out. If Cuff had been right about Rachel, would anyone have been grateful? If he had proved a case against Roseanna, would anyone have cared? More notice will be taken of him if he gets it wrong, for even detectives have reputations to lose.

Collins, then, has much sympathy for Cuff personally, but at the same time, through those remarks of Betteredge which are all the more effective for being put into the mouth of a servant, he conforms to the pattern by conveying a low opinion of detectives.

The distaste for detectives is repeated further up the social scale by the mistress of the house in *Wyllard's Weird*:

> Mrs. Wyllard was surprised and even horrified when . . . her husband told her that he had invited Distin, the criminal lawyer, to stay at Penmorval while he investigated the mystery of the nameless girl's death. The presence of such a man beneath her roof seemed to her like an outrage upon that happy home.

Her husband tries to set her mind at rest—at the expense of police detectives:

> . . . you confound the lawyer who practises in the criminal courts with the police agent you have read about in French novels. A man of low birth and education, with nothing but his native wit to recommend him; a man whose chief talent is for disguise, and who passes his life in a false beard and eyebrows, in the company of thieves and murderers, whom it is his business to make friends with and betray.

Mr Carter in *Henry Dunbar* is described as having 'an enthusiastic love of his profession', and as unaffected by any-

thing degrading in his job, but Miss Braddon still feels obliged
to justify his existence and methods, which she does in some
detail, on what are perhaps the only possible grounds—that it
is necessary for someone to do this 'treacherous' work. This
approach at least has the advantage of realism over the fairy-
godmother view of the detective that was to come. Mr Carter's
situation is summed up by the statement that perhaps his
'knowledge of his own usefulness was sufficient to preserve
his self-respect', but it is surely a negligible self-respect which
does not extend to his telling his wife that he is a detective:
'. . . to this day she don't know what my business really is. She
thinks I'm *something* in the City, bless her dear little heart!'
Given the close resemblance between Mr Carter and Mr
Bucket, Miss Braddon was perhaps anxious to ensure, by thus
excluding Mrs Carter from the proceedings, that in respect of
their wives at least there was to be a contrast, for Mrs Bucket, it
will be remembered, was 'a lady of natural detective genius'.
Or again, Miss Braddon may have thought that this rather
absurd touch added to the mysteriousness of her detective, but
that it could be thought of at all is once more a poor reflection
on the profession.

Gryce in *The Leavenworth Case* spells out even more clearly this
idea that the detective himself had no illusions about his status:

> 'Mr. Raymond,' cried [Mr. Gryce] at last, 'have you any idea
> of the disadvantages under which a detective labours? For
> instance now, you imagine that I can insinuate myself into all
> sorts of society perhaps, but you are mistaken. Strange as it may
> appear, I have never by any possibility of means succeeded with
> one class of persons at all. I cannot pass myself off for a gentleman
> . . . I am always found out . . . I can enter a house, bow to the
> mistress of it, let her be as elegant as she will, so long as I have a
> writ of arrest in my hand . . . but when it comes to visiting in
> kid gloves . . . and such like, I am absolutely good for nothing
> . . . But it is much the same with the whole of us. When we are
> in want of a gentleman to work for us, we have to go outside of
> our profession.'

Gryce is of course trying to get Raymond to act as his agent,
but his means to this devious end are, one feels, straight-

forward; he has chosen honesty this time as the best means of achieving his object, even though this involves him in admissions damaging to his standing and vanity. And that last remark of his is not without relevance to the acceptance of the amateur detective.[9]

The fictional detective also comes off badly in that he is often depicted as, at best, money-conscious and, at worst, a greedy mercenary. The factual background to this was mentioned earlier as lying in the reward and hire system and the economic necessity for a detective to supplement his meagre wages. The novelists ignored these causes and concentrated solely on the effects, with the result that detectives appear self-seeking, which was true but only half the story.

Carter approaches the financial side of his work in a very business-like manner, extracting from his employer, Clement Austin, a 'written engagement to pay the hundred pounds [reward] upon the day of the murderer's arrest'. With another hundred pounds on offer from the government Carter admits that this is 'a pretty high stake as the detective business went'. He is breezily blunt about his employer's obligations on expenses:

'I shall start for Winchester tomorrow morning.'
'Then I'll go with you,' Clement said promptly.
'So be it, Mr. Austin. You may as well bring your cheque-book while you're about it, for this sort of thing is apt to come rather expensive.'

Anna Katherine Green allows Mr Gryce's monetary considerations to be satisfied in more subtle style in this conversation with Raymond, who has allowed himself to be persuaded into service and who speaks first:

'. . . I have no selfish motive in this matter. If I succeed, the glory shall be yours; if I fail, the shame of defeat shall be mine.'
'That is fair,' [Mr. Gryce] muttered. 'And how about the reward?'
'My reward will be to free an innocent woman from the imputation of crime which hangs over her.'
This assurance seemed to satisfy him.

The tendency of the reward system to act against the ideal of co-operation between policemen is pointed up in the behaviour of Grimstone in *Aurora Floyd*:

> Now, the truth of the matter is, that Joseph Grimstone was not, perhaps, acting quite so conscientiously in this business as he might have done, had love of justice in the abstract and without any relation to sublunary [*sic*] reward, being [*sic*] the ruling principle of his life. He might have had any help he pleased from the Doncaster constabulary . . . but . . . Mr. Grimstone desired to keep his information to himself, until it should have brought him its golden fruit in the shape of a small reward from Government, and a large one from John Mellish. 'No,' he thought, 'it's a critical game; but I'll play it single-handed, or, at least, with no one better than Tom Chivers to help me through with it; and a ten pound note will satisfy him, if we win the day.'

Carter has the same selfish approach. His deliberate disregard of the telegraph has been mentioned, and he is even willing to forego his reputation to avoid dividing the reward. Some clothes have been found which Carter is sure will afford him a clue, but he pretends to agree with the local constable that they are valueless:

> The constable grinned as he took the sovereign which Mr. Carter offered him. There was something like triumph in the grin of that Winchester constable — the triumph of a country official who was pleased to see a Londoner at fault. I confess that I groaned aloud when the door closed upon the man . . .
> 'All this day's labour and weariness has been so much wasted trouble,' I said; 'for it seems to have brought us no step nearer to the point we wanted to reach.'
> 'Hasn't it, Mr. Austin?' cried the detective eagerly. 'Do you think I am such a fool as to speak out before the man who has just left the room? Do you think I am going to tell him my secret, or let him share my gains?'

Neither of this unprepossessing pair of Miss Braddon's can do without help altogether, so Grimstone is provided with the aforementioned Tom Chivers, and Carter has a Mr Tibbles, nicknamed Sawney Tom, 'not so much because he was clever, as because he looked so eminently stupid'. Gryce, too, has a familiar, revelling in the name of 'Q'—'an agent of mine [explains Gryce] who is a living interrogation point; so we call him Q, which is short for query'. Chivers and Sawney Tom do not seem to be official policemen, which may explain their apparent ignorance of the high rewards available and why they can be fobbed off with pittances such as the ten pounds which Grimstone mentally allocates to Chivers.

So taken up are Carter and Grimstone with thoughts of the reward in store that they spend as much time worrying about the possibility of failure and double-crossings by their henchmen as they do in detecting. Carter drifts out of *Henry Dunbar* apparently none the richer, but Miss Braddon is more generous to Grimstone, perhaps to encourage the others: 'It may be some comfort to the members of the force to know that John Mellish acted liberally to the detective, and gave him the full reward, although Talbot Bulstrode had been the captor of the Softy.'

However justifiable in terms of need, the attitude of these detectives towards money is scarcely that 'of the public servant rather than the paid hireling', or of men who 'eschew the vices of the mercenary and the blood-money man', as Ousby would have it in *Bloodhounds of Heaven*. Furthermore, the indications of these episodes, whether in relation to the detective's social standing or his financial motivation, is once again at odds with Ousby's theme of 'the considerable respect and affection with which Victorian writers and their audience had come to regard police detectives by the 1860s'.

Exception cannot be taken to Ousby's general argument that starting with Vidocq in the late 1820s the detective begins to emerge in literature as 'a defined . . . stereotype', and that from 'a suspect though often entertaining rogue, he finally becomes a hero of a less ambiguous sort; a solidly middle-class citizen whose values reflect those of the writer and his audience'. However, Ousby then adds: 'An important transition is thus effected. The detective moves from the world of the eighteenth century, of Jonathan Wild and Caleb Williams, to the world of Dickens' Inspector Bucket', implying that the detective's evolutionary process is well-nigh completed with the creation of Bucket. One wonders if Ousby has not got his timing wrong by some fifty years—that we have to go to the end of the century before it can be truly said that the detective of fiction is complete both in himself and in his reflection of the values of the writer and reader, that is, to Holmes. Ousby, it should be made clear, is far from denigrating Holmes, whom he sees as carrying 'the mid-Victorian respect for the detective to new heights of hero-worship'. In fact, from his outline one could construct a graph of detectival popularity. It would rise steadily to a peak in the 1850s and 60s with Bucket and Cuff (those two swallows, fifteen years apart), and plummet in the 1870s and 80s until revived and shot off the page by Holmes. Remembering, however, that Holmes is not a police detective, and given three worlds, those of Caleb Williams, Bucket and Holmes, that of Bucket seems much more akin to the former than to the latter, whether considered in terms of fiction or reality. Bucket as hero and stereotype still had some way to go.

Fluctuations in the popularity of detectives did exist and they may have run broadly in the pattern suggested by Ousby. Thus he might have quoted the *Saturday Review* of 1878 which felt that following the exposure of corruption at Scotland Yard 'distrust has now to a great extent replaced the confidence which was once felt in this branch of the police.' The article considers Dickens' role in the growth of this confidence and concludes that 'on such a subject his ideas were sure to reflect popular belief, although he might greatly exaggerate; and Bucket would never have been drawn if people had not been disposed to believe in the ability of the [detectives].' The *Saturday*, in this article on 'Detectives', 21 December 1878, adds a cautionary word, however: 'Probably the disbelief in detectives is nearly as exaggerated as the confidence in them formerly was', which reveals again that fund of sympathy for detectives that was to grow into the idea of allowing them greater and more secret power; it also bears out the suggestion made earlier that from the start belief in them was based more on hope than on tangible achievements.

Popularity is not so easily definable and quantifiable a characteristic that we can pin it down as precisely as we might like. Speaking of real-life detectives, Ousby himself points out that 'as early as 1868 the *Daily News* lamented: "Of late years the old confidence in the police has diminished. Whether as detectives or protectives, the public mistrusts them".' But, as we have seen, criticism, repugnance and distrust had dogged detectives and the police in general from their inception. The situation was too fluid for us to be too categorical; throughout the period of supposed enthusiasm generated by Dickens the real detectives were failing to check crime. Acceptance of detectives there certainly was, but whatever its extent, the motives behind this acceptance were rather more selfish than genuine 'respect and affection', if the outline in the preceding chapters is accurate. If there was respect, it was the respect born of hope, perhaps even of fear, rather than respect based on recognition of solid services rendered. And if there was affection, it sprang, on the part of writers, from gratitude for a good stock character, and on the part of readers from the pleasure of meeting such an interesting character—conveniently confined within the covers of a book. There is much more cynicism than affection in that parting shot at the end of *Aurora Floyd*.

NOTES TO CHAPTER 9

1 [Leslie Stephen], 'The Decay of Murder', *Cornhill Magazine*, December, 1869.

2 In *XIX Century Fiction* Sadleir describes Harwood as 'one of the minor mysteries of mid-nineteenth-century authorship'. His works published by Bentley have, says Sadleir, 'a look of importance. Yet, until finding him in the Bentley collection, I had never heard his name . . . nor seen a book of his in a second-hand shop'. Several of Harwood's novels were serialised in *Chambers's Edinburgh Journal*, including *Lady Flavia* in 1865. He is last heard of writing wild west serials for Cassell's *Saturday Magazine* in the 1880s.

3   Hawthorne, 'Riddle Stories', Introduction to *American Stories* (1909). (Wells, *The Technique of the Mystery Story*, says exactly the same, plus another page from Hawthorne without acknowledgement!).

4   [Donnelly], 'Crime and its Detection', *Dublin University Magazine*, May 1861

5   Dorothy L. Sayers, *Clouds of Witness* (1926).

6   [Geraldine Jewsbury], review of *Bleak House*, *Athenaeum*, 17 September 1853.

7   'Law and Police', *Guardian*, 26 July 1865.

8   Whicher has been identified as Dickens' model for Sergeant Witchem in his items on the detective police in *Household Words* in 1850.

9   Scotland Yard in fact experimented unsuccessfully with a direct entry system of 'gentlemen' detectives in the nineteenth century.

10
THE BEGINNINGS OF GREAT SURPRISES

There is no reason why the devil should have all the good sensation novels any more than all the good tunes to himself.

Saturday Review, 21 October 1865

Despite the many appearances and utterances to the contrary, the police detective was thus a far from indispensable character in sensation fiction. His advantages to an author writing a story with a secret—novelty, an aura of mystery and infallibility and his obvious relevance as a professional solver of puzzles— had to be set against his poor record, his mercenariness, his low social status and the general aversion to his job and the way he was believed to go about it. If we add to these drawbacks the technical points of authors' preference for Fate over rational proofs and for a final chapter devoted to matrimony rather than explanations, the balance swings against the detective's chances of inclusion in a story in any way but a passing role.

The riddle had still to be unriddled, however. Occasionally, as in Le Fanu's *Uncle Silas*, Providence alone was invoked to this end, but more usually the hand of God was allowed to work through men, and in the absence of an official detective, some- times in addition to one, the instrument was a character or combination of characters who had other, often more important, roles in the plot. The obvious choice was the hero, who then doubled as lover and detective, but a friend or relation of the hero or heroine was just as acceptable. In *The Moonstone* several people attempt to solve the problem of the missing gem after the departure of Cuff. In Collins' *The Law and the Lady*

(1875) it is the heroine herself who sets out to prove her husband's innocence. As might be expected, these part-time amateurs, with their better breeding and loftier motives, are more successful than their professional counterparts, though once again coincidence and Fate play a larger part than analysis. Tillotson points out that 'Robert Audley . . . feels "a hand drawing him on" in his inquiries—the hand being obviously Miss Braddon's.' In defence of these authors, however, it should be remembered that the elements of luck and of authorial omnipotence support many later detectives but are obscured by a smokescreen of impressive deductions from the essentially fortuitous discovery and by glib assertions that the clue was there for all to see but that only the expert appreciated its significance. Miss Braddon was followed by many another leading hand, and it is often only the cruder technique of the Victorian writer that leaves the coincidences and manipulations so much more obvious.[1]

Unlike police detectives, these amateurs figure more or less throughout the books in which they appear, but their detectival activities take up only part of their time, and the actual extent of their contribution varies considerably, from the relatively minor efforts of David Arden in *Checkmate* and of Walter Hartright in *The Woman in White* to the more substantial achievements of Heathcote in *Wyllard's Weird*. In this light they conform, as detectives, to the pattern of the professional and his minor role. Indeed, it is a moot point how far we ought to see some of these characters as detectives at all. A police detective, however ineffectual, is still a detective, but with amateurs one tends to assess their activities and abilities before awarding the title, and in making these assessments no two people, as was seen in the first chapter, will necessarily apply the same criteria or come to the same conclusion. Does the conducting of an investigation make the conductor a detective? Must the investigation be into a crime? For example, do Captain Wragge's enquiries on behalf of Magdalen Vanstone in *No Name* make him a detective? *Victorian Detective Fiction* says yes, but Magdalen herself is a more likely candidate for the title;

and a case could be made out for Mrs. Lecount, not forgetting Sergeant Bulmer of Scotland Yard and the private enquiry agent employed by Mrs Lecount. A glut of detectives, it seems, but only potentially so, because *No Name* is not primarily concerned with secrets and their unravelling.

Another problem where the romantic hero acts also as detective is that in the melodramatic atmosphere of Victorian sensationalism the disclosure of the secret was used more for a display of the hero's courage in standing up to the villain than of his cleverness in revealing him. And these characters would themselves be the first to refuse the award of the title 'detectives' and to disclaim any affinity with the men of Scotland Yard or the Rue de Jérusalem. 'I . . . I am not a detective,' stammers Robert Audley as the conclusive reason for refraining from questioning a child. And Goodchild Strange, in Sir Edward J. Reed's *Fort Minister, M.P.* (1885), uses the reputation of the law to bully a man into telling what he knows: 'Imagine me, please—you do not know that I am not—imagine me to be Chief Detective Strong . . . here . . . for the express purpose of arresting—you!' But as soon as the witness begins to talk, Strange encourages him by denying any link with the police: '. . . were I Chief Detective Strong I might arrest you without fear of consequences. But I am not a detective, and you are in no danger of arrest from me . . .' Yet Strange is patently the detective hero of this book. French authors and their heroes seem to have felt much the same way about detectives: '[Saint Briac] was by no means desirous of running up against him, for he could not have done so without confessing that he had just been tracking him like a detective, and it would have been distasteful to him to confess himself neither more nor less than a spy.'[2]

Yet even when allowance has been made for these factors, these melodramas still provide a nucleus of unalloyed detective work. It may be primitive and unsophisticated, it may be the product of legwork rather than brainwork, its leisurely pace may be frustrating, but as Sadleir puts it in *Things Past*, amidst the 'genteelisms and periphrases . . . the moralizings, the aggressive virtues, the unrelieved (but carefully selected) villainies', it is there. This nucleus, moreover, often leads directly to the dénouement and can be the most interesting part of the book. *Checkmate*, for example, perks up only when David Arden gets down, very late, to investigating Mr Long-cluse, and in Florence Warden's *The House on the Marsh* (1877)[3] the hero, Laurence Reade, is excruciatingly dilatory in doing something about his suspicions of Mr Rayner. The detection, however, is an integral part of the story, whereas the episodes featuring police detectives in sensation novels could be omitted or replaced, as suggested earlier, leaving the book perhaps the poorer but the plot intact. In this light, the part time amateurs of sensation fiction constitute the more immediate and important link with the explosion in this kind of writing in the next century.

And in one at least of these novels the detective and the detection—the words are applied in the strictest of Golden Age senses—form very much more than a nucleus. It was claimed earlier that *Lady Audley's Secret* was the sensation novel to begin all detective novels and the time has come to justify that assertion. The claim is of course exaggerated. It is no more possible to say which is the first detective novel than it is to say which of the chicken and the egg came first. Our personal favourite cosmogony will colour our preference. Miss Braddon herself admitted that this, her first successful work, owed much to *The Woman in White*, but this is an inspirational debt, not the imitative one of *The Notting Hill Mystery*. *Lady Audley's Secret* is more than able to stand on its own merits—as a second-rate sensational novel. Anthony Boucher's surprised delight over the book has been mentioned; and Norman Donaldson is also enthusiastic in his introduction to the 1974 Dover edition: 'A rare treat is in store for any reader who encounters *Lady Audley's Secret* for the first time.' If, therefore, you have not read it and your appetite has been whetted, I suggest you skip the rest of this chapter, as a plot summary follows. This is necessary mainly to show the extent of the detective work, but also to enable the correction of some misapprehensions about the story.

Lady Audley's Secret opens in Essex, where Lucy Graham, a

governess of unknown background, is wooed and won by a local landowner, the elderly Sir Michael Audley. The scene shifts to George Talboys who is returning to England from Australia where he has made his fortune. He is looking forward to reunion with his wife, Helen, whom he deserted three years previously because he could not support her and their infant son. At Audley Court, Phoebe, the new Lady Audley's maid, and her fiancé, Luke Short, find a baby's shoe in their mistress's jewel box. They keep this with a view to blackmail.

We are now introduced to Robert Audley, a briefless, idle barrister, who meets his old friend Talboys in London. The latter finds no letter from his wife at a prearranged place, but instead learns of her death on the Isle of Wight, whither the pair go to get confirmation from Helen's father, Lieutenant Maldon. A year passes during which Audley and Talboys visit Russia. Back in England, they decide to visit Sir Michael, who is Robert's uncle. Lady Audley takes elaborate measures to avoid them, beginning with a letter to Robert from Alicia, Sir Michael's daughter by an earlier marriage, saying that Lady Audley feels too ill to receive guests, and ending with a visit to London by the lady on a trumped-up excuse, when Robert insists on coming but staying at a nearby inn. During Lady Audley's absence Alicia lets the two men into her stepmother's room by a secret passage, and there they admire her portrait. The next day Talboys goes alone to Audley Court. He does not return to the inn and Robert can find no trace of his friend, though he does notice bruises on Lady Audley's wrists. The search is extended first to London and then to Southampton where Lieutenant Maldon is now living. Maldon claims that Talboys visited him before leaving for Liverpool and Australia. Off goes Robert to Liverpool, but he learns nothing except that there was a late passenger for Australia, a Thomas Brown with a broken arm. Robert can see no reason for Talboys to change his name and begins to suspect that his friend is dead. To help sort out his thoughts he compiles a 'Journal of facts connected with the disappearance of George Talboys, inclusive of facts which have no apparent relation to that circumstance'.

The clear implication of this list is the involvement of Lady Audley, so back goes Robert to Essex where he hints at his suspicions to her. Her reaction is to have her husband ask Robert, nicely, to leave. He goes, but only as far as the public house of Phoebe and Luke, now married and installed as inn-keepers at the necessary expense of Lady Audley. There he gets confirmation of his suspicion of blackmail and, meeting Lady Audley again, he tells her of this and of his determination to go through Talboy's effects which are at his London home. He is forestalled by a 'mysterious lady' who removes all Helen Talboy's correspondence, but Robert does find an inscription in a book by Helen Maldon—in Lady Audley's writing, as he can tell from a letter shown him earlier by Alicia. He seeks more evidence at Southampton and is told of the death a year or so earlier of Matilda, daughter of Maldon's housekeeper, but he does not immediately see the possibilities of this. Convinced in his own mind of what has happened, however, but reluctant to proceed because of his uncle, he visits Talboy's father who is unsympathetic to his story and suspicions, but Talboys' sister, Clara, persuades him to persevere, supplying him with letters from her brother, one of which includes a description of his wife, Helen.

Robert now tracks down Mrs Vincent who is Lucy Graham's only known antecedent before her arrival in Essex and who afforded Lady Audley the excuse for that trip to London. At Mrs Vincent's he finds a box labelled Lucy Graham with another label underneath naming Mrs G. Talboys. A visit to Wildernsea where the Talboys lived after their marriage produces a letter from Lieutenant Maldon showing that his daughter left him a day or so before Lucy Graham arrived at Mrs Vincent's.

Robert Audley now faces his aunt with this overwhelming evidence, but she is undaunted, realising that he is reluctant to bring disrepute on his uncle, and she threatens to have Sir Michael put him in an asylum. Robert retires once more to Luke's inn and sends Lady Audley a letter pointing out that he can produce witnesses to her previous existence as Helen

Talboys. The lady's retort is to burn the inn down. Her intended victim survives, however, saving Luke in the process, though the latter is seriously injured. At last Lady Audley breaks down and confesses all, including the fact that she has inherited her mother's madness and that she has killed George Talboys by pushing him down a well in the garden of Audley Court. On his deathbed Luke reveals that George is still alive, as Luke had rescued him from the well but kept silent to increase his hold over Lady Audley. George Talboys returns from abroad, Robert marries Clara and all ends happily—except for Lady Audley who dies in a mental asylum.

Lady Audley's Secret is by no means perfect. It lacks the subtleties of style and characterisation which mark Collins and Le Fanu at their best, and with the experience of a century behind us, the mystery and detection, the clues and the hints may appear at times laboured, but in actual presentation and dovetailing of her plot Miss Braddon need concede nothing to her contemporaries. For all its repetition in assessments of Miss Braddon, Thackeray's remark that if he could plot like her he would be the greatest novelist in the world, remains none the less appropriate, and this particular novel is all the more remarkable as the virtually maiden effort of a twenty-six year old woman.

When it appeared in 1862 the book was generally well-received by the critics. They could, it seems, stand a reasonable imitation of *The Woman in White*. The market of course could stand a lot more and, as we have seen, it was the flooding thereof with similar works (many by Miss Braddon!) that caused unfavourable reaction to set in. In 1865, before proceeding to lash Miss Braddon for 'making the literature of the kitchen the favourite reading of the drawing-room', the *North British Review*, in the person of W. Fraser Rae, took these earlier critics to task for their gullibility:

Almost as soon as *Lady Audley's Secret* appeared, it was lauded by distinguished critics . . . Daily newspapers which habitually neglected, or carped at works that fell short of a very high standard of excellence, became conspicuous for the exceptional compliments they paid to this authoress. Even a weekly journal which is noted for lavishing stinging sarcasms on the female novelists . . . has bestowed ungrudging praise on the writings of Miss Braddon . . . She has bewitched so many persons, that those who have the misfortune to be blind to her charms have had small chance of being listened to when pronouncing an adverse judgment.

Which judgement Rae duly pronounces, concluding:

Others before her have written stories of blood and lust, of atrocious crimes and hardened criminals, and these have excited the interest of a very wide circle of readers. But the class that welcomed them was the lowest in the social scale, as well as in mental capacity. To Miss Braddon belongs the credit of having penned similar stories in easy and correct English.

Which probably sent the less dedicated readers of the *North British* rushing to the nearest library.

Today, the mention of *Lady Audley's Secret* tends to elicit the same reaction as a reference to *East Lynne*—a smirk of condescending tolerance to Victorian melodrama. This reputation may explain its omission from the two main histories of detective fiction in English—Haycraft's *Murder for Pleasure* and Symons' *Bloody Murder*—and the solitary passing reference to it in Messac, but its reputation cannot or ought not to account for misrepresentations of it in some of those works on the genre which do allude to it.

Before looking at these, a confusion of longer standing is worth clearing up, namely, what is Lady Audley's secret? Is it the fact that she has killed or believes she has killed her first husband, or, going further back, is it her life before going to Essex, to conceal which the murder is necessary, or is it, going further back still, her hereditary insanity? Early commentators such as Mansel settled unhesitatingly on the first of these, and while deriding novels with secrets in general, found fault with the transparency of this particular secret. This error was compounded by the inclusion in the stage version of a scene actually showing Lady Audley disposing of George Talboys down the well, so that, as Tillotson says, 'the one thing everyone knows is what they suppose to be *the* secret'. There can be no doubt, however, that the primary secret is Helen Maldon's madness. This is made clear in the letter to her father which so mystifies Robert Audley and, this time, the reader: 'Forgive me if I have been capricious, fretful, changeable. You should forgive me, for you know *why* I have been so. You know the *secret* which is the key to my life' (author's italics). This madness is used by Miss Braddon partly as a means of winning sympathy at the end for Lady Audley, but most importantly, within the plot, as a way of preventing a miscarriage of justice, since her husband is not really dead. The stigma of bigamy, her ambition and her first husband's rather heartless desertion are sufficient motives for her actions, but none of them would have saved her from the gallows. Only insanity, serving as both reason and excuse, can do this. The other secrets are not to be discounted of course, at least from Lady Audley's viewpoint, since she has to live with their cumulative effects. A more accurate though somehow less apposite title might have been 'Lady Audley's Secrets'.[4]

That Lady Audley has done away with George Talboys seems too obvious too early, and this fact, coupled with the book's reputation, may have caused later readers, looking for a whodunit, to give the story up at this point, thus contributing to its decline in popularity and hence apparently to what can only have been the most cursory of readings by some recent commentators. For example, in *The Collector's Book of Detective Fiction*, Eric Quayle states that '[Lady Audley] is brought to justice more by the long arm of coincidence than by the exercise of any detective skill, but there are elements of logical deduction in the story, especially in her elderly husband's methods of proving her guilt.' This last phrase is so patently wrong that no more need be said here. In *The Development of the Detective Novel* Murch makes a more equivocal statement: 'eventually she meets retribution through the efforts of a former victim'. Who is this 'former victim'? Surely not Talboys, who has no more to do with Lady Audley's downfall than has Sir Michael. This leaves only Robert Audley, but here again, apart from the fact that the concept of a *former* victim bringing retribution has something of the supernatural or the contradictory about it, at the time of her attempt on his life, he has already assembled incontrovertible proofs of her guilt, and it is her realisation of this that causes her to try to kill him as the only means left of re-establishing her security. Whatever her meaning, Murch goes on to say that this former victim's 'success is due to coincidence and good luck, rather than to any detective skill' (was Quayle paraphrasing Murch?), and she concludes of Miss Braddon's novels in general that the author 'never makes it the function of one particular figure to view the puzzle as a whole, or to collect and co-relate evidence in the manner of a detective'. On the validity of these statements the reader must judge for himself from my summary or from the book itself, but abjuring the linguistic games of my first chapter I must declare that if Robert Audley is not a detective and *Lady Audley's Secret* is not a detective story by any Golden Age definition, then we must surrender to Humpty-Dumpty's approach to language: 'When *I* use a word . . . it means just what I choose it to mean—neither more not less.'

Quite apart from its conformity to the purist's definition, *Lady Audley's Secret* is a continual source of amusing examples of what was yet to be. If you look for a surprise ending in your detective story, you have it here in Talboy's reappearance. If you like the personal involvement of the detective, the irony of Robert Audley's inability to bring his case home without breaking his uncle's heart must appeal. There is even tabulation in the best tradition of the 1920s and 30s, and if loose ends annoy—how did Dupin see both sides of that letter at the same time?—you can rest easy with this book; everything is neatly parcelled at the end, and one can visualise Miss Braddon smiling as she tied the last knot which pre-empts any complaint that Talboys might have let Audley know he was safe: Talboys did write, but he gave the letter to Luke, the one man who could not deliver it, for he would then lose his hold over Lady Audley. Finally, if you like Holmes-style deductions, Miss Braddon provides, not perhaps with Doyle's technical perfection, but she does score off that scientifically trained author by using the correct word, 'induction':

'I am a barrister, Miss Alicia, and able to draw a conclusion by induction. Do you know what inductive evidence is, Miss Alicia?'
'No', replied Alicia . . .
'I thought not. I dare say Sir Harry [Alicia's suitor] would ask if
it was a new kind of horseball. I knew by induction that the
baronet was going to make you an offer; first, because he came
downstairs with his hair parted on the wrong side, and his face
as pale as a tablecloth; secondly, because he couldn't eat any
· breakfast, and let his coffee go the wrong way; and, thirdly,
because he asked for an interview with you before he left the
Court.'

These parallels extend to the personality of the detective.
Robert Audley, Miss Braddon tells us, is regarded by others as
'an inoffensive species of maniac' and 'a generous-hearted
fellow; rather a curious fellow too, with a fund of sly wit and
quiet humour under his listless, dawdling, indifferent,
irresolute manner. A man who would not get on in the world;
but who would not hurt a worm'. The facts seem to bear out
these opinions. With a private income of £400 a year, he has
been advised to supplement it by becoming a barrister, which
he did because he found it easier than opposing his advisors,
'but he had never had a brief, or tried to get a brief, or even
wished to have a brief.' He is the friend of all the stray dogs in
London, his hunting is confined to a quiet trot on a horse of
outlook similar to his own, and his first and only attempt at
skating ends up with him 'lying placidly extended on the flat
of his back until such time as the bystanders should think fit
to pick him up'. His favourite amusements are smoking German
pipes and reading French novels.

The hero thus described was not new in 1862 but thereafter
he proliferates as the good-natured, uncomplex layabout who
becomes involved in a mysterious situation, sometimes reluctantly, sometimes accidentally, but always in the end effectively.
He is Max Wedmore in Florence Warden's *The Mystery of
Dudley Horne* (1897), for example: '. . . a good-looking fellow of
five-and-twenty, with a reputation as a ne'er-do-well . . . his
father had a great idea of bringing a young man up to some
useful calling, to keep him out of mischief. Max preferred the

mischief . . . Mr Wedmore was always finding mercantile situations for his son, Max was always taking care to be thrown out of them after a few weeks, and taking a rest which was by no means well-earned.' He will be found again in William Le Queux, E. Phillips Oppenheim, Sapper and John Buchan. He is the clubland hero. He may appear as spy, rogue or detective or as all three. He may save himself, his friend or his country, but he will always emerge a better man as the result of his experiences. As Robert Audley is forced into seriousness in his determination to track down Talboys' murderer, Miss Braddon changes the tune. She 'doubts if, had he ever taken the trouble to get a brief, he might not have rather surprised the magnates who underrated his abilities', and finally ,of course, he conforms. Happily married, he 'has had his first brief and . . . the meerschaums and the French novels have been presented to a young Templar'. The presentation is symbolic. That young Templar will be the hero of the next novel we read.

And if the authors named above are considered outside the pale of *detective* fiction, Robert Audley reappears, as reliable as ever, in the 1920s. In A. A. Milne's *The Red House Mystery* (1922) he steps off the train as Antony Gillingham, who 'has come to Woodham for a holiday, because he liked the look of the station'—and, needless to say, finds a body; Antony Gillingham, who also has £400 a year (those were the days of stable prices) and whom his friend, Bill, addresses as 'Dear Madman'. Then there is Philip MacDonald's *The Rasp* (1924) which introduced Anthony Gethryn who 'read for the bar; was called, but did not answer'.

But most of all there is Reggie Fortune, the creation of H. C. Bailey and perhaps the most popular detective creation of the period between the wars. Mr Fortune is a doctor with semi-official connections with the police and he appears most often in short stories, the first volume of which, *Call Mr. Fortune*, appeared in 1919. The first story, 'The Archduke's Tea', opens with Reggie's father complaining: 'You only do just enough . . . Never brilliant. No zeal. Now, Reginald, it won't do. Just enough is always too little.' And Reggie describes himself as doing 'nothing more thoroughly than anybody I know'.[5] Bailey's hero has the same easy-going, comfort-loving approach to life as Miss Braddon's: 'Nobody . . . had ever liked him too much, but everybody liked him enough; he got on comfortably with everybody from barmaids to dons,'[6] and when disturbed, he laments: 'Lomas, you have waked me up. That was my after-lunch sleep. And it isn't time for tea . . . You have no heart, Lomas. I believe you want me to work.'[7]

Behind the façade of studied lethargy Reggie really likes his work, just as Robert Audley, despite his disclaimer about being a detective, betrays the Victorian ambivalence to that trade:

'. . . you ought [says Lady Audley] to have been a detective police officer.'
'I sometimes think I should have made a good one.'
'Why?'
'Because I am patient.'

This leads to a deeper similarity between the two authors in that both try to put over a real concern for the victim and, however contradictory it may seem, the criminal; they are concerned, too, about justice in the abstract and as they feel it ought to apply in particular cases. This is why, for example, Miss Braddon allows the murderer in *Henry Dunbar* to live out his life in peace, and it is one reason why Lady Audley is in the end almost exonerated. Written today, *Lady Audley's Secret* would probably be hailed as a brilliant study of a psychopath.

It is not, as one might expect, that Miss Braddon's efforts are swamped in melodrama. There is melodrama, but it is not *bad* melodrama:

She hated herself and her beauty.
'I would laugh at you and defy you if I dared,' she cried; 'I would defy you and kill myself if I dared! But I am a poor pitiful coward, and have been so from the first—afraid of my mother's horrible inheritance; afraid of poverty; afraid of George Talboys; afraid of *you*.'

The melodrama was to come later and is perhaps best exemplified by the style of chapter-heading which she often adopted—

'Touch Lips and Part with Tears', 'Who Knows Not Circe?', whereas the chapter titles in *Lady Audley's Secret* are all straightforward statements of fact.[8] Despite her popularity, Miss Braddon must rest her claim to lasting fame on this one book alone; she was well-advised to have most of her later books published as 'by the author of Lady Audley's Secret'. This is a tragedy, however, because, as Michael Sadleir has pointed out in his chapter on her in *Things Past* (1944), Miss Braddon was unable to develop her very real talents—even her worst detractors such as the *North British Review* and the *Eclectic* admitted these—partly by having to write, literally, for her life and that of her lover, John Maxwell, the publisher, to save him from debt in the years following *Lady Audley's Secret* (in spite of its success), but mostly because her public demanded books on the sensational, not on the psychological or moral. Miss Braddon was a victim of her own success.

Bailey also wanted to write seriously and tried to do so. As far from favourable commentaries on upper-class life in the years following World War I, Bailey's books will be prized by future sociologists as much as they were once appreciated for their restrained, if rather oblique, approach to detection. Some of these stories are concerned less with detection than with that other aspect of police work—prevention. In 'The Silver Cross', for example, a theft is the prelude to a procured suicide, which Reggie vaguely divines but is too late to prevent; in 'The Face in the Picture' he does succeed in preventing a murder, and in 'The Rock Garden' he forestalls an extortionist. All these three stories in *Mr Fortune Explains* (1930) are really exercises in detection forwards—predetection, as J. C. Masterman later called it in his experiments in similar vein, for example in *The Case of the Four Friends* (1957). Bailey is out of favour at the moment. Many find his style trying; it is often as oblique as his detection, and Reggie's staccato speech can be wearing. He must be taken in small doses. In *The Shadow on the Wall*, Reggie remarks: 'Nothing has a taste of its own. Except the cheeses. I grant you them. But I am not strong enough for cheese today.' Substitute these stories for the cheese and ourselves for Reggie and his occasional reluctance to partake and we have the situation of even the willing reader. Symons describes Bailey's writing as facetious and whimsical, and the opening of *Black Land, White Land* (1937) explains why:

> In the opinion of Mr. Fortune, this case was his first masterpiece. He will explain, when allowed, that he had not before matured the confidence in his own ability to rearrange the wicked world which is the birthright of the natural man.

Yet Bailey, to judge from his writing or at least from between its lines, did believe in the possibility of rearranging this wicked world. 'Shall not the Judge of all the earth do right?' asks a character in 'The Silver Cross', to which Reggie replies: 'Yes. Yes. I believe that too . . . But it has to be done through men.' However, Bailey himself never seems to have matured the confidence in his own ability to write about his beliefs in a straightforward, unselfconscious manner. Perhaps he chose the wrong medium and found himself in a Catch 22 situation: detective fiction is non-serious; you may write seriously about detectives and detection, but it will still be called detective fiction—which by definition is non-serious. Much the same position as Miss Braddon and that author, already mentioned, whose attempt to say something important in the thriller went unrecognised because the story itself was so entertaining.

Returning to *Lady Audley's Secret*, Robert Audley does differ from later detectives in the style of his detective work. It is not of the inspirational variety of most of these gentlemen, but more in the manner of Inspector French, with the patient build-up of evidence, the deliberate progress to a solution (distance no object), and also, let it be said, the occasional laboriousness. It must be stressed, however, that it is due solely to Audley's efforts, not coincidences, that Lady Audley is brought to book. Indeed, it could be argued that the only feature of later detective fiction lacking in this novel is the requisite number of coincidences. That Helen Talboys should take a job near Audley Court, that Robert Audley should know George Talboys and that the latter should be rescued by Luke Short are situations easily digested by those (and I am one of them) who accept that in Agatha Christie's *The Mysterious Affair at Styles* (1920) Hastings should be visiting the Inglethorpes, who have provided a home for some displaced Belgians, who include Poirot, who is a detective, who can then investigate Mrs. Inglethorpe's murder, because Hastings knows him. The one debatable coincidence of *Lady Audley's Secret*, the availability of the dying Matilda as a substitute body to allow Helen Talboys to 'die', is no better or worse than the availability of a suitable unknown pauper to Sir Julian Freke in Dorothy Sayers' *Whose Body?*, and the actual process of Matilda's substitution is a digestive molehill compared to the manoeuvring of corpses in Sayers' book. Finally, Talboys' failure to die is eminently plausible against the famous resurrection from the Reichenbach Falls, as well as a pleasant change from the inevitable success, at least initially, of the most outlandish fictional murders.

For *Lady Audley's Secret* is not a whodunit. If this is a fault, then so be it. The interest lies in the gradual clarification of the half-known, not the sudden revelation of the hitherto unfathomable. It lies, as Murch herself says, in the reader's 'mounting suspense aris[ing] out of his uncertainty as to whether her schemes will succeed and how, if at all, her guilt can be proved'. But so far from precluding detection this suspense springs largely from the detective work of Robert Audley, at first tentative then gathering momentum. Virtually no sensation novels with detectives and secrets are whodunits and nothing else. *Bleak House* has a whodunit sub-plot only; *The Moonstone* is a better example, except that its author would rightly object to the description. The identity of the criminal, however, is usually the principal and often the sole theme of much later detective fiction, and it is perhaps the presence of this feature in these two earlier books that has entailed their classification in this century as detective stories. But in most sensation novels the question is not 'who?' The answer to that is often obvious. The question is rather 'how did he do it?' (*Checkmate*), or 'how can it be proved?' (*Lady Audley's Secret*), or 'where is the missing document?' (*The Dead Secret*) or 'can this innocent man be vindicated?' (*The Law and the Lady*).

We come here to a difference between sensation fiction and later detective fiction, but again it is a difference of emphasis only. Detective fiction may also ask questions like these, but it tends—there are always exceptions—to ask them as supplementaries to the basic one of who did it: 'Who killed X, plus, how did he manage it in a sealed room?' Most of John Dickson Carr's stories are of this type. More generally, the only supplementary questions to the 'who?' is 'aren't we having fun finding out?'

In Victorian fiction, however, the culprit and sometimes even the secret are obvious to us; so they ought to be—we have had more practice. They were just as obvious, probably, to the Victorian reader—often deliberately so. But they were not obvious to the characters in the book and the author's stress was on the effect of the secret on the characters. Of course if the secret was so obvious that even the characters ought to have seen it, the Victorians themselves rejected the book. Thus the *Athenaeum* in its review describes *Lady Flavia* as 'a poor mystery to sagacious readers', but in the better sensation novels the reader would be caught up with the floundering characters and their reaction to the mystery, how they were affected by it and how all was eventually revealed to *them*. Collins' *The Dead Secret* is a good example of this approach. Published in 1857, this was Collins' first attempt at mystery and secrets. It seems that he was never destined to win on the critical front. Later to be scourged for his concentration on secrets, he was taken to task by some critics of this book for letting the secret out too soon, but back came Collins at them in typical fashion in his preface to the second edition of 1861:

> I was blamed for allowing the 'Secret' to glimmer on the reader at an early period of the story, instead of keeping it in total darkness till the end. If this was a mistake (which I venture to doubt), I committed it with both eyes open. After careful consideration, and after trying the experiment both ways, I thought it most desirable to let the effect of the story depend on expectation

rather than surprise; believing that the reader would be all the more interested in watching the progress of 'Rosamund' and her husband towards the discovery of the Secret, if he previously held some clue to the mystery in his own hand.

It is tempting to hear in this statement rumblings of the fair play principle, and this general approach of Collins might just be deemed to constitute theft of R. Austin Freeman's thunder as inventor of the 'inverted' detective story, in which the reader is shown first the detailed commission of the crime and then the detective's reconstruction of events.

This is not the case, however. In discussing the twentieth-century rule of fair play, we saw how Collins would have preferred Dickens to insert some clues at the beginning of *A Tale of Two Cities*. In a letter to Collins, Dickens rejected this proposal on the grounds that 'the business of art is to lay all that ground carefully, not with the care that conceals itself . . . but only to *suggest*, until the fulfilment comes. These are the ways of Providence, of which ways all art is but a little imitation.' These words might seem to cast Collins further into the role of a rabid fair player, but if we recollect how he deliberately revealed the secret half-way through *No Name* and couple that with his thoughts on the construction of *The Dead Secret*, it will be seen that he was simply experimenting in the writing and plotting of fiction generally and in the best ways of handing his speciality —the secret.

It was the Victorian and Edwardian over-reliance on 'the ways of Providence' which caused the balance in the problem of how best to treat the mystery element to swing in favour of laying the ground 'with the care that conceals itself', so that the dénouement is a *total* surprise. Freeman can rest easy on his laurels. Collins is really much closer to Dickens in this than to the twentieth century. His books show that he was not a devotee of the shock ending and his final chapters are never devoted to detailed explanations any more than are Dickens'. His disagreement with Dickens is one of degree within the principle of foresight and commonsense in plotting, and he would, I think, have agreed with Dickens when the latter wrote to him

(6 October 1859) that the ideal ending would 'show, by a backward light, what everything has been working to', in other words, that there should be no need of explanations for the whole effort of the author has been aimed at gradual unfolding of his secret.[9]

If this is correct, then to ask at what point in the introduction of actual detectives and palpable detection a sensation novel becomes a detective novel seems a futile question. It makes as much sense to ask at what stage in the introduction of sensation a detective story becomes a sensational one. We have come full circle to the essential identity of the two. One asks who did it, the other asks how or what or where; the one asks its question ostensibly of the reader, the other directs its questions at the characters, but both are asking variations on the elementary common question: what has happened? And the existence of *Lady Audley's Secret*, which came 'into the world determined to make "a sensation"'[10] yet is admitted by Barzun and Taylor in *A Catalogue of Crime*, which holds no brief for pre-Doyle efforts, to contain 'much mystery and more detection than is found in many a modern thriller', demonstrates the artificiality of any attempt to distinguish sensation novels from detective novels except in differences of detail and of emphasis.

NOTES TO CHAPTER 10

1 Moreover, things were not quite as bad as Ousby would have us believe; in discussing the novelists' reliance on the 'guiding hand of Providence' he asserts that 'Joseph Wilmot, the murderer who eludes Carter's clutches at the end of *Henry Dunbar*, is conveniently drowned in a storm at sea.' In fact, Wilmot escapes altogether with the help of his daughter, and the critics took Miss Braddon severely to task for her failure to arrange for his punishment on this earth.

2 Fortuné du Boisgobey, *The Angel of the Chimes* (1885?).

3 The usual date given for this book is 1884, but both the British Museum Catalogue and the National Union Catalogue give 1877. The English Catalogue for 1884 states that the edition of that year is a 'new' one.

4   Elaine Showalter in *A Literature of Their Own* (1977), suggests that 'As every woman reader must have sensed, Lady Audley's real secret is that she is *sane* and, moreover, representative.' As a mere male, I will never be able to appreciate this subtlety.

5   H. C. Bailey, *The Shadow on the Wall* (1934).

6   Bailey, 'The Archduke's Tea', in *Call Mr. Fortune* (1920).

7   Bailey, 'The Missing Husband', in *Mr. Fortune, Please* (1927).

8   In a way I am Satan condemning sin; all the chapter titles of this book are taken from detective novels.

9   For a discussion of this point in connection with *Edwin Drood* and Poe's criticisms of *Barnaby Rudge*, see Felix Aylmer's *The Drood Case* (1964).

10 Review of *Lady Audley's Secret*, *Athenaeum*, 25 October 1862.

11

THE ADJOURNED INQUEST

'All my pipes appear to be the wrong shape. Buy me one with a bend in it.'

R. C. Woodthorpe, *Silence of a Purple Shirt* (1934)

Yet if we are looking for detective heroes in sensation novels, *Lady Audley's Secret* is a rare provider. Most aspects of the book were immediately imitated: 'The Baronet—the maiden fair, The Panther with the yellow hair', as W. S. Gilbert puts it, but not its creation of an amateur detective hero nor its concentration on detection. No one, not even Miss Braddon herself, was prepared to recognise what she had created in Robert Audley, and by the time the amateurs arrived in force in the 1920s *Lady Audley's Secret* was despised where not forgotten. This fate of the solitary, full-time amateur detective of mid-Victorian fiction, with all his social advantages, underlines the remoteness of the official policeman's chances of rising above his secondary role. In a sense it would be true to say that sensation fiction was detective fiction except for a detective. Despite the examples of Dupin, Waters, Bucket, Cuff and Robert Audley, the Great Detective with his miraculous abilities, plausible deductions and overweening vanity was yet to come. There are foreshadowings of these traits, but in the event sensation detectives are condemned to hard grind and a chase and not even Bucket is remembered in the winding up of everyone's fate in the last chapter.

By far the most striking point in the foregoing sketch of the detective of Victorian fiction is its astonishingly close resemblance in many respects to the earlier profile of the real detective of the time. The low social status, the overall lack of success, the money consciousness are coupled, however paradoxical it may appear, with attributions of a mystique which promises great things but never quite achieves them. It seems that at least in their depiction of police detectives sensation novelists fulfilled the requirement of contemporary critics that characters should be true to life, and this compliance was repeated with the amateurs in their distaste for their own detectival activities.

This realism was of course relative, because novelists were subject to the same moral constraints that we saw operating on the writers of short stories about detectives. These portraits of detectives in novels were similarly toned down to suit contemporary taste, but there was little toning up compared with what was to come and this unexpected adherence to at least some of the facts perhaps explains why one gets the impression, admittedly fleeting and insubstantial, that the critics' reaction to the detective's arrival on the literary scene is a little less vicious in tone, a little less absolute in its condemnation than their treatment of sensation fiction in general. Not that there is much that is positively favourable, and what there is is often qualified in the same way as the occasional apologist for sensation fiction never quite let go his hold on the fence.

The *Athenaeum's* likening of Bucket to a jewel is a rare straightforward comment. Robert Louis Stevenson's teenage reaction to Cuff in a letter to his mother—'isn't the detective prime?'—is offset by his maturer reflections on detective stories in the postscript to *The Wrecker* (1892), where he and his co-author Lloyd Osbourne talk of being 'repelled by that appearance of insincerity and shallowness of tone'. *The Times* reviewing *The Moonstone* accepts that fictional detectives may merit graded certificates of realism from Scotland Yard, but it adds that 'we cannot affect to love the police court flavour these characters infuse into modern tales'. Absolution is often conditional as in the *Westminster Review* on Miss Braddon ('Contemporary Literature' 1864): 'If it be good to stimulate our predatory instincts . . . while we trace the dodgings and doublings of an accomplished scoundrel matched with an adroit detective, then let all praise be given to Miss Braddon.' There is a great deal more that is positively unfavourable, but it is amusing to note in these and other remarks the glimmering realisation and almost shameful admission that detection just might be fun.

So faithful to the real thing was the presentation of the detective in novels that some critics perversely condemned him as too real; this sordid character had no place in their concept of reality. Other critics, again, picked on the one facet of the detective that could be labelled unreal—his supposed infallibility.

Sensation fiction doubtless contributed to the popular conception—misconception we should perhaps say—of the omniscient detective, but even here, in so far as the myth had a basis in fact and a definite existence in the minds of many people as a sort of reassurance against the incoming tide of crime, authors were being accurate in reflecting this aspect of the detective. When we recall the *Athenaeum's* preference for the fictional variety after McLevy had revealed the truth about the vagaries of real-life detection, it might be argued that the novelists were doing society a service. The reviewer of *The Silver Cord* (1861) in the *Saturday Review* goes so far as to condone these extravagances:

There is . . . much in this story itself which is in itself improbable, but which only makes it more interesting. A large portion of the action turns on the proceedings of the French police. When once we are launched on the dire mysteries of a system where a superhuman ingenuity and vigilance plays with and regulates a machinery that is represented as embracing and penetrating everything, the more wonderful things are, the better we are pleased. We like to hear how the officer of each grade has all his subordinates in his power, knows the minutest incidents of their lives from their earliest infancy, and is always behind a wall or door if ever they have a secret he is not meant to hear . . . we are avowedly in the region of mysteries, and the police would have no interest for us if they could not see through a stone wall and be in twenty places at once.

221

A few years later, however, the *Saturday* was seeing things rather differently. When in 1864 it wrote that 'there is little scope for ingenuity in the detection of crime, because, if there is evidence, it is almost always easy to produce it; and if there is none, it is altogether impossible to get it', it was doing more than defending the police on the grounds of the frequent hopelessness of their task. The article's main purpose was to attack the writers of sensation fiction who distorted the truth: 'these remarks are intended to discredit, not the police, but the novelists' who 'think that the only striking incident that ever varies the monotony of every day life is the discovery of a mysterious murder by a consummate detective,' and who hold as 'a cherished belief' that 'an *atra cura*, or rather a *caerulea* or dark-blue cura, sits behind every criminal, and hunts him down in a second-class railway carriage with the sagacity of a Red Indian, the scent of a bloodhound, and an unlimited command of all the resources of modern science.'

The *Saturday's* contention in this and other articles is that the detective of fiction is to be treated with caution—'condemned' would be too strong a word—because stories of his powers are based on a fallacy, and their uncritical acceptance is not only misleading but positively harmful to society's fight against crime by engendering complacency. The fallacy has been looked at already in connection with the humbug of detective fiction of the Golden Age. It is the fallacy of basing inevitable conclusions on circumstantial evidence, of accepting authors' assertions as incontrovertible facts. As the *Saturday* says, however, 'the person who invented the riddle and knows the explanation is of course able to pretend to discover it by almost any steps . . . and thus he can easily convey the impression of the exercise of any amount of sagacity on the part of the person who is supposed to make the discovery', whereas 'in real life, and especially in the real life of policemen, such discoveries are hardly every made . . . the simple truth is that . . . there is very little scope for the sort of cunning with which the novelists delight to credit the normal detective of a sensation novel'[1].

This attempt to counterbalance the extravagances of the novelists by putting the detective in his proper perspective resembles the efforts of real policemen in their memoirs, and in most of its articles on the problem of crime and its detection the *Saturday* includes a sideswipe at the detective of fiction if only to stress the real detective's limited ability and, to be fair, his limited opportunities. Poe figures in this discussion as the instigator of the fallacy and suffers accordingly:

> In the various articles which have appeared upon the Road murder, as well as in those which were written about the Waterloo Bridge carpet bag, wishes were expressed that some decipherer of riddles, like Mr. Edgar Poe, would present himself and put the world in possession of the secret. In fact, however, no such art exists ... In [the case of 'Marie Roget'] the facts really occurred, but there is nothing except the assertion of Poe's editor to show that there was any truth at all in the interpretation which he put on them.[2]

The *Saturday's* strictures on detectives of fiction, enjoying as they do the advantage of validity (though not, thank goodness, of enforceability) are rarely exaggerated or overstated. Condescension, not vituperation, is often the keynote of its approach: 'this detective-worship appears one of the silliest superstitions that ever were concocted by ingenious writers'; condescension mixed with a piece of prophecy calculated to turn Hamlet's soul green with envy: 'It may perhaps be a little ungracious to object to what may be described as a well-tried, serviceable, common form which has sold a considerable number of popular novels, and which, in the natural course of things, may be expected to sell several more.'[3]

Much more vehement than the *Saturday's* disapproval of the detective on social and logical grounds was the criticism which saw the presentation of detectives in novels as too realistic and attacked the impropriety, nay, immorality, of introducing into books men of such a treacherous profession and of such an unsavoury background. Typical of this approach is Mrs Oliphant, writing in *Blackwood's* in 1862:

> We have already had specimens, as many as are desirable, of what the detective policeman can do for the enlivenment of

literature; and it is into the hands of the literary Detective that this school of story-telling must inevitably fall at last. He is not a collaborateur whom we welcome with any pleasure into the republic of letters. His appearance is neither favourable to taste nor morals.

Her prediction of a rosy, if infernal, future for the detective of fiction reveals Mrs Oliphant as a rival to the *Saturday* in the soothsaying business. Her next statement, however, is on the face of it rather confusing, for having drawn attention to the ubiquity of the detective, she goes on to suggest that both in reality and in their fiction people have more sympathy for the hare than for the hound:

> It is only in rare cases, even in real life, that bystanders side with those conspirators of justice; and in fiction it is almost a necessity that the criminal who is tracked through coil after coil of evidence should become interesting, as we see him thrust into a corner by his remorseless pursuers . . . Mr. Wilkie Collins . . . has given a new impulse to a kind of literature which must, more or less, find its inspiration in crime, and, more or less, make the criminal its hero.

Mrs Oliphant is referring here to *The Woman in White*, particularly that 'new type of the perennial enemy of goodness', the villainous but appealing Count Fosco, and while in the immediate future the incorruptible detective dominated sensation fiction, Mrs Oliphant's long-range forecasting was accurate. The story of the clever rogue, going back in recognisable form much further than Poe's detective stories, has never lost its appeal—witness Raffles, Blackshirt, the Saint and Mr Ripley—and today the modern Fosco enjoys a greater vogue within sensation fiction than the detective.

Mrs Oliphant's apparent slip from the predominant detective to the predominant criminal is instructive. The overlap between rogue and detective began with each acting in the capacity of the other, Vidocq being the outstanding example, and Mrs Oliphant's attitude indicates the continuing identification of the pair. For her at least, the world of Jonathan Wild and Caleb Williams and the world of Bucket are much the same.

And this identification is no quirk on her part alone, but has remained with us in varying degrees over the years in both fact and fiction. Taking fiction alone, it is one of the sources of confusion surrounding the word 'detective' and it explains the ease with which authors such as E. W. Hornung and Maurice Leblanc, creator of Arsène Lupin, can switch their rogues into detectives or even combine the two activities in one episode.

In Mrs Oliphant's case, her failure, if such it be, to distinguish between the criminal and the detective can be appreciated when her overall purpose is remembered. It is in another article written for *Blackwood's* in 1863, just over a year after the one quoted above, that she uses the term 'detectivism', and in the earlier discussion of this it was suggested that by this word she intended less the person of the detective than the activities which he stood for—squalid work, devious methods—and the atmosphere of crime which he brought with him. 'Police-Court' was the adjective of the time for these stories not 'detective', and it was with the immorality of these sensational novels of crime that Mrs Oliphant and others like her were concerned. It was as an *habitué* of police-courts and hence an obvious character for such novels that the detective is a contributory factor to the 'confused moral world' of which Mrs Oliphant speaks. As such, he, or at least his effect, is to be condemned, but he is by no means the principal or only source of immorality. Indeed, at one point Mrs Oliphant admits that these stories do not 'spring from any natural bloodthirstiness on the part of the English literary mind, but apparently from a lively appreciation of the advantages of a good police, mingled with certain conceptions of the picturesque'. Could it be that even Mrs Oliphant is betraying a flickering of enjoyment of detective stories? Probably not; her point is more that what makes a police force good at its job is often the opposite of what is morally correct, for she goes on to add that 'the science of the detective . . . is by no means founded on truthtelling.'

The Victorian fiction so far considered has revealed the detective as policeman and amateur. The former was the more common, certainly the more easily recognisable of the two.

Both had made their *début* in the 1850s and had become regular, though not inevitable, let alone pivotal, features of sensation fiction in the 1860s. They rose, then, with the sensation novel and, if we accept some contemporary and later opinions, they fell with it. The decline of sensation fiction into a rut in the 1870s and the critical calm of that decade—calm, that is, relative to earlier outbursts—have been noted; much the same seems to have applied to the detective as the microcosm of sensation. As we have seen, in 1869 the *Cornhill* was already complaining that the intelligent detective was a drug in the market, and it was no doubt hoped by his critics, as they hoped of sensation fiction as a whole, that he would go away if ignored or as people came to their senses. These are, of course, critics' opinions and sensation fiction with or without detectives continued to be written and to sell. But still no novel appeared in English with a deliberately contrived detective hero in action as such throughout the story. The concept of detective fiction as the conscious intention of writing a novel about detectives and detection was still lacking.

It would now be easy and obvious to say that Conan Doyle arrived and rescued, some would say created, detective fiction by his device of a highly acceptable third type of detective, the superior private professional, the 'consulting detective'.

After all, do not virtually all commentators agree that the 1870s and 1880s was a doldrums period for the fictional detective? Thomson, Symons and Haycraft have been heard on this (see page 34); Murch also makes the point:

> In the period that followed the publication of *The Moonstone* and *The Mystery of Edwin Drood* detective fiction continued to be written in England, without reaching any notable heights until the final decade of the nineteenth century.

And Ousby:

> . . . the fiction of the 1870s and 1880s . . . is something of an interregnum . . . Indeed, reviewing the fiction of this period with the benefit of historical aftersight, one finds it difficult to resist the impression that authors were merely marking time until the publication of Doyle's Sherlock Holmes stories.

These are probably correct assessments of the development of detective fiction in England, but the appearance of Holmes against this desultory background is rather sudden, perhaps just too opportune, and in the history of detective fiction as a whole these assessments may be over-eager in casting Doyle as the saviour or creator of the genre. One senses that historians, having made a good *hors d'oeuvre* of Poe, are straining at the leash to sink their teeth into the meat of Holmes. Haycraft, for example, is only one-eighth of the way through *Murder for Pleasure* when he can write:

> Gaboriau, Collins, Dickens. Each contributed something *toward* fictional detection. Jointly, they kept the form alive: saved the theme, perhaps, from premature extinction . . . But the creation of a really great detective character, the writing of full-length detective stories concerned with detection and nothing else, was still two decades away—locked in the questing brain of a red-cheeked school-boy in Edinburgh.

In *The Puritan Pleasures of the Detective Story*, Routley dismisses the pre-Holmes period altogether—for reasons which may not exclude unfamiliarity:

> Behind Holmes stands Aristide [*sic*] Dupin. Edgar Allan Poe published *The Murders in the Rue Morgue* in 1841, and that began it all. He was quickly [*sic*] followed by the primitive French school of detection writers, Gaboriau, Leroux [*sic*] and the rest . . . Any Englishman who knows the literature to any extent [*sic*] is content to see in these the heralds of Doyle—the anabaptists who stand behind he true puritans. There is nothing in them that Doyle did not do better.

There are various explanations for the appearance and popularity of Holmes in the last years of the nineteenth century, ranging from the purely literary through the social and economic to the psychological. A persuasive version is Routley's, if only because he includes in it elements of pretty well all the others. He suggests that the detective story began to flourish when it did because three conditions were being met: 'a tradition of integrity in the police force . . . a readiness in the reader to accept a "hero" played perfectly straight, a detective who never fails and . . . an eagerness in the reader to take pleasure in the special activity of observation'; detective literature of the Holmes variety was particularly acceptable because it satisfied the precepts of what Routley calls 'secular puritanism'. These precepts are intellectualism, by which he means 'a love of just and rational conversation', morality in the sense of 'a passion for social justice which leaves room for individual development and distinction', and 'acceptance of the values of the city', meaning 'a denial that in order to live the good life you must live in the English countryside'. This summary does less than justice to Routley's book which, despite his cavalier dismissal of anything before Holmes and an unwarranted reliance on memory,[4] is both humane in its general approach and perceptive in its detailed appreciations of individual authors.

There is also, I believe, much truth in his thesis, though one of his conditions for the growth of the detective story—the tradition of police integrity—is at variance with the findings in this book, at least in respect of police detectives. Their very venality might of course be urged as a powerful factor in the acceptance of the supersleuth of fiction who is always above corruption; add ineffectiveness to venality and there is much to be said for this opposite view of Routley's of the evolution of the Great Detective, not least its simplicity. However, in the light of the ambivalence in the Victorian attitude to detectives it might be more accurate to say that it was not the ineffectiveness of the detective police but the hope for their effectiveness that led people to welcome the Great Detective of fiction. If there had not been a nucleus of goodwill towards real detectives, revealed, for instance, in the muted condemnation of the bribery affair of 1877 and the wary support for the C.I.D. and the Special Branch, as well as in the flirtation with the authoritarian French system; if there had been only public apathy, despair and derision (and there were all three), then surely a fictional figure like Holmes would have stood much less chance of success. But given this fund of goodwill, which is almost the total progress of the detective thus far in both fact and fiction, and then given, in fiction, a choice between portraits of potentially successful but currently dubious characters very like the real thing and portraits of highly successful ones like Holmes, the public is not to be blamed for preferring the latter, if only as a sort of wish-fulfilment only slightly anticipating, it was hoped, the reality to come. The Great Detective was a mental short-cut to the eventual success of the detective system, not a permanent substitute for it.[5] Bearing this idea out to a certain extent is the fact that as the reputation of Scotland Yard waxed after World War I so in fiction the Great Detective of the Holmes variety waned, and the police heroes and procedural stories of such writers as Freeman Wills Crofts and Henry Wade began to take his place.

All these factors and others, including the skill of Doyle himself as a writer, must have contributed in some degree to the success of Holmes. But they are *post facto* explanations. It is inconceivable that Doyle took careful account of them, even supposing they were recognisable at the time, and divined that the iron was at the correct temperature. They leave certain pertinent questions unanswered.

Why, for example, did Doyle choose to write on the apparently moribund subject of detectives? What, apart from Scottish obdurateness and Irish sanguinity, made him think he might succeed? And why, if he was the first to succeed in concentrating on the detective aspects of sensation fiction, was the expression 'detective fiction' in use before his first, relatively unsuccessful venture into the genre in 1887?

It is time—at last!—to answer the question posed many pages back: why the 1880s?

NOTES TO CHAPTER 11

1   'Detectives in Fiction and in Real Life', *Saturday Review*, 11 June 1864.

2   'The Detection of Crime', *Saturday Review*, 22 September 1860.

3   'Detectives in Fiction and in Real Life', op. cit.

4   For example, besides getting Dupin's forename wrong and making Gaboriau (died 1873) a contemporary of Leroux (born 1868), Routley gives Holmes' first appearance in the *Strand* as 1887 and confuses Leo Bruce's *Case for Three Detectives* (1936) with Christopher Bush's *The Case of the Fourth Detective* (1951).

5   In an article entitled 'The Detective as Metaphor in the Nineteenth Century' (in *The Mystery Writer's Art*, ed. Nevins, originally in *Journal of Popular Culture*, Winter 1967) E. L. Gilbert puts forward the following interesting idea: 'It is, of course, extremely satisfying to view the detective—that apostle of pure reason— as the product and even the symbol of a reasonable age. But if reason had its triumphs in the nineteenth century, it also had its failures, and the detective was a product of those as well . . . Man's shaping mind, which had set out to build Jerusalem in England's green and pleasant land, had built Tom-all-Alone's instead. And from the dark and terrible slums of Tom-all-Alone's there sprang a new kind of crime—impersonal, anonymous—that required for the first time great hordes of impersonal, anonymous policemen for its detection, policemen who, simply by undertaking to solve these crimes, became themselves unwilling dwellers in the slums that reason had built.' An editorial note in *The Mystery Writer's Art* states that Gilbert hopes to expand this article to a full-length study, but I have been unable to trace anything to date.

12

THE READER LEARNS MUCH THAT
HE HAS GUESSED

It is obvious that current fiction is suffering from a revival. The tales of mystery and murder which went out of fashion as art came in are beginning to captivate once more . . .

Review of *Wyllard's Weird*, *Athenaeum*, 21 March 1885

The answer is an open secret: Gaboriau. In the best tradition of the classic detective story, though without commitment to it as an article of faith, I have tried to obey the rule of fair play by dropping his name at regular intervals, beginning with the intriguing and very relevant hesitancy of the *Saturday Review* in 1886 as to whether this 'great and increasing' genre should be called 'detective fiction' or 'the Gaboriau novel'. That he gave his name for a time to this kind of story is a measure of his importance. 'For more than two decades from 1870 onwards', writes Murch, who alone of recent commentators gives Gaboriau something approaching his due weight, 'English literary critics were using the term "in the style of M. Gaboriau" as a sufficiently informative description of new fiction.' But for the advent of Holmes and Gaboriau's nationality we might still be using his name today, whereas unless one is a specialist or a collector, the question now being asked is who was this Gaboriau.

He is virtually unknown and almost certainly unread today. Even in 1935, despite a brief revival in the late 1920s at the instigation of Arnold Bennett through his influential column in the *Evening Standard*, *The Times Literary Supplement* was obliged to open an article commemorating the centenary of

231

the Frenchman's birth with the words: 'Emile Gaboriau, like some other literary pioneers, is today probably more venerated than read.' The article continues: 'Everybody knows that he was a master of detective fiction and that he created Monsieur Lecoq.'[1] Forty years on, even that knowledge is doubtful. As if to reinforce the shadowy nature of Gaboriau's influence, *The T.L.S.* was three years late with its centenary article. Etienne Emile Gaboriau was born, not in 1835, or 1834 or 1833, all of which have been categorically proposed, but in 1832 on 9 November. This is asserted on the strength of a copy of Gaboriau's birth certificate kindly supplied by the authorities of Saujon where he was born.[2]

Gaboriau's father was a *'receveur de l'Enregistrement'*, a sort of census-taker who 'administered the civil, military, or religious life of the country' and whose 'ranks varied from prefects to petty judges to mayors and other local authorities'.[3] Saujon, a town about sixty miles north of Bordeaux, near the mouth of the Gironde, has a street named after Gaboriau, but it was not his permanent home. His father's work took him and his family all round the area of Charente-Maritime, but when his mother died in 1851 his father settled in Jonzac, some miles inland from Saujon, and it was there that Gaboriau was buried in 1873.

Destined by his father for the law, he was articled to a solicitor, but not finding this to his taste he joined the army in 1852 and served for four or five years before going to Paris in 1856 or 1857, probably to the great disappointment of his father. In Paris Gaboriau seems to have drifted into journalism by way of a carrier's office and the writing of slogans and songs for the pastry firms to which the carrier made deliveries. During 1858 and 1859 he contributed pieces to several papers and 1860 found him writing a daily editorial letter for the *Journal de la Guerre*, devoted to reporting the war with Italy which had begun in 1859. He quitted this when his impartiality offended his republican editor, to whom he gave notice by writing: 'You can hardly bring yourself to pay me a hundred francs [a month], yet you ask of me three hundred francs-worth of republicanism. Get yourself another writer.'

Gaboriau's self-dismissal may not have been quite the altruistic gesture it seems, for he was already making more promising contacts in the literary world, notably his future publisher, Dentu, through whom he doubtless met other writers, and in that same year, 1860, he began to work as an assistant to Paul Féval, a well-known *feuilletoniste* or serial writer of the time. A *feuilleton* was a leaflet containing an instalment of a serial and was appended to a daily newspaper as an inducement to buy. With its 'interrupted meetings, abductions . . . [and] startling openings', to quote Messac, it was in many respects the French equivalent of the English sensation novel; but as a daily requirement it obviously put much greater pressure on authors, to whom the English weekly, let alone fortnightly or monthly, serial must have seemed a rest-cure, and the strain of *feuilleton* writing may well have contributed to Gaboriau's early death.

Contact with these writers must have inspired Gaboriau to novel writing, for between 1861 and 1863 he produced seven books, none of which was particularly successful and all of which are now forgotten. Then in 1865 he wrote a *feuilleton* called *L'Affaire Lerouge* which catapulted him to fame. It ran first in the evening paper, *Le Pays*, without making much impression, but it did attract the favourable attention of Eugène Chavette, editor of another paper, *Le Soleil*, and his patron, Polydore Millaud, who republished it in their paper between April and July 1866. It created a sensation. Gaboriau's success can be gauged from the fact that the 300 francs Millaud paid him for the second serial rights became 20,000 francs for the retention of his services plus a present of gold chimney ornaments worth 7,000 francs. Gaboriau himself went on to write the other three novels which contain his detectives Tabaret and Lecoq and which constitute his claim to fame: *Le Crime d'Orcival* (1867), *Le Dossier No. 113* (1867) and *Monsieur Lecoq* (1869); to these may be added *Les Esclaves de Paris* (1868),[4] though Lecoq does not appear until the finale. Gaboriau has to his credit other novels featuring detectives, professional and amateur, and these might have had some historical interest had not those named swept the others into the background by going far beyond mere featuring; they surmounted the hurdle at which virtually all contemporary English writers baulked—they unreservedly made the detective the hero.

A pertinent question in the light of this outline is the relevance of Gaboriau to the England of the 1880s, given that he was writing some twenty years earlier. His works were certainly known in England as soon as they were published. The *Saturday Review* devoted a full-length article to *L'Affaire Lerouge* as soon as it appeared in 1866. Collins is known to have owned and is said to have been influenced by Gaboriau's writings. Even Dickens may not have been immune to the Frenchman's influence. Referring to *Edwin Drood*, Andrew Lang has suggested that 'in the mechanical construction of a puzzle plot (a low branch of the art of fiction) he [Dickens] could not shine, but unhappily he was ambitious of laurels such as Gaboriau wears.'[5] But the reviewer in the *Saturday* and Collins and Dickens and any other interested party were reading Gaboriau in the original French. Those were the days when translations were not absolutely essential. It was not until the early 1880s that home-produced translations began to appear, giving Gaboriau to a much wider audience and mothering the necessity of inventing an umbrella word for the kind of book he had written.

The build-up of Gaboriau's reputation to its peak in the 1880s probably began with that review of *L'Affaire Lerouge* in the *Saturday Review* for 15 December 1866, which is couched in astonishingly favourable terms:

> The story is well told, and is full of those fine and delicate touches, those epigrammatic sentences and incisive phrases, so peculiarly French; the ingenuity of the evidence is very clever, and the analysis of character and motive subtle and true. It is not ghastly and immoral like . . . some others of recent production, but it is neat, careful, well sustained and interesting; and, if criminal, is also decent.

In 1867 a brutal eleven-page abridgement of this book appeared in *Bentley's Miscellany*, but the first full translations of Gaboriau were done in the United States where they were printed as serials in Sunday newspapers and then in volume form, often with more lurid titles. *L'Affaire Lerouge*, for example, became *Crimson Crime*, and *Les Esclaves de Paris* changed cities to become *Manhattan Unmasked*.

Copies of these translations no doubt found their way across the Atlantic, helping to enhance Gaboriau's reputation and encourage imitators—so many, it seems, that in 1879 *Blackwood's Magazine* felt obliged to warn budding authors against following in their footsteps or, rather, rut:

> There are men whose names will occur to everybody, who have lost reputation prematurely, because they are fast fixed in a groove . . . In some respects they may be said to have been English Gaboriaus. Working backwards . . . they put together most cleverly intricate puzzles . . . [but] these feats of art and skill are not to be multiplied indefinitely; and yet, though each subsequent repetition of them has been falling flatter and flatter, it never appears to occur to the authors that it would be well to change their vein.

Not that this writer was complaining about Gaboriau, who he admits was 'a master of his particular craft'; it was the poor quality of his imitators that worried him, and his only complaint about Gaboriau, interestingly enough, is that in his later books he had deserted his detectives: '. . . subsequently, he wandered away more and more from his criminal courts and the Rue Jerusalem and its detectives, into the commonplace world of dissipated Paris.'[6]

A year earlier in an article on 'Modern Novels' the *Saturday Review* was positively urging would-be novelists to use the best mystery novels as a guide to the construction, if not the topic of their plots. And the example it gives? 'The most successful author of novels of mystery was, beyond all doubt, the late Emile Gaboriau . . . [and] *L'Affaire Lerouge* is perhaps the most successful novel of its kind ever written.' On the principle that any advertisement is good advertisement, these articles, despite their reservations, can only have advanced the cause of Gaboriau in England.

It was suggested earlier that the tenor of critics towards fictional detectives was a shade less vehement than towards sensation fiction generally, and that the possibility of their providing entertainment was hinted at ever so reluctantly. Gaboriau and his detectives seem to have found these chinks in the critics' otherwise impenetrable armour and to have prised open gaping holes. Reservations there may be, but the 'problem' with Gaboriau is to find an unqualified adverse comment. And when in 1881 Vizetelly launched his shilling series of 'Gaboriau's Sensational Novels', followed quickly by similar issues of works by Gaboriau's disciples such as Du Boisgobey, France was seen as the home of a school of detective fiction far superior in its products to anything being written in England. The *Saturday* had noted the trend in 1874, in its article on 'Edgar Allan Poe',: '. . . such stories as the *Murders in the Rue Morgue* show a capacity for ingenious construction unequalled by anyone who has not written in French', and it remarked on it again in 1886: 'The detective stories apparently most popular with the British public are of French or American origin.'

The 1870s and 1880s may thus have been a doldrums period, but it was only so for those writers who were trying in vain to emulate Gaboriau. It was far from dull for English readers:

> If the abundance of supply affords any accurate test, the demand for the detective novel is great and increasing. Novels of this class must surely be counted amongst the greatest successes of the day. It is a book-stall success, so to speak; that achieved by extensive, sometimes phenomenal, sales at low rates, and meaning a widespread dissemination far exceeding anything the circulating libraries could accomplish.

So wrote the *Saturday* in that article of 1886 and it goes on freely to admit, as we have seen above, the dominance of the 'foreign importation'. Nor was there any doubt about the source and leader of this influx.

Gaboriau reigned supreme. He had—this was to become *de rigueur* for all the best detective fiction writers—his elevated readership in Bismarck and Disraeli, and his influence extended into real life, as Doyle's and Freeman's is said to have done later, '. . . on the occasion of a memorable murder', noted the *Saturday* in 1883, 'which has remained a mystery to this day, English detectives were advised to study the methods described by Gaboriau.' More specifically, A. E. Gathorne Hardy, a lawyer by profession, underwrote the authenticity of Gaboriau's cases in an article entitled 'The Examination of Prisoners —Emile Gaboriau' published in the *National Review* in 1884:

> To those who are desirous of becoming acquainted with the French criminal procedure, and have not the leisure or inclination to study abstruse legal text-books, I pass on the advice given me many years ago by the late Mr. Justice Willes . . . 'Young man,' he said, 'you mean to practice at the Bar, and you will find it useful to know the French criminal practice; you had better read Gaboriau's novels, and they will give you a thorough insight into it.'

The object of this article is to question 'whether the exceptional privileges accorded to the British criminal are really advantageous to the community, or even to injured innocence', and Hardy goes on to advocate a restructuring of British criminal procedure along lines similar to the apparently more effective and efficient French practices as illustrated in Gaboriau's novels. This is yet another instance of the movement already noted in the 1880s to import some form of the more totalitarian French system, and while it would be going too far to suggest that Gaboriau was the source of this, he was obviously a contributory factor, and the emergence of this movement, coinciding with the appearance of translations of his works, must again have helped increase his popularity.

What kind of book was Gaboriau writing that it was accepted by both readers and critics and that it succeeded where English sensation novelists, treating the same topics of crime, mystery and detectives, were left far behind? In what did he differ so greatly from Miss Braddon and Collins that he overcame the critical hostility to this kind of novel and won readers in a country already well-catered for in the field of sensation?

That Gaboriau had achieved something both different and more acceptable is clear from the critics' broadly favourable reaction to him, though of course they had no reason at first to suspect that he was instituting a sub-division of sensation fiction which was to become so extensive and in some respects so apparently different as to be able in time to deny its parent. To begin with, Gaboriau's superiority and the grounds for his critical acclaim were indicated more by favourable comparisons than by positive appreciations. He was good because the rest were bad—and bad often in a moral sense. This is seen in the *Saturday's* comment, already quoted, that *L'Affaire Lerouge* 'is not ghastly and immoral, like . . . some others of recent production', followed in haste and surprise at commending a book dealing with crime by, 'if criminal, [it] is also decent'. The same paper (June, 1869) back-pedals a little in its review of *Les Esclaves de Paris*, but provides another reason for preferring Gaboriau:

> If we must have sensational stories full of horrors and improbabilities, we should prefer applying to writers who, like M. Gaboriau, aim at nothing else but excitement pure and simple. *Les Esclaves de Paris* has no pretensions to teach philosophy or to recommend Red Republicanism; it does not form part of a trilogy destined to illustrate a grand social thought. M. Gaboriau's sole purpose is to amuse and he does so thoroughly.

In 1878 the *Saturday*, writing on 'Modern Novels', reverted to the moral issue:

> *L'Affair Lerouge* and *Le Crime d'Orcival* have gone through twelve editions, and *Le Dossier No. 113* through ten. A greater success could hardly be desired for any novelist; but it might perhaps be urged that nevertheless it is not one to be envied, inasmuch as Gaboriau's works are of a demoralizing nature. The criticism would, however, be unfounded, for, though he usually dealt with crime, he was totally free from any morbid sympathy with it, and he never failed to make his criminals utterly odious. The success of his books, then, was certainly not due to any degrading characteristics.

The reviewer of *Les Esclaves de Paris* obviously has in mind novels with a purpose, still very much in fashion at the time, as the sufferers in comparison with Gaboriau. The second writer (perhaps he is the same one) admits that he is advocating Gaboriau as relief from all sorts of contemporary terrors—'deeply sentimental fiction . . . the more vividly passionate story . . . the analytic novel, perhaps the most terrible of all . . . [and] the works of authors who are totally unable to invent a plot'. Terrors, one notes, not confined to the nineteenth century. There are worse things, it seems, than pure sensation novels, but this writer also brings out one fundamental difference between Gaboriau and English sensation novelists when he says that 'though he usually dealt with crime, he . . . never failed to make his criminals utterly odious.' As we have seen, one of Miss Braddon's favourite devices was somehow to contrive volume three sympathy for her villains, no matter what horrors they had perpetrated in volumes one and two. Lady Audley and Joseph Wilmot are obvious examples. Collins, too, allows Fosco to go unpunished and he makes Magdalen Vanstone's ill-fortune at the hands of the law the justification for her subsequent dubious tactics to right this legal wrong. This tendency of sensationalists to exalt or exonerate evil was a sticking point for many critics, who saw themselves as the guardians of moral as well as of literary taste. In Gaboriau they seemed to find an author of whom they could approve even though he dealt in the hitherto reprehensible subject of crime. Black, in Gaboriau, was black, and white was white: the bad were punished and the good lived happily ever after; there were no complications except in the plot, no lessons except in detection, and analysis was confined to clues. So was born the ideology of the detective story.

So much for the critics' reasons for accepting Gaboriau. The reaction of ordinary readers reveals a more interesting and relevant reason. The following is from the biography of Edward Burne-Jones by his wife:

At one time Edward read many detective stories—Gaboriau especially—the bookstall at Victoria Station being ransacked for them whenever he went down to Rottingdean. But he wanted to hear them also. 'Rookie, you must read a Gaboriau and tell it to me. He's the most wonderful inventor of detective business that has ever been. Do you remember that wonderful chase through Paris that lasts a whole day—by the police, a detective and a woman?'

'Didn't Dickens do good detectives?' asked Mr. Rooke.

E. 'Yes, but it's quite a different kind of invention that I am thinking of: the clever tracking out of intricate mysteries.'[7]

Then there is Gathorne Hardy's comment, perceptive at any time but of mephistophelean astuteness for 1884, expressing as it does what one feels the critics of the day were trying to say about Gaboriau, and what the critics of the future were to single out as the feature distinguishing detective fiction from the sensational:

> The reader must be prepared for murder, thefts, bigamy and other crimes, and 'moving accidents in flood and field'; but if Gaboriau wishes, like the fat boy in *Pickwick*, 'to make your flesh creep', judging from my own experience he does not in the least degree succeed. My feelings are never at all harrowed by the woes of bereaved relations, plundered bankers, and betrayed damsels, who all seem to me as lay figures constructed to set off to advantage the life-like personalities of the real heroes, the marvellous detectives.

The detective business and the marvellous detectives; here is the essential contribution of Gaboriau. He was the first novelist deliberately, consistently and completely to swing the criminal romance away from the crime and the criminal and to focus on the detective. The 'completely' needs qualification, as we shall see, but not in a way that affects the validity of this statement. Before Gaboriau there were novels with detectives, not novels about detectives or novels about detection. There are odd examples of works which approach Gaboriau's concentration on these themes—*The Notting Hill Mystery*, *Lady Audley's Secret*, *The Moonstone*—but even these lack that vital intention of exalting these elements. Again, none of these books was followed by others in quite the same vein or using the same characters, and their popularity was due at least as much to other factors as to their detectives and detection—the thrill of a beautiful murderess in *Lady Audley's Secret*, the interplay of character in *The Moonstone*, and even though *The Notting Hill Mystery* is presented from the investigator's point of view, the interest is centred on Baron R. But Gaboriau sets the detective in the centre of the stage, turns the limelight on him and puts him through his paces. And both author and character come through with flying colours.

In one direction Poe is Gaboriau's obvious inspiration. It may safely be assumed that he had read Poe in Baudelaire's translation which enjoyed immense success in France. It seems that Gaboriau hoped to write a series of short stories to be entitled *Récits Etranges*, which smacks of Poe and of which perhaps 'Le Petit Vieux de Batignolles' is the only one to have been written. But as Valentine Williams points out in 'Gaboriau: Father of the Detective Novel', *National Review*, 1923, quoting from an un-named French writer:[8] ' "He derived from this class of story [Poe's] . . . a new type, and impressed his own particular quality upon it so well that, instead of being a servile and insignificant plagiarist, he stands out as an original and fertile creator".' This assessment accords ill with Haycraft's conclusions about Gaboriau in *Murder for Pleasure*: 'he blazed no really new trails, but he tilled in honest peasant fashion a great deal of virgin soil.' In *Bloody Murder*, Symons rightly takes Haycraft to task for his condemnation of 'the tawdry puppetry, the fustian, the cheap sensationalism, the dull and irrelevant digressions [and] the dreary and artificial verbiage' of the Frenchman's writings. Haycraft's first remark may be ascribed to native pride, for it is no mean feat to have been wise enough to be the first really to profit from Poe, and in any case tilling the soil is more beneficial and productive, perhaps, than careering wildly into the unknown. A compromise may be found in Williams' comment that 'Poe was the scientist who produced the text-book; Gaboriau seized upon his exposition and dramatized it.'

In another direction Gaboriau's stories have their roots firmly planted in a French tradition. Just as novels with detectives were being written in England for many years before Doyle, so too in France Gaboriau could draw on a wealth of fiction replete with mysteries and detectives, and just as Doyle fits into the English sensational tradition, so Gaboriau is part of the French. Balzac and Dumas are obvious influences, but the undergrowth was no less thick than England's—Zevaco, Decourcelle, Ponson du Terrail and Gaboriau's employer, Féval, to name but a few, 'turned out' as Williams says, 'their thousands of words a day, year after year, throughout their writing career, a never-ceasing stream of thrills and surprises whirled along in a rolling river of verbiage'.

Without the efforts of these predecessors Gaboriau might never have conceived and executed his detective stories. There is probably more of Balzac than of Poe in Gaboriau, from his habit of using the same characters over a series of novels and of modelling his aristocrats along Balzac's lines (of necessity, as Messac points out, since he would have little opportunity to mix in such circles) to his eminently Balzacian declaration in *Le Dossier No. 113*:

> 'But how can such rascalities take place in Paris, in our very midst, without—'
> 'Parbleu!' interrupted the fat man [Lecoq], 'you are young, my friend! Are you innocent enough to suppose that crimes, forty times worse than this, don't occur every day? You think the horrors of the police-courts are the only ones. Pooh! You only read in the *Gazette de Tribunaux* of the cruel melodramas of life, where the actors are as cowardly as the knife, and as treacherous as the poison they use. It is at the family fireside, often under the shelter of the law itself, that the real tragedies of life are acted; in modern crimes, the traitors wear gloves, and cloak themselves with public position; the victims die, smiling to the last, without revealing the torture they have endured to the end. Why, what I have related to you is an every day occurence.'

Gaboriau's achievement was to produce something new from the old formulas, the old characters and the old plots of sensation fiction. This he did by arranging his people and events round the detective—the detective who had always been there but in the background. Nothing changed except the emphasis. As Gathorne Hardy says, there are still crimes of all sorts, but now they are seen from the standpoint of the 'marvellous detectives'.

In the light of the elaborate theory developed so far of the unacceptability of detectives, especially police detectives, as fictional heroes, it is ironic—not to say deflationary—that Gaboriau should have created in Lecoq a successful police hero. It is tempting to say that this could only have happened in France, but this would only be following in the fallacious footsteps of the many authors from these islands who, reared in the tradition of 'it couldn't happen here', seek plausibility for their more improbable or *risqué* episodes by setting them across the channel where anything, so they believe, can happen. It is good for the English soul to note that Gaboriau regarded London as 'the most corrupt capital in existence'.

A police hero in France of the 1860s was in fact a more un-likely creation than in England. That country had at the time an even stronger preference than England for the rogue-cum-detective—Balzac's Vautrin, for example, Ponson du Terrail's Rocambole and the prime equicovator himself, Vidocq. The tradition continued in France with Maurice Leblanc's gentleman-thief, Arsène Lupin, and the dreadful Fantômas stories of Souvestre and Allain. Indeed, with the exception of Tabaret and Lecoq and Gaston Leroux's Rouletabille (and Maigret if Simenon's are detective stories) France did not indulge in Great Detectives, whereas the Anglo-Saxon countries made them into a minor industry while also maintaining a regular output of Raffles-like characters.

The unpopularity of the French police system has been mentioned, and Messac shows in the following how antagonism towards detectives comes out as strongly in French fiction as in English:

In a chapter of *The Mohicans of Paris* entitled 'The Talking Well', Dumas introduces an ex-convict named Gibassier who has fallen down a well after his escape from prison. He is discovered by M. Jackal, and there, at the bottom of the well, the prisoner and the head of the *Sùreté* exchange deep philosophical opinions on the police: 'A country without police is a great vessel without compass or rudder,' says Gibassier. But—and this is both curious and deplorable—'the police, instead of concerning themselves with important affairs of state, look into the most trivial matters, and allow themselves to become preoccupied with activities which are quite unworthy of their attention . . . You have degraded the word police by setting its best minds, not to watch over state security, but to catch thieves . . . But what have these unfortunate thieves done to you? Can't you let them go about their business in peace? . . .'

These ironic reflections are clearly an allusion to the sort of activities in favour under the Restoration. That was the time of the *agents provocateurs*, more concerned with sniffing out conspirators, real and imaginary, than with chasing thieves. These practices, and the use of ex-convicts such as Vidocq and Coco Lacour, explain why the police force became discredited, with consequences which were felt for a long time afterwards. We know that Balzac showed only a limited sympathy for his 'spies'; Hugo made Javert a wise dog; wise, no doubt, but still a dog. In a collection of short stories published around 1856, Charles Barbara introduces a policeman who spends his day spying on a suspect through a hole bored in a partition . . . He is astonished to see him having a good wash every morning: 'Such a passion for ablutions is a new one on me. I hardly ever wash except on shaving days. It's a good twenty years since I was in a river or a bath and I'm none the worse for it".'

This statement, put into the mouth of a policeman, bears out the popular idea of the informer, linking as it does moral and physical uncleanliness. M. Jackal himself, although portrayed as quite spick and span . . . nonetheless conveys a certain repugnance. Salvator, obliged to get into a carriage with him, hesitates to sit beside such a person: 'Only with difficulty did Salvator seem to overcome the repugnance which the policeman aroused in him.' But M. Jackal himself has no illusions: he is as repelling to himself as he is to others. When he discovers . . . M. Gerard's double crime, instead of arresting the murderer, who has powerful political connections, he goes so far as to explain what Gerard must do to avoid arrest: '. . . so be on your guard, and don't be caught unawares. Deny everything, deny it boldly, deny it to the death, even before the royal procurator; as need be, I will support you; I'm good for that.' It is impossible to convey the tone in which M. Jackal pronounced these last words. It was as if he despised himself as much as he despised M. Gerard.' We are still a long way from the debonair detectives to whom we have grown accustomed in contemporary novels. The policemen of the old school are almost always greedy and servile, when they are not grotesque, even if they are English.

Apart from breaking with a long line of rogue heroes expected to outwit their pursuers, Gaboriau was thus also flying in the face of a deep-set and equally long-established prejudice against the police when he created his detective heroes. So powerful were both these elements that Gaboriau's books bear strong traces of them—'the first man you might meet [says Lecoq]—a fraudulent bankrupt just out of jail, or a notary who gambles on 'Change with his client's money—would feel himself compromised by walking up the boulevards with me! A police agent?—fie! However, as old Tabaret used to say to me, the contempt of such people is but one form of fear' (*Le Crime d'Orcival*, pp. 234-5).[9] It would only be surprising if passages like this did not exist; the inheritance of several generations is not to be shrugged off overnight. Gaboriau in fact devotes several pages of 'Le Petit Vieux de Batignolles' to showing that in the Paris police there are, besides the 'obnoxious, political *mouchards*', 'detectives of a very different stamp—men like the great Monsieur Lecoq and the eminent Monsieur Méchinet, who in their whole career never do one day's political service' ('Petit Vieux', p. 127).

It is probably to his judicious intermingling of the new with the old that Gaboriau owes some of his success. In *Monsieur Lecoq*, for example, the man known as Mai, whose identity Lecoq spends most of the first part of the book trying to establish, is not the villain of the piece but the object of a plot. It is vital to Lecoq's pride that he find his answer; it is equally vital to Mai and his friends that his true identity is not established or the honour of his name will be compromised. The reader, however, is free to adopt either the interesting new angle of following with the hound—*in detail*, which had not happened before, or the edifying variation on the well-proven old angle—running with the *innocent* hare. Whichever the reader chooses, Gaboriau wins; of course the reader chooses to do both and Gaboriau doubles his winnings.

With his detectives, too, Gaboriau did not do a complete *volte-face*. His favourable presentation of Tabaret and Lecoq must be set against his portraits of their lesser brethren. Gevrol, in *L'Affaire Lerouge* and *Monsieur Lecoq* is the boastful-bungler type. He may even be the original of this now hackneyed character, pre-dating Collins' Inspector Seegrave by some two years; and other early English detectives, while often ineffectual, were not set up, as is Gevrol, as Aunt Sallies and, worse, Benedict Arnolds, for it is hinted in *Monsieur Lecoq* that Gevrol was bribed to aid the unknown prisoner. Then the sly Fanferflot who, ambitious but inept, first investigates the robbery in *Le Dossier No. 113*, also comes off badly, being described by a colleague as a 'smooth-tongued imbecile', and eventually given a strong hint by Lecoq: 'A man can shine in the second rank, who would be totally eclipsed in the first'. Père Absinthe—his name tells his story—who is Lecoq's Watson in *Monsieur Lecoq* fares worst of all:

> . . . he had seen prefect succeed prefect, and he might probably have filled an entire prison with the culprits he had arrested with his own hands. Experience had not, however, made him any the shrewder or any the more zealous. Still he had this merit, when he received an order he executed it with military exactitude, so far as he understood it. Of course if he had failed to understand it, so much the worse.
>
> *Monsieur Lecoq*, p. 16

Bumptious, corrupt, over-ambitious, incompetent drunkards. The composite picture shows that Gaboriau was far from enamoured of all detectives or blind to their faults. This technique of course helps to emphasise the abilities of Tabaret and Lecoq, but even with these two Gaboriau could not or did not completely avoid touches of that embedded repugnance. He may have created Tabaret an amateur to try to overcome this difficulty, but in the event we are told that Tabaret conceals his calling from his friends and neighbours, preferring his late excursions and odd hours to be put down to an old roué's debauchery rather than admit his association with the police.

Lecoq himself starts off, in *L'Affaire Lerouge*, as an ex-convict, a Vidocq-like character, who is described as 'an old offender, reconciled to the law'. Gaboriau must have regretted these words when, for some reason—realism perhaps, or preference for a hero younger and more attractive than Tabaret—he chose to concentrate on Lecoq. His motive may have been less deliberate. In the haste of *feuilleton* writing he may simply have forgotten those words in his previous book. He noticed them, however, or had them pointed out to him, for he is at pains both in *Le Crime d'Orcival* and in *Monsieur Lecoq* to give Lecoq's 'true' background. Lecoq, we are informed in the first of these books, had not actually broken the law, but had devised several schemes, all illegal, to enrich himself and so escape the drudgery of his existence as a calculating machine for an astronomer. 'I should frighten you if I were to tell you half the ideas I entertained in those times. If many thieves of my calibre existed, you'd have to blot the word "property" out of the dictionary.' (*Le Crime d'Orcival*, p. 82). His innate honesty, however, and fear of becoming a criminal drove him into the police service. This whitewash is second-coated in *Monsieur Lecoq*, where Gaboriau begins by using Waters' method of attracting sympathy for the exponent of a despised profession:

> The son of a respectable, well-to-do Norman family, Lecoq had received a good and solid education. He was prosecuting his law studies in Paris, when in the same week, blow following blow, he learned that his father had died, financially ruined, and that his mother had survived him only a few hours. He was left alone in the world, destitute of resources, obliged to earn his living. But how?
>
> *Monsieur Lecoq*, p. 12

He obtains work with the astronomer who is now given a name —Baron Moser. One day he explains his latest theoretical crime to the Baron who points out that 'when one has your disposition, and is poor, one may either become a famous thief or a great detective. Choose.' (*Monsieur Lecoq*, p.13).

Once again, the rogue and the detective are being seen as sides of the same coin. A similar mentality is required for both pursuits, and this potential for development in either (or both) directions is repeated in later detective fiction. Holmes amuses himself by planning crimes and Edgar Wallace's Mr Reeder has a 'criminal mind'; Thorndyke must as usual out-Holmes Holmes and goes about the business much more methodically:

> I employed [my leisure] in considering the class of cases in which I was likely to be employed, and in working out theoretical examples . . . For instance, I planned a series of murders, selecting royal personages and great ministers as the victims . . . the particulars of these crimes I wrote out at length, in my private shorthand . . . After completing each case, it was my custom to change sides and play the game over again from the opposite side of the board; that is to say, I added, as an appendix to each case, the analysis with a complete scheme for the detection of the crime.
>
> R. A. Freeman, *The Red Thumb Mark* (1907)

This variation on setting a thief to catch a thief may have been in Gaboriau's mind as a joke on his employer, Féval, for he seems to have borrowed the name Lecoq from Féval's *Les Habits Noirs* (1863), the Lecoq of which is an accomplished robber.

To return to his background, Lecoq thinks the Baron's advice excellent:

> Police service did not inspire him with repugnance—far from it. He had often admired that mysterious power whose hand is everywhere, and which, although unseen and unheard, still manages to hear and see everything . . . He considered that the profession of detective would enable him to employ the talent with which he had been endowed in a useful and honourable fashion; besides opening out a life of thrilling adventure with fame as its goal.
>
> *Monsieur Lecoq*, pp. 13–14

With the Baron's help he is enlisted in the police, but 'a cruel disenchantment awaited him. He had seen the results, but not the means'. With this case, however, Lecoq believes his opportunity for advancement has come.

At one level, then, Gaboriau had no illusions about detectives, their work or their reputation. A remark in *Le Dossier No. 113* sums up his attitude: 'If the commissary of police is a sceptic, the detective has faith; he believes in evil.' This cynicism is only to be expected from a man who in the course of his

duties frequented the police courts and the Rue de Jérusalem.
Valentine Williams paints an imaginary picture of Gaboriau

> sitting on the hard benches of the squalid little courts of the
> sombre Palais, soaking up 'atmosphere' for his chief or kicking
> his heels about that gloomy corridor, so often described in his
> books, La Galerie de l'Instruction, where the examining magis-
> trates have their rooms. We can see him in those little cafes that
> border the Seine in the vicinity of the Palais and the Prefecture,
> yarning with one or other of the remarkable galaxy of types
> which the Paris detective force has always provided.

A romanticised account, but I think we can accept that as a
journalist-cum-secretary Gaboriau was in an excellent position
to judge the difficulties of persuading readers to believe in a
detective hero—a 'good' detective. This awareness shows itself
in his attempts to present Lecoq and Tabaret in a favourable
light—even if it means abandoning all other detectives to the
devil. Here is Gaboriau's description of Lecoq's arrival at
Orcival:

> At this moment hearing the door open, M. Courtois turned round
> and found himself confronted by a man whose features were
> scarcely distinguishable, so deeply did he bow with his hat
> pressed against his chest. 'What do *you* want?' sternly asked
> M. Courtois. 'What right have *you* to come in here? Who *are*
> you?' The newcomer drew himself up. 'I am M. Lecoq', he
> replied, with a gracious smile. 'M. Lecoq of the detective force . . .'
> The announcement clearly surprised everyone, the examining
> magistrate as much as the others, for M. Lecoq whom none of
> them had ever met before, in no wise resembled the conventional
> French detective. The latter is commonly depicted as a tall
> fellow, with heavy moustaches and 'imperial', wearing a military
> stock collar, a greasy silk hat, and a threadbare frock-coat
> buttoned up to the throat so as to conceal either the complete
> absence of linen or at all events the extreme dirtiness of a calico
> shirt. Such an individual will have immense feet incased in heavy
> Wellingtons and will carry in his right hand a powerful sword-
> stick or bludgeon. Now M. Lecoq, as he appeared in the dining-
> room at Valfeuillu, had nothing whatever in common with this
> familiar type.
>
> *Le Crime d'Orcival*, p. 38[10]

And so was born another convention of detective fiction: the Great Detective is to be raised from the ruck by certifying him to be as unlike a detective as possible.

Lecoq is not only different, in a superior sense, but he is also honest. The popular notion of the detective as corrupt was perhaps Gaboriau's greatest stumbling-block in making him a credible hero. One of the first points made about Tabaret in *L'Affaire Lerouge* is that he plays detective, not to 'augment his revenues' as the commissary insinuates, but for the glory of it all, so much so that he often spends money from his own pocket to further an investigation and he has arranged for the institution of an annual prize 'to be bestowed on the police agent who during the year had unravelled the most obscure and mysterious crime' (*L'Affaire Lerouge*, p. 32). The offer of a bribe in *Le Crime d'Orcival* affords Lecoq (and Gaboriau) the opportunity for a disquisition on detectives, temptation and reality:

'Yes, yes, you wished to pay me. Oh, don't excuse yourself, don't deny it. There are professions, I know, in which manhood and integrity seem to count for nothing. Why do you offer me money? What reason have you for judging me so mean as to sell my favours? You are like the rest; you can't fancy what a man in my position is. If I wanted to be rich—richer than you—I could become so in a fortnight. Don't you see that I hold in my hands the honour and lives of fifty people? Do you think I tell everything I know? I have here', added he, tapping his forehead, 'twenty secrets that I could sell tomorrow, if I liked, for a plump hundred thousand francs apiece.' He was indignant, but beneath his anger one could detect a sentiment of resignation. He had often to reject such offers. 'I grant you readily enough', he resumed, 'that people would laugh in your face if you tried to destroy this idea which has existed for ages; if you said that a detective is honest and can't be otherwise—that he is ten times more honest than any merchant or notary, for he has tenfold their temptations, without any advantages for his probity . . .'

Le Crime d'Orcival, p. 234

Yet Gaboriau chose to risk this scornful laughter—and succeeded. His success in France cannot be attributed solely to his extension and elaboration of Poe's themes. His success in England cannot be attributed solely to a sneaking admiration for the French police system. It is also doubtful if the critic's belief in his more moral approach to crime is valid, and even it it were, whether this caused people to read his books. The critic who wrote that his sole purpose was to amuse was much nearer the mark. The bitterness and cynicism which have been noted are interesting but rare. They indicate what Gaboriau might have achieved as a serious novelist, which he hoped to become and which his early death prevented. We can judge him only by what he did, and this was to amuse. It is his means which make him outstanding. Here are detectives who not only promise great things; they achieve them. Here at last the myth of ability and the aura of magic are realised, if only in fiction—and if only for our amusement.

NOTES TO CHAPTER 12

1 'Emile Gaboriau', *The Times Literary Supplement*, 2 November 1935.

2 Inordinate pride in this 'discovery' was deservedly dashed when I read in Nancy Curry's unpublished Ph.D. thesis (see 3 below) that a French writer, Emmanuel Car, worried by the variety of birth-dates, had procured a copy of the birth certificate from the long-suffering *mairie* of Saujon as long ago as 1932 and cleared up the question in an article, '*Le Centenaire de Gaboriau*', published in *Le Club des Masques*, 15 January 1933—except that, such is the fate of much research, no one seemed to notice Car's contribution to knowledge. Curry mentions several post-1933 French references with the wrong date, and in English writings it is only in this decade with Curry's reference taken up by Bleiler in his introduction to the 1975 Dover reissue of *Monsieur Lecoq* that Gaboriau's birth-date is being correctly stated, for example in the *Encyclopedia of Mystery and Detection* (1976).

3 Nancy Ellen Curry. *The Life and Works of Emile Gaboriau*, Ph.D. thesis, University of Kentucky (1970). It is to this thesis that I am indebted for most of the details of Gaboriau's life.

4 These are the dates of volume publication; the serial version usually appeared a few months earlier.

5 Quoted in Aylmer, *The Drood Case*.

6 [A. I. Shand], 'Contemporary Literature: IV. Novelists', *Blackwood's Magazine*, 1879.

7 G. B-J, *Memorials of Edward Burne-Jones* (1906).

8 Presumably Marius Topin whose *Romanciers Contemporains* (1881) includes material on Gaboriau.

9 Editions of Gaboriau's books quoted are Belford, Clarke of Chicago and New York, published undated, but probably 1880s, except: *File No. 113*, Downey, London, 1901 (*Le Dossier No. 113*); 'Le Petit Vieux de Batignolles' in *The Bedside Book of Great Detective Stories*, ed. Herbert Van Thal (1976). French titles have been retained here as there are several English variants, but the relevant Belford, Clarke titles are: *The Lerouge Case*, *The Crime of Orcival* and *Monsieur Lecoq*.

10 The 1929 Gollancz edition gives a slightly different version with certain omissions and certain additions, though the net effect is the same.

13
IN WHICH AN IMPORTANT ACT OF RESTITUTION IS MADE

'Well', said the Vicar, 'to go back to what we were saying about
the perfect criminal. Reverse the question. Is there such a thing
as a perfect detective?'

V. L. Whitechurch, *Murder at the Pageant* (1930)

On Thursday, the 6th of March 1862, two days after Shrove
Tuesday, five women belonging to the village of La Jonchère
presented themselves at the police station, at Bougival. They
stated that for two days past no one had seen the widow Lerouge,
one of their neighbours, who lived by herself in an isolated
cottage. They had several times knocked at the door, but all in
vain. The window-shutters as well as the doors were closed; and
it was impossible to obtain even a glimpse of the interior. This
silence, this sudden disappearance alarmed them. Apprehensive
of a crime, or at least an accident, they requested the interference
of the police to satisfy their doubts by forcing the door and
entering the house.

These are the opening words of *L'Affaire Lerouge*. They leave
little room for question about the subject-matter of the story,
and any doubts that police, crime and mystery are the themes
are soon dispelled, for within two pages the widow Lerouge is
found dead in her cottage, brutally murdered. It is the same
with Gaboriau's other detective stories. There is no lingering
introduction into polite society, with, at most, undertones of
troubles and mysteries to come. From the start of a Gaboriau
novel we are plunged straight into the mysteries and their
investigation by what Carter would approve of as 'proper
detectives'. Gaboriau's precise, journalistic openings are indeed

almost tedious in their uniformity. *Le Crime d'Orcival* reads thus:

> Just as daylight was breaking, at three o'clock, on the morning of Thursday, the 9th of July, 186–, Jean Bertaud and his son, well-known as poachers and marauders among the inhabitants of Orcival—one of the pleasantest villages in the vicinity of Paris— left their cottage bound on a fishing expedition.

One can easily guess what they found. *Le Dossier No. 113* actually begins with an excerpt from a newspaper:

> In the Paris evening papers of Tuesday, February 28, 1866, under the head of *Local Items*, the following announcement appeared: 'A daring robbery, committed against one of our most eminent bankers, M. André Fauval, caused great excitement this morning . . .'

The vicissitudes of *feuilleton* writing are shown by a new date for the robbery—7 February—appearing later in the story. Finally, *Monsieur Lecoq* is faithful to the pattern:

> At about eleven o'clock in the evening of the 20th of February, 186–, which chanced to be Shrove Sunday, a party of detectives left the police-station near the old Barrière d'Italie to the direct south of Paris.

Again, one can anticipate their discovery. Whether Trollope read Gaboriau is not known, but it is doubtful if he did, for if he was put out by Collins' habit of always seeming 'to be warning me to remember that something happened at exactly half past two o'clock on Tuesday morning', then Gaboriau must have driven him mad.

Going back to *L'Affaire Lerouge*, the stage soon fills with the men charged with the investigation of the widow's murder; M. Daburon, the magistrate, Gevrol, the celebrated chief of the detective police and his jealous and ambitious assistant, Lecoq. Gevrol has no doubts about the correct line of inquiry: 'We must find the tall, sunburnt man, the gallant in the blouse . . . the miscreant has taken his measures with great precaution; but I will catch him.' Daburon points out, that in material clues they are no further forward than when they started, which affords Lecoq the opportunity of annoying his chief by mentioning old Tirauclair, the nickname of an elderly gentleman who has helped the police in the past and whose proper name is Tabaret. 'What could he do more than we have done?' snarls Gevrol, but the magistrate is interested and sends Lecoq back to Paris in search of this Père Tabaret.

Lecoq soon returns with him and the new arrival brushes aside offers of advice and background detail from the others: 'Lecoq has told me the principal facts, just as much as I desire to know . . .I prefer to proceed without receiving any details, in order to be more fully master of my own impressions.' And assisted only by Lecoq he sets about his investigations:

> He did not allow Lecoq to have a moment's rest. He wanted this or that or the other thing. He demanded paper and a pencil. Then he wanted a spade; and finally he cried out for plaster of Paris, some water and a bottle of oil. When more than an hour had elapsed, the investigating magistrate began to grow impatient, and asked what had become of the amateur detective.
>
> 'He is on the road,' replied the corporal, 'lying flat in the mud, and mixing some plaster in a plate. He says that he is nearly finished, and that he is coming back presently.' He did in fact return almost instantly, joyous, triumphant, looking at least twenty years younger . . .
>
> 'I have solved the riddle!' said Tabaret to the magistrate. 'It is all clear now, and as plain as noon-day . . .'
>
> *L'Affaire Lerouge*, pp. 19–20

He then announces, contrary to the others' theory, that the robbery of the widow had nothing to do with her murder and that the assassin 'is a young man, a little above the middle height, elegantly dressed. He wore on that evening a high hat. He carried an umbrella, and smoked a trabucos cigar in a holder.' Tabaret goes on to justify these assertions from the evidence he has found, and to elaborate on the method of murder as if he had been present.

'Why this is romance,' Gevrol explodes, but needless to say Tabaret's inferences are all proved correct. Of course we have heard it all before, but no one had dreamed of it when Gaboriau wrote it. These are Poe's happier moments stripped of aridity and re-clothed in amusement. This was the pattern for detective fiction as it was to be written for many years to come. If Ousby is right in dismissing Tabaret as 'a comic zany', then in logic Doyle ought to have submitted his stories about Holmes to *Comic Cuts*. There is no room for half measures here. If we dismiss Tabaret, we dismiss detective fiction. We cannot have Holmes without Tabaret and, of course, Lecoq. For without them we would not have had Holmes. The two Frenchmen are the only really strong men before Agamemnon.

Doyle made two well-known comments about Gaboriau. The first is in *A Study in Scarlet* (1887) where Holmes describes Lecoq as 'a miserable bungler'. The second is in his autobiography, *Memories and Adventures* (1924): 'Gaboriau had rather attracted me by the neat dove-tailing of his plots'. There is a whiff of contradiction here, but since the first was written by Doyle in his capacity as a literary agent and the second by Doyle *qua* Doyle, I think we are justified in taking the autobiographical comment as nearer his true opinion.

Doyle does not elaborate on what he means by 'neat dove-tailing', but the structure of his own long stories leaves little doubt. Thus in both *A Study in Scarlet* and *The Valley of Fear* (1915) Doyle faithfully follows Gaboriau's system of a first part concerned with a crime, its investigation and virtual solution, then a second part in which time is turned back and a new story started which from remote beginnings brings the reader to the commission of the crime discovered at the opening of the book. A few pages are then devoted to what must be the 'neat dove-tailing' of the two strands. Thus in *A Study in Scarlet* we are transported from Victorian London, where Holmes has been investigating the murder of Drebber and Stangerson, to the open spaces of Utah in the Country of the Saints, where the source of these murders lies. The same idea applies to *The Valley of Fear*, and this parallels exactly Gaboriau's technique in *Le Dossier No. 113*, *Les Esclaves de Paris* and *Monsieur Lecoq*. In *L'Affaire Lerouge* and *Le Crime d'Orcival* the explanation of the crime—for that is what these apparent digressions are—is worked into the parent story without a complete and unexplained change of scene. Doyle also achieved this in *The Sign of Four* (1890), where Jonathan Small's story is longish but comes in the natural course of the story, as does M. Plantat's in *Le Crime d'Orcival*. If continuous, consecutive, coherent narrative is the touchstone, then Gaboriau's best effort is *L'Affaire Lerouge* and Doyle's is *The Hound of the Baskervilles* (1902).

This similarity of construction is a very obvious common factor in Gaboriau and Doyle, and is generally condemned in both, a point to be considered shortly. The point for the moment is the equally obvious, though less often mentioned, influence in detail which Gaboriau seems to have had on Doyle. Thus *A Study in Scarlet* progresses on very similar lines to *L'Affaire Lerouge* with only slight changes in sequence and emphasis. The latter opens with a crime, an unsuccessful investigation by the authorities, a successful one by Tabaret, with his background filled in during a conversation with the magistrate, Daburon. The former begins with Holmes' background, then comes the crime, the perplexed police and the sending for the amateur who puts them to shame. It may be said that this is one recognised pattern for developing a detective story, but when Doyle was writing *A Study in Scarlet* in 1886 there was no recognised pattern—except Gaboriau's. It may be said that essentially this is the only possible pattern; essentially, yes, but surely not to the extent of this similarity of detail:

L'Affaire Lerouge

'Great crimes are now so rare. The race of strong fearless criminals has given place to the mob of vulgar pick-pockets. The few rascals who are heard of occasionally are as cowardly as foolish. They sign their names to their misdeeds, and even leave their cards lying about. There is no merit in catching them. Their crime found out, you have only to go and arrest them.' (p. 30)

A Study in Scarlet[1]

'There are no crimes and no criminals in these days . . . There is no crime to detect, or, at most, some bungling villainy with a motive so transparent that even a Scotland Yard official can see through it.' (pp. 23–24)

257

[Gevrol] is really an able man, but wanting in perseverance, and liable to be blinded by an incredible obstinacy. If he loses a clue he cannot bring himself to acknowledge it, still less to retrace his steps . . . The subordinate Gevrol had brought with him was a smart fellow in his profession, crafty as a fox, and jealous of his chief. (p. 7)

'Gregson is the smartest of the Scotland Yarders . . . he and Lestrade are the pick of a bad lot. They are both quick and energetic, but conventional—shockingly so. They have their knives into one another, too. They are as jealous as a pair of professional beauties.' (p. 27)

'I prefer to proceed without receiving any details, in order to be more fully master of my own impressions.' (p. 19)

'It is a capital mistake to theorize before you have all the evidence. It biases the judgement.' (p. 28)

. . . he darted into the inner chamber. He remained there about half an hour; then came out running, then re-entered and then came out again; once more he disappeared and reappeared again almost immediately. The magistrate could not help comparing him to a pointer on the scent, his turned-up nose even moved about as if to discover some subtle odour left by the assassin. All the while he talked loudly and with much gesticulation, apostrophising himself, scolding himself, uttering little cries of triumph or self-encouragement . . . the investigating magistrate began to grow patient, and asked what had become of the amateur detective. 'He is on the road,' replied the corporal, 'lying flat in the mud.' (pp. 19–20)

As he spoke, he whipped a tape-measure and a large round magnifying glass from his pocket. With these two implements he trotted noiselessly about the room, sometimes stopping, occasionally kneeling, and once lying flat on his face. So engrossed was he with his occupation that he appeared to have forgotten our presence, for he chattered away to himself under his breath the whole time, keeping up a running fire of exclamations, groans, whistles, and little cries suggestive of encouragement and hope. As I watched him I was irresistibly reminded of a pure-blooded, well-trained foxhound as it dashes backwards and forwards through the covert, whining in its eagerness, until it comes across the lost scent. (p. 35)

'If you are not minute in your investigations I cannot help it; anyhow, I am. I search and I find.' (p. 21)

'They say that genius is an infinite capacity for taking pains . . . It's a very bad definition, but it does apply to detective work.' (p. 35)

'The assassin . . . is a young man, a little above the middle height, elegantly dressed. He wore on that evening a high hat. He carried an umbrella, and smoked a trabucos cigar in a holder.' (p. 21)

'There has been murder done, and the murderer was a man. He was more than six feet high, was in the prime of life, had small feet for his height, wore coarse, square-toed boots and smoked a Trichinopoly cigar.' (p. 36)

'By Jove!' exclaimed the corporal. (p. 21)

'You amaze me, Holmes,' said I. (p. 37)

After which we begin to suspect that Doyle owed rather more to Gaboriau than the histories tell us, a suspicion borne out by another, less well-known, reference to Gaboriau in Doyle's diary. John Dickson Carr mentions it in his biography of Doyle:

'I have read Gaboriau's *Lecoq the Detective*', he wrote; the first reference to Gaboriau in all his papers, '*The Gilded Clique*, and a story concerning the murder of an old woman, the name of which I forget.' Looking this up, he inserted *The Lerouge Case*. 'All very good. Wilkie Collins, but more so.'

Could Doyle have re-read *L'Affaire Lerouge* when he looked up its title? At the least, we now know that the book was in the forefront of his mind when he was toying with ideas for a detective story. And when he came to write it—well, even Fergus Hume, self-confessed admirer and emulator of Gaboriau, though a much less talented writer than Doyle, went about his imitation, *The Mystery of a Hansom Cab* (1886), rather more subtly—and without finding it necessary to belittle Gaboriau. Hume openly acknowledged his debt to the Frenchman in a preface to a later edition of *The Hansom Cab*, and goes so far as to pay him a compliment in the story itself:

259

'Fact is, don't you know,' observed Mr. Rolleston, wisely, 'there's more in this than meets the eye, . . . think 'tective wrong myself—don't think Fitz killed Whyte . . .'

Then, of course, after such an observation, a chorus, chiefly feminine would arise: 'Then who killed him?'

'Aha,' Felix would retort . . . "tective fellers can't find out; that's the difficulty. Good mind to go on the prowl myself, by Jove.'

'But do you know anything of the detective business?' some one would ask.

'Oh, dear, yes,' with an airy wave of his hand; 'I've read Gaboreau [sic], you know; awfully jolly life, 'tectives.'

No absolute disparagement of Doyle is intended here; only a suggestion that the distribution of recognition within detective fiction could bear some reorganisation. Doyle freely admitted his debt to Poe. Gaboriau, I am sure, would have admitted a similar debt. Nor can we doubt Doyle's sincerity when he wrote: 'As to work which is unconsciously imitative, it is not to be expected that a man's style and mode of treatment should spring fully formed from his own brain',[2] but it was Poe alone that he seemed to have in mind here. Given the foregoing, one feels that he owes, for his start in life, a more immediate debt to Gaboriau, not for showing him that stories about detectives and detection could be written—Poe did that—but for showing him that they could become alive. That was the achievement of both Gaboriau and Doyle, and if in the long run Doyle did it better, could he have done it at all without Gaboriau's lead?

One can now appreciate why Doyle tried his hand at a detective story in 1886: they were all the rage—thanks to Gaboriau. One can also understand why he had difficulty in having his story accepted: it was not the most novel of variations on Gaboriau. 'It is nearly six years since the death of Emile Gaboriau, and no one has succeeded as yet in imitating him even tolerably, though he had struck into a line that was as profitable as it was popular.' This comment of A. Innes Shand's on 'French Novels' in *Blackwood's*, June 1879, still held good in 1887. T. W. Speight, Hawley Smart, Hugh Conway and B. L. Farjeon (to name but a few) were doing their best, but somehow they seemed to miss the source of Gaboriau's success—his concentration on an interesting detective. The last-named must have been pleased to see the *Westminster Review* ('Contemporary Literature, November 1887), at least link his name with the master: 'Mr. Farjeon has three distinct manners . . . Dickens . . . high-flown, mystical . . . and, third and best, his Gaboriau or detective manner.' Sir Edward Reed did rather better with his creation of Goodchild Strange in *Fort Minster, M.P.* (1885), the Watson-narrator of which describes Strange as 'distinguished by clear, direct, and penetrating power of thought, undisturbed by heat or passion of any kind. Indeed, the one defect of my friend's character was a want of sufficient warmth of temperament to generate at all times the working force necessary for actual life in this competitive era'. And when the narrator lays the facts of the case before Strange, the detective answers in the statutory manner:

> 'I am not surprised . . . to find you doubting Kilmaine's guilt, for the man no more committed the crime than I did . . . all the facts brought to light are inconsistent with the foolish theory of the police and the people.'
> 'Inconsistent . . .!' cried I . . .
> 'This only proves,' said Mr. Strange . . . 'that you have not yet begun to view the facts calmly, and that you have not done unwisely in seeking someone to help you to do so.'

In many respects, it seems, Sherlock Holmes was joining a well-established fraternity.[3] And Dorothy Sayers' proposition that 'in 1887 *A Study in Scarlet* was flung like a bombshell into the field of detective fiction' is seen to be the exaggeration it was earlier suggested to be. Indeed, anyone celebrating 1887 as a turning point in detective fiction is four years premature. In 1890, when Doyle had *The Sign of Four* to his credit, *Blackwood's Magazine*, in August, managed to devote an article to 'Crime in Fiction', by A. Innes Shand, without mentioning him except very indirectly—and detrimentally: 'It was reserved for Gaboriau to strike out the new line which has been followed since he wrote "*L'Affaire Lerouge*" by hundreds of his countrymen and of course . . . his superiority in his special department is undeniable.'

Doyle's true medium in detective fiction, as has been pointed out often enough, was the short story. 1891, when the first Holmes short story appeared in the *Strand*, is the date for those who wish to pinpoint anniversaries. His two earlier long stories are not bad novels, but they contributed nothing to detective fiction that was not there already. Gaboriau wrote only one short detective story, 'Le Petit Vieux de Batignolles', so it is difficult to compare them in this sphere. Suffice it to say that Gaboriau's solo effort can rank as one of the great detective short stories of all time. How many of Doyle's short stories rank above it must be a matter of personal preference. Where Doyle is outstanding is in his maintenance of a high standard over a long period in the field of the short story.

Even after Holmes' debut in the *Strand*, however, it is interesting that for several years many, perhaps a majority, of the few critics who wrote about detective fiction preferred Gaboriau to Doyle.

In the *Bookman* (American) of May 1902 there is a little jingle by Carolyn Wells called 'A Ballade of Detection', part of which runs:

> Sherlock, thy subtle powers I know,
> Spirit of search, incarnate quest,
> To thee the laurel wreath I throw . . .

Wells' allegiance is thus pinned to the masthead, but her poem is immediately followed by an article, 'The Detective in Fiction' by A. B. Maurice, who is intent on bestowing the wreath elsewhere:

> The deductions of Dupin and of Sherlock Holmes we are ready to accept, because we feel that it is romance, and in romance we care to refute only what seriously jars our sense of what is logical; we take those of Lecoq, because they convince beyond all question, because when one has been forced upon us, we are ready defiantly to maintain that no other is possible.

I am not sure that Lecoq's deductions are either less romantic or more necessarily true than Holmes', but they are at least as impressive. My favourite is Lecoq's exposition to Père Absinthe

—and us—of the meaning of a cry uttered by a man the police have captured in a murderous brawl in a drinking-shop; the man was seeking to escape by the back door but was forestalled by Lecoq's anticipation of this manoeuvre:

'And now,' [Lecoq] continued, 'what would you say if I showed you that this young man [the prisoner] had received an excellent, even refined education.'

'I should reply that it was very extraordinary . . . but . . . you have not proved it to me yet.'

'But I can do so very easily. Do you remember the words that he uttered as he fell?'

'Yes, I remember them perfectly. He said; "It is the Prussians who are coming." '

'What do you suppose he meant by that?'

'What a question! I should suppose that he did not like the Prussians, and that he supposed he was offering us a terrible insult.'

Lecoq was waiting anxiously for this response. 'Ah, well; Father Absinthe.' he said gravely, 'you are wrong, quite wrong . . . allow me to explain. You have certainly heard of a terrible battle which resulted in one of the greatest defeats that ever happened to France—the battle of Waterloo?' . . .

'Yes . . . I have heard of it.'

'Very well; you must know then that for some time victory seemed likely to rest with the banners of France. The English began to fall back . . . when suddenly on the right, a little to the rear, a large body of troops was seen advancing. It was the Prussian Army. The battle of Waterloo was lost.'

[Father Absinthe] exclaimed. 'I understand. The man's words were only an allusion.'

'It is as you have said,' remarked Lecoq, approvingly. 'But I had not finished. If the emperor was thrown into consternation by the appearance of the Prussians, it was because he was momentarily expecting the arrival of one of his own generals from the same direction—Grouchy—with thirty-five thousand men. So if this man's allusion was exact and complete, he was not expecting an enemy, but a friend. Now draw your own conclusions.'

Father Absinthe was amazed but convinced . . .

'Wonderful! Prodigious!' [he] exclaimed.

Monsieur Lecoq, pp. 18–19

Lecoq's deduction here is a masterpiece because it is so obvious when you see it, and when it is compared with Holmes' conclusions about Jabez Wilson's tattoo, one can appreciate Maurice's point.

Four years after Maurice's article Cecil Chesterton, writing in *Temple Bar* on 'Art and the Detective', came down even more heavily for Gaboriau against Doyle:

> They [the Holmes tales] were excellent stories, admirably conceived, and in the great majority of cases admirably executed. But their charm was not wholly or even mainly the charm of the pure detective story. One or two, like 'Silver Blaize', for instance, were admirable even from the technical point of view, but for the most part,—well, you have only to compare them with Gaboriau to feel the difference. The fact is that Sherlock Holmes was too perfect a detective for the stories of which he is the hero to be perfect detective stories . . . This idealization of the detective is in a way fatal to the art of the detective story. That the true solution may be absolutely hidden from the reader it is necessary that it should be only slowly and partially revealed to the detective. Holmes sees everything in a moment, and so leads us to see too much. That is where Gaboriau's hero has the advantage of him. In one of his conversations with Watson, Holmes is, I remember, very severe on Lecoq, whom he pronounces 'a bungler'. Certainly Lecoq had no pretence to the faultless insight of his critic. He was a clever and energetic detective, but no miracle worker. He made mistakes, he followed false scents, he led the reader astray. And so he made the story. In a word Lecoq was a bungler because Gaboriau was an expert.

If this had been written anonymously, it might easily have been attributed to Cecil's brother; the same love of antithesis and paradox are there. G.K. would also, it seems, have accepted his brother's opinion. Pressed to give the best detective story, he once placed 'The Murders in the Rue Morgue' first, and *L'Affaire Lerouge* and *Trent's Last Case* equal second, with Holmes still running.[4]

In 1913 we can still find Gaboriau being backed against Doyle—by B. E. Stevenson, himself the author of detective stories, in an article entitled 'Supreme Moments in Detective Fiction'. These moments, according to the writer, belong only to Dupin, Tabaret, Lecoq and Holmes. The choice is fairly obvious, with both Gaboriau's detectives earning a place, and the group is interesting as much for its omissions, which by 1913 included Baroness Orczy's Old Man in the Corner, Thorndyke, Leroux's Rouletabille and E. C. Bentley's Philip Trent, who might have deserved a place for getting it wrong. Holmes, indeed, seems only to have scraped into fourth place:

> Twenty years after Poe's death, Emile Gaboriau began that series of detective stories which still remain, on the whole, the best of their class. There is probably no scene more satisfying than that in which Tabaret arrives at the place of the murder in *The Lerouge Case*, and, after a short investigation, proceeds to reconstruct the crime. Here, plainly, is the genesis of Sherlock Holmes, and yet Holmes never quite rose to this height . . . Lecoq, though inferior to Tabaret, is far greater than Holmes—more picturesque, more subtle, more resourceful—and with a sense of humour . . . In so far as detective work goes, Gaboriau's stories are far better than Conan Doyle's . . . which brings one to Sherlock Holmes—whom one does not love. Indeed, it is not always easy to respect him. Wholly deplorable are those puerile 'deductions' with which so many of the stories open.

These opinions have been given, not because I believe them necessarily correct—far from it in some respects, though in others they bear out my conclusions about the primacy and quality of Gaboriau and the depth of Doyle's unacknowledged debt to him—but to show that the Frenchman was not a flash in the pan of the 1880s and quickly doused by Doyle. They show that Gaboriau was a principal factor in detective fiction and ahead of Doyle in some hierarchies even after the turn of the century. These writers would have been astonished at the relatively rapid decline of Gaboriau's readership as the century wore on. As a matter of historical fact, however, as opposed to literary preference, Stevenson badly misjudged the future when he claimed that the Holmes stories 'do not wear as well as Gaboriau's', and one suspects that in 1913 Stevenson was flogging a dying horse. Ronald Knox had written his 'Studies in the Literature of Sherlock Holmes' in 1911 and this was to spark off[5] the cult of 'finding out what we aren't meant to find out' about Holmes, to use Knox's own words.

Re-issues of Gaboriau's books became less frequent, and though never quite forgotten at least by authors in search of a variation on the inevitable reference to Holmes, Gaboriau was by the early twenties well on the way to a position within detective fiction similar to that occupied today by Sir Walter Scott within fiction as a whole—honoured on the shelf.

To appreciate one reason for this demise one has only to look at a book by Gaboriau, particularly any pre-World War I edition. An average volume of his runs to at least 300 pages of close-set type and mis-type. Unless one is able and willing, like his first English admirers, to read him in the original French, one must also contend with what the *Saturday Review* euphemistically called 'not always irreproachable translations'. *Monsieur Lecoq* must approach 300,000 words and *Le Crime d'Orcival*, Gaboriau's shortest detective novel exceeds 100,000. Compare these with the 75,000 of, say, *The Mysterious Affair at Styles* and one can appreciate the reader's preference for the latter if only on the grounds that light reading ought to conform to its description physically as well as mentally. This discouraging thickness is due to his habit of writing in the same book not only a detective story but also a historical romance much longer than the second parts of *A Study in Scarlet* and *The Valley of Fear*. Let Messac speak for all those who have drawn attention to this feature, almost invariably to condemn it—and that means virtually everyone who has written about Gaboriau:

> The plan almost always adopted in Gaboriau's *romans policiers* is a very attractive first part: mystery, inquiry, 'deduction'; the detective performs marvels. Then abruptly, just on the verge of a solution, the narrative thread breaks. The reader suddenly finds himself taken back some twenty years and a long, rambling history is recounted: The Honour of the Name (the second part of *Monsieur Lecoq*), The Secret of the Champdoces (the second part of *Les Esclaves de Paris*). When this history has lasted long enough, the main thread of the story is taken up again, and Lecoq is able to uncover in six pages all that has been laboriously told to us in two hundred. It is clear that this approach is against the princi-

ples of good story-telling. It would have been better to allow the reader to follow Lecoq's investigations without interruption and to discover with him, step by step, the secret of the Sairmeuse, the Champdoces and the Tremorels.

Another point often urged against Gaboriau stems directly from this technique: the virtual solution of the mystery by the end of the first part precludes any rise to a grand *finale* with the unmasking of the surprise villain.

These criticisms are only valid, however, in the context of detective fiction as it developed in the 1920s. On the question of length, for example, short novels were then the order of the day, particularly in this field. A publisher would hesitate at 90,000 words and boggle at 100,000, but his nineteenth-century counterpart, who on occasion had to squeeze extra chapters out of reluctant authors[6] in order to fill three volumes, or, failing that, had to resort to resetting with larger type and fewer lines per page,[7] would have welcomed with open arms Gaboriau and his hundreds of thousands of words. A limit of around 90,000 words in itself precludes discursiveness, if discursiveness was Gaboriau's sin, but its introduction avoided for later writers of detective fiction what Gaboriau may have found a problem—that a tale concerned only with detectives and detection could not be made to run efficiently for much beyond that limit. Messac points out that as a *feuilletoniste* Gaboriau was expected to complete a large given number of episodes and that, since detection did not provide enough, the extra were found in the device of an extended flashback, though whether this is to be seen as a fault or a virtue stemming from necessity is open to argument. Certainly an important factor in the survival of the detective novel and the re-birth of the detective short story towards the end of the nineteenth century was a happy series of coincidences: the decline of the three-decker, the rise of the shorter, single-volume novel and the advent of popular magazines, like the *Strand*, which wanted short stories as much as extended serials.

Doyle began writing just as these events were occurring, and his relative lack of success with his first detective novels can to some extent be traced to the difficulty of reconciling the tradition of the long three-decker with the brevity which a detective story seems to demand. James Payn summed up this problem when he rejected *A Study in Scarlet* because he felt that it was at the same time too long and too short. It was only when Doyle abandoned the novel format and concentrated on the short variety that he really found his feet. Brevity in the twin sense of short story and economic style was a major source of Doyle's success and perhaps his most lasting contribution to detective fiction. It is a pity that his admirers could not similarly curtail their researches to the relevant or even the possible and eschew the fatuous and the puerile. As with Shakespeare and the Old Course at St. Andrews, so with Holmes—one keeps hoping that the last word has been written. Be that as it may, this new-found brevity helped to render Gaboriau out of date.

Surprise, as the deliberately contrived culmination of the plot, is also a twentieth-century innovation. Thomson and Haycraft, amongst others, take Gaboriau to task for premature release of the cat, and it is true that at least in *Le Crime d'Orcival* the culprit is fairly clear early on to modern readers, and also that in *L'Affaire Lerouge* he is available by simple elimination to those who can be bothered to eliminate. But these are faults only if one regards surprise as an end sufficient and necessary in itself. Nineteenth-century writers were well aware of the value of surprise in a story, but they tended to see it as only one means among many of achieving their wider aim of entertainment on a broad canvas, which surprise alone could never hope to fill. Collins may have believed in making us wait, but he gave us something to fill the time—and it was not another murder or two. We have returned to the issue already discussed of the relative unimportance in the nineteenth century of 'who did it' against 'how it was done' and how people were affected by the secret.

This 'failure' of Gaboriau to conform to the 1920s vogue of detective fiction caused some commentators to ask if it was not possible that of the two approaches Gaboriau's was to be preferred. Was it not possible, they asked, that Gaboriau was right in expanding his stories to give the full drama behind the detection, and that later detective fiction had strayed from the better path in confining itself to mechanics? Such stories are often very good, but does it follow that other types are very bad? The unease was of course on a much wider front than just Gaboriau versus the rest. This was the time of the revival of *The Moonstone* and the claims of detective fiction on *Bleak House*, but it is nevertheless interesting how often Gaboriau's name crops up. T. S. Eliot, for example, reviewing *The Mystery of Orcival* for the *Criterion* in 1929, casts doubt on the need to keep the cat in the bag and is, into the bargain, rather more accurate than B. E. Stevenson on Gaboriau's durability: 'Lecoq, when one knows the dates, does wear extremely well. One of the merits of this story [*Le Crime d'Orcival*] is that we know the criminal very early; the only difficulty is to prove the crime and catch the culprit.' And A. E. W. Mason, introducing *Inspector Hanaud's Investigations* (1931), gives us the middle-ground view of a writer trying to extract the best from each of these worlds:

> I . . . still think that the best detective novel ever written is the first volume of Gaboriau's *Monsieur Lecocq* [*sic*] taken with the last chapter of the second volume. All the long explanation between seems to me tedious, pretentious and laboured . . . One is provided with a set of new characters and distant causes and the close narration of the actual story is lost . . . At the same time I was haunted by a desire to make the story of what actually happened more intriguing and dramatic than the unravelling of the mystery and the detection of the criminal. I wanted, in a word, that the surprise which is the natural end of a detective story should come in the middle and that the victims and criminals should between them, when brought into the witness-box, tell a story which, while explaining, should transcend in interest all the doubts and even the alarms which a good mystery is able to provoke.

These are eminently Victorian ideas, yet Mason was also haunted by contemporary insistence on categories and divisions within sensation fiction, for he goes on: 'I wanted, in a word, to use Miss Tennyson Jesse's division, to combine the crime story which produces a shiver with the detective story which aims at a surprise.' Haunted, too, by the current requirement for strict fair play, which, if he was to implement his ideas, was the first 'rule' to be ruthlessly discarded. But instead we find him apologising in this Introduction to an omnibus volume of his Hanaud stories for his failure to play fair with readers in *At the Villa Rose* (1910), the very book in which he arguably comes closest to achieving his ambition.

Another Gaboriau-based questioner was Arnold Bennett who gave intermittent attention to detective fiction in his influential weekly column, 'Books and Persons', in the *Evening Standard* between 1926 and 1931. The pattern of his discussion of the genre over these years curiously prefigures and parallels the much better known—and much more venomous—pieces by Edmund Wilson in the early 1940s. Thus, in an article entitled 'No Really First-Rate Detective Stories', Bennett remarked that 'of the present school of idolised mystery-mongers, I think that they are over-praised',[8] which earned him an increased postbag with, he tells us, 'many spirited protests of passionate admirers of the said school of novelists, and many injunctions to read various supreme modern masterpieces—named by name—and then humbly to reconsider my views in the light thereof. Every correspondent chose a different supreme modern masterpiece.' Such a reaction, of course, was to play straight into Bennett's hands. Wilson's article, 'Why Do People Read Detective Stories?', was a much more deliberate goad and proponents of the genre were again easily caught out with their claims that if only he would read such-and-such a book, his eyes would be opened. Wilson obliged by selecting Dorothy Sayers' *The Nine Tailors*, Ngaio Marsh's *Overture to Death* and Margery Allingham's *Flowers for the Judge*, but proved himself impervious to the combined charm of the three ladies, each book being shredded in turn. A similar fate awaited any book he might have chosen, for there is nothing easier to destroy critically than a detective story. With hindsight, one can see that silence, utter and complete, was the only weapon with which to combat Wilson's outburst. But at the time people had forgotten that Bennett had done it all years before, though more politely; people had also forgotten or never learned that detective fiction *is* second-rate stuff.

Replying to his readers in an article entitled 'I take up the Challenge of Detective Fiction Lovers', 17 January 1929, Bennett chose from the books recommended to him J. J. Connington's *The Case with Nine Solutions*, which was duly deflated, gently but firmly. Connington, whose real name was A. W. Stewart, was one of the many academics (he ended his career as professor of chemistry at The Queen's University, Belfast) who have dabbled in detective fiction. His best known detective was Sir Clinton Driffield, and in his day he had a considerable following. His stories are by no means the worst produced between the wars, but they were not built, more than any others, to withstand Bennett. It is the grounds of deflation, however, that are interesting here:

> . . . before reading it I took the precaution of re-reading an older masterpiece of detection—Emile Gaboriau's *L'Affaire Lerouge*. I read this work in English as a youth, I read it again in French in 1910, and now I have read it a third time. It is over sixty years old. You can judge its antiquity by the fact that one of the characters is saved from a nervous breakdown by running into a doctor's and getting himself bled. It held me once more. The basis of the plot is far older even than the book: substitution of infants soon after birth, in this instance one half-brother for another half-brother! . . . The dénouement is delayed because, out of regard for a girl's honour, the accused man would not establish an alibi! What is even worse, the plot depends on two enormous coincidences. The amateur detective . . . happens to live in the same house as the assassin! And the examining magistrate happens to be madly in love with the aristocratic girl, who is madly in love with the accused man! A trifle thick, or steep? Yes. And further, the murder is insufficiently motivated. Nevertheless, the narrative sweeps you swiftly and irresistibly along, because, the coincidences and the one defect of motivation being condoned, it shows a consistent logic, and also it has a powerful human interest, which interest is worked out with extreme thoroughness—perhaps with excessive thoroughness.

The characters are conceived with some originality, and convincingly drawn. The amateur detective, the examining magistrate, the two half-brothers and their astounding patrician

father, the noble girl, the expensive wanton, and the dying
mother of the assassin, are *created*. You are genuinely concerned
about their destinies.

The scene of the discovery of the crime, and the first activities
of the amateur detective, are brilliantly presented. All the detective parts are indeed excellent. But in the scheme of the book
they are not more important than the human drama; nor are
they developed at such length as the human drama. Take away
the entire business of detection, and the book would remain a
good, sound, old-fashioned emotional novel. Gaboriau was a
novelist, not merely a clever amateur detective.

Is this the same author whom Haycraft accused of tawdry
puppetry and cheap sensationalism? There is a double standard
at work here. Bennett is judging this particular book and
detective stories generally against the backdrop of literature
while Haycraft and Thomson judge mainly, sometimes solely,
on detective qualities as prescribed by the twentieth century.
The two standards are as east and west. This is nowhere more
apparent than in Thomson's comments on that last paragraph
of Bennett's. Having quoted it, Thomson writes in *Masters of
Mystery*:

> Mr. Bennett implies that in the detective story detection should
> be subordinate to the human drama. He does not take into
> account the fact that the two should be mutually dependent on
> each other: and that what we look for first in a detective story is
> surely detection. The weakness, not the strength, of *L'Affaire
> Lerouge* lies in just this separation. This human drama did not
> need a detective at all.

Time has told against Thomson's isolationist view of detective
fiction, but not in favour of Bennett's or at least not in a way of
which Bennett, one feels, would have approved. Bennett is in
fact reversing the Golden Age's method of assessment; he is
judging contemporary detective fiction in the light of earlier
works: 'I had set a high standard for Mr. Connington to reach,'
Bennett goes on, 'But of what use is a standard if it is not
high?' And Connington, despite 'unusual and satisfying
ingenuity', does not reach Bennett's standard:

. . . the human repercussions of . . . events are simply not handled; and . . . only one character has any life, the chief constable of the borough. He lives. The rest do not. The book is inhuman. If a jig-saw puzzle has emotional quality, then *The Case with Nine Solutions* has emotional quality. If not, not.

The story is flat; it has no contours. And the writing is as flat as the story. I do not deny that the thing can be read. It has some attraction, but no attraction of emotion. It has employed the invention of the author, not his imagination. A tragedy is not a tragedy until it moves you. This book has four tragedies, and you do not care two pence.

This is of course the standard formula for demolishing a detective story. As if to emphasise the identical nature of sensation fiction and detective fiction, Bennett could be the *Spectator* slanging *The Moonstone* in 1868: '. . . we have no person who can in any way be described as a character, no one who interests us, no one who is human enough to excite even a faint emotion of dull curiosity as to his or her fate . . . Collins put together the pieces of his puzzle with little trouble and no interest.' In a way, Bennett is being as unfair to the detective story as Thomson is to Gaboriau—or, indeed, the *Spectator* to Collins. Perhaps the only answer to this kind of criticism is given, oddly enough, in *The Case With Nine Solutions*: 'All three of them were experts in death, and among them there was no need to waste time in polite lamentations. None of them had ever set eyes on the victim before that night, and there was no object in becoming sentimental over him.' To the attitude of these three can be added those of detective fiction fans *en masse*, and one can begin to appreciate that, given these sentiments, the only defence against the Bennetts of this world is to attribute to the genre specialized motives and objects—leading, as we have seen, to specialized problems.

The importance of Bennett's criticism in the present context, however, is not his attitude to Connington but his attitude to Gaboriau. He does not seek to hide or defend the latter's faults, but uses him, despite his faults and, I think, quite fairly, as the criterion by which to judge his successors. This, Bennett is saying, is how it has been done and how it should be done, and

273

his views are a blunt, perhaps extreme, expression of the under-current of disquiet below the euphoria of the period and of the question which nagged at the minds of even the most overtly enthusiastic, Kipling's question, 'It's clever, but is it Art?' Or, as Bennett himself put it, 'The mystery-mongers of 1929 ought to understand that detective-novelists are subject to the same great principles as other novelists.' Bennett obviously saw Gaboriau as adhering to these principles while writing about detectives and detection.

That Gaboriau was a great favourite of Bennett's is clear not only from these references in the *Evening Standard* but from his correspondence and from one of his least known works, *Hugo* (1906), for which Gaboriau was at least an indirect inspiration. *Hugo, A Fantasia on Modern Themes*, to give it its full title, is a detective story only in the *Victorian Detective Fiction* sense of the term; fantasia is much more accurate. Hugo's is a Harrod's-style store, priding itself in stocking every conceivable item of merchandise and in providing a service second to none. There are ructions when the eponymous Hugo discovers that his shop does not carry handcuffs:

> 'Lamentable!' he ejaculated—'lamentable! You will tell Mr.—Mr. Banbury this morning to procure some handcuffs, assorted sizes, at once, and to add them to the—the—Explorers' Outfit Department.'

One of the store detectives, Albert Shawn, is presented by Hugo with a copy of *Le Crime d'Orcival* following a botched disguise. At the end of the book Albert claims to have learned a lot from it, and he has even spread the gospel to his wife: 'I brought Lily along with me . . . She's read Gaboriau, too, sir, and she's mighty handy.' Bennett's partiality to Gaboriau was sufficiently well-known for it to be satirized in D. B. Wyndham Lewis's *The Roaring Queen*, written in 1936, but not published until 1973, because of possible libel suits following his descriptions of various literary personalities of the 30s, some of whom (I will *not* say *sic transit*) are unidentifiable for certain today. Bennett's remarks on detective fiction are, however, no more than occasional gauntlets flung down to galvanise authors into improving quality, and his references to Gaboriau have the same give-away air.

It was left to the writer of 'Emile Gaboriau', the article in *The Times Literary Supplement* mentioned earlier, to present a fuller and more coherent case for Gaboriau. The article is sub-titled 'The Detective Novelist's Dilemma', which dilemma is presented by analogy with those crossroads at which sensation fiction has been at regular intervals represented as standing since birth:

> . . . the present is a very good moment at which to ask ourselves whether . . . there is, in fact, any active principle behind the lip-homage we offer to Gaboriau. Mystery fiction is standing now at much the same crossroads as in Gaboriau's time. In the interval it has made a circular tour and come back on its tracks; and it will need to make a fresh start in a new direction if it is not to commit suicide and remain for ever at the crossroads with a stake through its heart.

The author feels that 'Gaboriau may serve as a direction-post in this dilemma.' Admitting his failure to match, in brevity, unity and general technique, the standards of the twentieth century, the writer tries to go beyond the ostensible historical and literary reasons behind this and to suggest that Gaboriau nevertheless has other points in his favour:

> He is a ferocious moralist, pursuing the sins of youth with savage retribution, but at least he is allowed to persuade us that the sins have been committed . . . What Gaboriau . . . has, which his successors have not, is breadth of treatment and, in a large sense, seriousness of aim.

Gaboriau may never have 'quite succeeded in synthesising the intellectual and the emotional', but he was aware of the problem and at least tried to combine them. We may not approve of the great length and the dual plots, but,

> if we make the effort we are to some extent rewarded by the greatly increased richness and significance of the book as an interpretation of life. We see the passions and interests which led

to a sordid murder, not foreshortened into a paragraph but spread over a prospect as wide as life itself, and moving ineluctably through a real time and space to a predestined end behind the grisly glass cases of the Morgue and under the chill light of a police investigation. Here is the case as Lecoq sees it; there were the passions as the people felt them.

This is as good a justification as any, if justification is necessary. The writer is hoping that Gaboriau's broad approach will be taken up while his construction is improved. Only the problem of Gaboriau's technique *vis à vis* later detective fiction remains to be considered, and the writer exonerates him on precisely the same grounds as earlier I denied that Collins and Poe and sensation writers in general were writing detective fiction: lack of intention—

The truth is that neither Collins nor Gaboriau aimed at writing what we should call detective stories. What we look upon as their defects were due to no failure of method, but rather to a difference of purpose. With all their passion for secrets and puzzles, they were novelists, and they aimed at writing novels. They can certainly never have dreamed that the detective problem could come to stand as a book by itself, cut off from the great stream of human and literary tradition.

Now all this is, I believe, accurate. But it is not, in Gaboriau's case, the whole story. Gaboriau, we are told, 'aimed at writing novels', but it is reasonable to ask what kind of novels—what did he write about. And the answers to these questions, despite Bennett's and Thomson's opinion of their role, must be 'detectives'. 'Crime', 'secrets', 'puzzles' and the like must also figure, but only in a longer answer and then some way below detectives. These other words would do for Collins, but not for Gaboriau. In a positive and deliberate sense, Gaboriau set out to write about detectives, their successes, their failures, to have them as his centrepieces, to propose them as superior alternatives to rogues and criminals. No, he was not writing 'detective fiction', but to say this is now to quibble. What he did write was, twenty years later, considered so distinctive and influential as to be worth the invention of the term. This is where Gaboriau differs from Collins and all the other writers of the time who employed detectives. To them—and to many later writers—the detective was useful. To Gaboriau he was vital.

So fascinated was Gaboriau by detectives that he set himself to render the unacceptable attractive. Beside Gaboriau's interest, Dickens' and Collins' appears negligible. We cannot know that Valentine Williams' picture of Gaboriau haunting the police courts is authentic, but the following passage from *L'Affaire Lerouge* provides strong circumstantial evidence for it:

> 'In reading the memoirs of celebrated detectives, more attractive to me than the fables of our best authors I became inspired by an enthusiastic admiration for those men, so keen scented, so subtle, flexible as steel, artful and penetrating, fertile in expedients, who follow crime on the trail, armed with the law, through the brushwood of legality, as relentlessly as the savages of Cooper pursue their enemies in the depth of the American forests.'
>
> *L'Affaire Lerouge*, p. 29

That is Tabaret speaking, but it could well be Gaboriau. More plainly autobiographical still is 'Le Petit Vieux de Batignolles', which Gaboriau presents as the only available part of the memoirs of one M. Godeuil, who starts off life intending to become a doctor but switches to detection after his adventures in Batignolles with Méchinet of the detective service. The story is prefaced by a few words from Godeuil including a dedication which aptly sums up Gaboriau's whole object in writing not just this short story but all his accounts of detectives:

> Need I speak of the nature of these memoirs? They will describe the struggles, efforts, defeats, and victories of the few devoted men to whom the security of the Parisians is virtually entrusted. To cope with all the criminals of a city, which, with all its suburbs, numbers more than three millions of inhabitants, there are but two hundred detectives at the disposal of the Prefecture of Police. It is to them that I dedicate this narrative.
>
> 'Le Petit Vieux', p. 106

One other clear indication of Gaboriau's intention to write something different from the run of the mill crime story of his time is his own description of his tales as *'procédés de raison-*

nement en matières judiciaires', which his publisher, Dentu, changed to '*romans judiciaires*'. As Williams points out, Dentu knew his public. But did he quite appreciate what Gaboriau was trying to do?

Up to Gaboriau, no novelist—and Poe only in the short story—had taken a detective and thrust greatness upon him. Gaboriau differs radically from all the writers we have so far considered in that he starts with a detective and finishes with a detective. Even Poe ends with a dissertation, and Robert Audley is a detective in spite of himself. With his long, historical flashbacks Gaboriau gives us rather more than we have come to expect, and it is in this sense that my assertion of the completeness of his concentration on the detective needs qualification. The qualification, however, relates to over-completion, not under-completion. Thomson is less than accurate when he says that 'Gaboriau's novels . . . are not so much detective stories, as stories in which a detective has helped, but only helped, to unravel an entangled skein of events . . . and even from a grossly material point of view the detection occupies only a fraction of the whole.' Thomson is here describing the sensation novel with a detective, not Gaboriau; and in speaking of fractions Thomson is thinking of the proper variety—one over two—but Gaboriau actually gives us a bonus by way of an improper fraction—two over one! Yes, as twentieth-century detective stories *Monsieur Lecoq* and *Le Dossier No. 113* are too long, but the detective parts are complete in themselves. Indeed, the first part of the former, *L'enquête*, is so self-contained that it has been published on its own on several occasions with no mention of its second part, *L'honneur du nom*.[9] The 'digressions' in *L'Affaire Lerouge* and *Le Crime d'Orcival* are much more closely linked with the detective plot; they may seem long-winded, but they are Gaboriau's way of doing something that had never been done before. Moreover, the romances which make up the second parts of the other two books, especially that in *Le Dossier No. 113*, are entertaining in themselves if the reader can disabuse himself of the notion that the problem of who did it is necessarily central to the detective story.

Of course Gaboriau did not obey the rules. He was making them, or at least one, and that a much more basic one than anything to follow and on which all that followed depended; the rule, simply, that detective stories could be written and enjoyed. We can accept or reject, as we please, any or all of the explanations of his faults, or we can agree with Bennett that his faults do not matter when set against the verve of his tales. But whatever we do, we cannot deny that the intention to write novels about detectives and the achievement of that intention are Gaboriau's lasting contributions to literature.

NOTES TO CHAPTER 13

1 Edition quoted: *Sherlock Holmes, Long Stories*, Murray (1929).
2 A. C. Doyle, preface to Collected Edition of his works, 1903, quoted in *Quarterly Review*, July 1904.
3 See also E. F. Bleiler, Introduction to *Monsieur Lecoq* (1975).
4 G. K. Chesterton, 'The Best Detective Story', in *Detection Medley*, ed. Rhode (1939).
5 The conflagration really began after this piece was included in Knox's *Essays in Satire* (1928).
6 In *Mudie's Circulating Library* (1970) Guinevere Griest recounts Mrs. Gaskell's troubles with her publishers over the failure of *Mary Barton* to fill two volumes: 'in spite of her repeated remonstrances and her offer to reduce her price, Chapman and Hall insisted on more text. She finally added Chapter 37, which contains "Details Connected with the Murder".'
7 Bentley, for example, had to reduce the number of lines per page in the third volume of Lytton's *The Last Days of Pompeii* from twenty-four to twenty-two, giving twenty more pages (see J. A. Sutherland, *Victorian Novelists and Publishers* (1976).
8 Re-published in *Arnold Bennett: 'The Evening Standard' Years*, ed. Andrew Mylett (1974).
9 e.g. *Monsieur Lecoq*, Hodder & Stoughton, 1917, contains only *L'enquête*. Downey published both parts separately in 1901 without any indication that they were halves of the same novel. The Dover edition of 1975 consists of the first part and the last pages of the second, as if to comply with Mason's opinion. (see p. 269).

14
ELUSIVE CLIMAXES

'I,' said Anthony, opening the door, 'I am Dupin, I am Lecoq, I'm Fortune, Holmes and Rouletabille. Good-night.'

Philip MacDonald, *The Rasp* (1924)

When in *L'Affaire Lerouge* the examining magistrate is persuaded by Lecoq to send for Tabaret, Gevrol warns what will happen:

As soon as [Tabaret] finds himself in the presence of a crime . . . he pretends he can explain everything on the instant. And he manages to invent a story that will correspond exactly with the situation. He professes, with the help of a single fact, to be able to reconstruct all the details of an assassination, as a savant pictures an antediluvian animal from a single bone.

L'Affaire Lerouge, p. 13

These words symbolize at once the service and the disservice which Gaboriau rendered to English sensation fiction.

The service consisted in the simple but far-reaching fact that Gevrol's prognostications are absolutely correct. Tabaret comes along and astonishes not only officialdom and his own Watson, but also—and this had not been achieved since Poe —the reader. Earlier fictional characters had been amazed at the detective's skill, but we usually have only the author's word for this. Here in Gaboriau's stories the willing reader has no difficulty in joining with the characters and accepting the author's claims for his detectives. This is the true birth of the Great Detective, not the miscarriage which followed Poe's attempt to thrust him full-grown into an unprepared world. Gaboriau's detectives had the benefit of a gestation period in the womb of sensation fiction. They were born into a hard world, but not an impossible one. They could and did make their way. To stress the point made in the foregoing chapter, the detective's role in novels up to Gaboriau was auxiliary or accidental, but with Gaboriau he was enabled to occupy the position of 'captain of the ship', as Hanaud is fond of describing himself.

So successful was Gaboriau's apotheosis of detectives that it is tempting to conclude that the term 'detective fiction' was invented in the 1880s specifically to denote fiction about detectives, as opposed to any other connotations of 'detective'. That this would not be wholly justified is shown by the application, remarked on already, of 'detective' to the involved plots of sensation fiction in the 1860s, that is, several years before the decade which saw the popularization of Gaboriau's works on this side of the Channel. The truth, or as near the truth as we are likely to get, is that the concepts of the detective-person and the detective-act were inextricably mixed in the mind of the person or persons unknown who introduced the term. Yet the impact of those 'marvellous detectives' could well have been the deciding factor which ended the search for a generic term with the acceptance of this particular one.

Advocates of the primacy of detection in detective stories may have both history and logic on their side, but very often they have boredom as well. Detection in real life, it has been said often enough, is a ninety-nine per cent boring affair, and however cleverly authors may sugar the pill, most detective stories of novel length suffer at some stage from the no doubt necessary but nonetheless yawn-provoking questions and leg-work—where else or better to conceal that vital clue! Some writers make us wade through the morass without apology; others, more humane or guilt-ridden, try to soften the blow; Ellery Queen, for example, in his best Euphuistic:

> The loose and vasty association of crime investigators and criminal-hunters, when they foregather on some fantastic afternoon in the capital city of the Fifth Dimension, might do worse than adopt as their organisation's war-cry that immortal device

on the national aegis of Vraibleusia: viz., *Something will turn up* . . .
Statistics are uncertain, but it is not fanciful to say that half the
sleuths in this world are waiting for something to turn up, while
the other half are busily nosing along the trail of something that
has already turned up. In either event the spirit of the motto
holds. The waiting period, however, is not necessarily a period of
inaction. On the contrary, it is a period of frenzied activity which
is termed 'waiting' only because it accomplishes nothing and
arrives nowhere . . . Ellery Queen recognised the signs from afar,
and settled down—having no conventional requirements of duty
to satisfy—to wait in a stoical serenity. The worthy Inspector,
however . . . was compelled to go through the motions . . . The
conventional things had to be done.

The American Gun Mystery (1933)

The very brief account of the inspector's work that follows is
dwarfed by the length of this excuse for mentioning it; but the
thought was there. Nor does simple honesty always make for
good reading as when the policeman in J. S. Fletcher's *The
Kang He Vase* (1924) admits that 'this business . . . consists
largely of the question-and-answer system' and then unfortunately goes on to prove it. Ernest Bramah, creator of the blind
detective, Max Carrados, cloaks the grind under a well-turned
compliment:

'But you have some idea of the method adopted—some theory,'
persisted Mr. Ing. 'You can tell us what to do.'

'Even there I can only put two and two together and suggest
investigation on common-sense lines.'

'It is necessary to go to an expert even for that sometimes,'
submitted the old gentleman with a very comical look. 'Now, Mr.
Carrados, pray enlighten us.'

'May I put a few questions then?'

'The *Virginiola* Fraud' in *The Eyes of Max Carrados* (1923)

Good writing like this, and Bramah's is consistently so, would
excuse much in tales of peripatetic interrogators, which can
pose problems for authors who are attracted by the supposed
authenticity of the question and answer technique, while conscious of its potential unattractiveness as literature. In an
attempt to enliven the wearisome routine of detection, some

writers tend to concentrate on their heroes' personal problems, which are rarely relevant to the mystery in hand except by one of those coincidences supposedly eradicated many years ago from sensation fiction, a development about which Barzun rightly complains, 'Am I a couch?' Not that Carrados is one for physical grind. A couple of pages later in the same story he reveals his membership of the guild of Great Detectives: 'The temptation to be oracular was irresistible. Carrados smiled inwardly. "I should try to find a tall, short-sighted, Welsh book-dealer who smokes perique tobacco, suffers from a weak chest, wears thick-soled boots and always carries an umbrella".' A hint, at most, as to the true facts of detection is to be preferred, and is sufficient salve, if such be needed, to the consciences of reader and writer alike. Thus Dorothy Sayers in *Whose Body?* uses the same method as Queen of having the professional do the work and report to the amateur, but makes the point with exemplary succinctness and more real humour: ' "It affords me, if I may say so, the greatest satisfaction", continued the noble lord, "that in a collaboration like ours all the uninteresting and disagreeable routine work is done by you".' And off goes Parker into the hard, real world of detection and shoebills.

So widespread, however, did the tendency of detective novels towards mere recital of facts become that even Haycraft, most Christian of critics except towards Gaboriau, felt obliged to protest, albeit in parenthesis, in *Murder for Pleasure:*

> . . . a transcript of evidence is not fiction. Don't seat your detective at a table and parade the witnesses before him. Move him around, mix evidence with events—or else you will have a yawning reader on your hands. (British writers please note!)

In 'Not "Whodunit?" But "How?"' (the article written in response to Emund Wilson), Barzun makes a case for the primacy of detection over the detective, taking detection in a sense different from walk-and-talk routine. His definition of detective fiction in this article was given in the first chapter but it is worth quoting again in order to consider it more fully:

'a detective story is a narrative of which the chief interest lies in the palpable processes of detection', and Barzun tells us that this palpable process 'takes in much more than the main idea around which the particular story has grown', such as haemophilia in Sayers' *Have His Carcase* and high voltage cables in Bramah's short story 'The Tragedy at Brookbend Cottage'. Barzun continues: 'All the little unregarded details of daily life must be treasured up and used by the authors as matters of interest and significance. That is why floor plans, maps, timetables, the habits of the deceased and of his butler are so perennially alluring.' But are any of these things *detection?* Not one of them—from haemophilia to butlers—is unique to detection or to detective stories even. Haemophilia could form the basis of a torrid romance and numerous text-books thrive on high voltage cables. Indeed, as Barzun admits elsewhere, in an article called 'Detection in Extremis', these 'entrancing facts about *rigor mortis* or the onset of arsenic poisoning [are] data which the author [has] conscientiously copied from texts on forensic medicine or marshalled out of his or her experience as archaeologist, trained nurse, cryptanalyst, railway engineer, or collector of first editions'. And very properly, too; any author will research his subject and use his experience for his purposes, just as he will treasure up the little unregarded details of daily life; but his purpose need not be detection. There is nothing uniquely detectival in these processes which Barzun describes. They are facts of life and as such are available to all novelists. When integrated into a particular story they may be the appurtenances of detection, but scarcely its actual process. A process implies activity and activity implies people, and if anything is to distinguish detective fiction it is the person who deals in these 'entrancing' facts in the context of a mystery: the detective.

One wonders if Barzun is not mistaking means for ends, for if a detective story is essentially these processes, if they are the end to which the efforts of writer and reader are directed, then frankly detective fiction deserves the fate meted out to it in David Holloway's splendid back-handed compliment—that if he were condemned to a desert island with only one book, he would choose, not Shakespeare or the Bible or Dickens, but *A Century of Detective Stories*, 'an endless stream of monumentally unmemorable short stories. I could read them for years, and might well have to'.[1] I do not think Barzun in 'Not "Whodunit" But "How?" ' is making this mistake, but is deliberately over-emphasising his case in a hopeless effort to explain the inexplicable to Edmund Wilson. But Barzun thereby comes very close to sabotaging the whole genre when he excludes from it *The Moonstone*, Father Brown, Agatha Christie, Rex Stout, half the Wimsey books and 'a good many other able yarn-spinners who borrow the atmosphere of detection while cheating us of the substance'. As a general rule, however, I do not feel cheated by Father Brown, Wimsey, Poirot and these others, because they constitute what can be seen as the different but complementary substance of detective fiction—the detective. Barzun's substance, the palpable processes of detection, seems to come down to originality and skill in manipulating everyday facts of life. He is right to stress these aspects, but as mere facts, however entrancing, they are liable—I put it no higher than that—to end up as recitations or lectures, putting the story on a par with the semi-documentary, police-procedure variety. What may—and I put it no higher than that—rescue them from their inherent dullness is the presentation and behaviour of the man who deals in the processes.

And if this detective is to be, in A. E. W. Mason's words, 'an outstanding person, actual, picturesque, amusing, a creature of power and singularity', then he must be something more than an Inspector French or a Thorndyke or a Thinking Machine, as Jacques Futrelle actually called his detective. '[I] am diappointed,' says J. B. Priestley, 'when I am handed over to an ordinary police inspector',[2] and one sympathises. Thus there is a feeling of disappointment, of authorial incompetence even, when, in *The Duke of York's Steps* (1929), Henry Wade's Inspector Poole is stymied by the problem of how to establish whether a man is left or right-handed or ambidextrous, and has to admit that 'the brilliant detectives of fiction—Holmes,

Poirot, Hanaud (not French, he was too true to life) would have devised some simple but ingenious trick by which the unsuspecting Hessel would have been tested in both hands simultaneously.' Realistic, Wade's detective may be, but the ingenious yet simple trick is exactly what we do want; demanding fireworks, however, we get a damp squib: 'Poole could think of nothing better than to put a plain-clothes man on to shadow the banker and watch his unconscious hand action.'

There are of course engaging fictional policemen—Mason's Hanaud, for example, though I would be obliged to make an exception of him since his creator's views on the detective are one of the mainsprings of this book, but Hanaud is in his own right fantastic enough to be remote from the realistic policeman, French or English. The policeman's great contribution to the fiction of the Great Detective is as a foil, not the butt which ceases to amuse after a time, but as the devil's advocate for the obvious solution, a role entirely foreign to the Great Detective, who must make the straight crooked before final realignment:

> 'Well, it's the easiest theory', said Campion. 'Not wishing to give offence, Stanislaus. You are always hot on the easiest scent.'
>
> 'You won't offend me', said the Inspector, bridling . . . Something in Mr. Campion's manner had made him slightly uncomfortable, however. In the last case they had worked on together, Mr. Campion's fantastic theory had been correct, and the Inspector, who was a superstitious man in spite of his calling, had begun to regard his friend as a sort of voodoo who by his mere presence transformed the most straightforward cases into tortuous labyrinths of unexpected events.

Thus Inspector Oates in Margery Allingham's *Death of a Ghost* (1937). H. C. Bailey makes the same point in 'The Little Milliner', one of the stories in *Mr Fortune Explains* (1930):

> 'If some fellow's been playing tricks with the girl, that'd account for everything', Bell pronounced. 'Take it like that, and we've got a regular, ordinary case.'
>
> 'Oh, my aunt!' Reggie moaned. 'Why do you fellows want to make every case an ordinary case.'

Why, indeed; except that otherwise the *raison d'être* of the Great Detective would disappear and with him much of detective fiction.[3]

It is significant but not surprising that the word 'fantastic' has begun to figure prominently in the discussion. For fantasy is the keynote of the Great Detective. Priestley exactly conveys the requirement when, having dismissed the ordinary police-man, he adds that he prefers his detectives 'with a touch of the high fantastical'. He goes on to express a weakness for those detectives 'who appear very stupid to everybody concerned but myself, fat men from Denmark Hill, old professors with shawls and steel spectacles, all "masking an almost superhuman skill and courage" under a most unpromising exterior'. This brings us down to cases, where personal preferences and prejudices must hold sway. 'From Father Brown to Peter Wimsey the range is wide', comments Barzun in a later, more moderate article—'Detection and the Literary Art', in the *New Republic* for April 1961—in which he readmits these two and Nero Wolfe into the fold; wide enough indeed to satisfy in some manifesta-tion anyone willing to accept that touch of the high fantastical which is the only barrier to enjoyment in store. Hence Barzun would probably accept Priestley's broad dictum, but he takes specific exception to those 'amiable bumblers' as he calls them:

> There is in fact but one limit that must not be transgressed: the detective cannot be a fool. I have no use for these intellectual little men who are always mislaying their belongings and nursing a head cold, yet manage to track down desperate murderers . . . They are as unconstitutional in their ways as the 'poison unknown to science' which kills before the cork is out of the bottle.

I hesitate to take sides here, but there are dangers in being as specific as this; mislaid belongings are altogether too remi-niscent of Father Brown, and forgetfulness is a time-honoured gambit to allow the detective a second visit.

What is certain, however, is that the detective, while dealing in facts and arguments, must not be simply a medium or a soap-box through whom they are presented. He must be a character attractive enough in his own right to engage and hold our interest over and above the particular story in which he figures. This is what Gaboriau achieved with Lecoq and despite the profusion of emulations it is an achievement which, bearing in mind the times and conditions, has rarely been equalled. And Gaboriau did more. He gave sensation fiction that gale of wind which it needed to escape from the doldrums into which it had drifted.

For taking over from Gaboriau and leading this escape we must thank Doyle, who, riding the crest of the wave, took certain aspects of the Frenchman's writings and created a legend. The problems of detective fiction can be ascribed to his leaving other aspects behind. The evolution of detective fiction can be read in any history of the genre, but it is a development dominated by the Colossus of Holmes, and discounting the insular vanity typified by Routley, it is easy to appreciate why Holmes is the Mecca of historians. At one blow Doyle transformed the fictional detective of English literature from suspect public professional to endearing amateur or, strictly, private professional and in doing so created and popularised, in an age of hard realism, a romantic character who could fill the role of both wish-fulfiller and idol. The surface of the historical background to Doyle's success has occupied much of this book. The factors against a super-sleuth—the unpopularity of detectives of any type, the immorality of writing about them, the immorality of the men themselves on occasion and, let it be admitted, the generally poor quality of what was written— were considerable; at the same time there were favourable portents—the desire for reassurance in the battle against crime, the interest in science and scientific discovery and, let it not be forgotten, the success of Gaboriau. The odds, had he but known it, were against Doyle, but he gambled and won.

Once Holmes was accepted the route of the detective story through the twentieth century may have been, and looking back only as far as Holmes, probably was, inevitable. The difficulties in portraying venal, greedy and socially unacceptable characters, especially as heroes, disappeared; these erstwhile monopolists of the fight against crime could become butts for the wit of the Great Detective who put the world to rights with a glance at the parsley or your bootlace. This introduction of the private and, later, the amateur detective, and the temporary relegation of Scotland Yard may have been essential for survival of sensation fiction; certainly his presence as a virtual necessity in a detective story was not seriously questioned until after World War II, nor was any serious attempt made to explain the background to his acceptance until Murch's book in 1958. And whatever the ostensible changes in the Great Detective in the years after Holmes, he was essentially the same man for half a century at least. As he tells us in *Those Days* (1940), E. C. Bentley may have seen in his creation of Philip Trent a detective who 'was recognisable as a human being, and was not quite so much the "heavy" sleuth', and in his plot of *Trent's Last Case* (1913) he may have proposed 'not so much a detective story as an exposure of detective stories'. But with his 'new' detective what he in fact succeeded in doing was to emphasise the genuine amateur as opposed to the professional and not the amateur against the private consultant of the Holmes variety; Trent and Holmes have more in common than in contrast. Bentley's story itself served to revitalise detective stories, particularly those of novel length, not to debunk them; as Bentley admitted in his autobiography, not many saw his book as the exposure he intended. Bentley's influence really came to the fore after World War I and an interesting monograph could be assembled on the similarities between *Trent's Last Case*, A. A. Milne's *The Red House Mystery* (1922) and Philip MacDonald's *The Rasp* (1924), of which not the least instructive conclusion might be the non-existence of that war as far as detective fiction and the Great Detective were concerned. Again, while the private eyes of Hammett and Chandler may seem, in their mock-hero roles, to be the complete antithesis of Holmes, they are still privateers, more at odds with the police than Holmes ever was and eventually emerging, despite or because of those mean streets, as even more moral and upright characters. Even police heroes of the 1920s and 30s, such as Inspector French and Sir

Clinton Driffield, although intended as a serious challenge to the reign of the non-professional, were too heavily tarred with Holmesian attributes in a slow-motion way ever to be complete breaks, while other police heroes like Michael Innes' Appleby and Ngaio Marsh's Alleyn, with their erudition and good connections, were no more than Great Detectives in government pay.

The usual justification—some might say rationalisation—for the Great Detective is that he is the only *dramatis persona* whom the author can mould into a real character, the others being almost of necessity puppets—'deliberately superficial', in Barzun's defiant phrase. Whether the puppetry is necessary or deliberate, many detective stories do stand or fall, as far as characterisation is concerned, on the person of the detective. Moreover, the acceptance of the Great Detective into fiction as a leading but often lonely character, however justifiable and however pleasurable, brought with it problems, not the least of which was how to work into a criminal investigation such a fantastic, not to say unofficial character and then how to persuade readers that such a travesty of known police procedures might occur. This was a problem typified very early in the history of the genre—by none other than Gaboriau.

Which brings us to the disservice.

Let us go back to Gevrol on Tabaret: ' . . . he manages to invent a story that will correspond exactly with the situation. He professes, with the help of one single fact, to be able to reconstruct all the details of an assassination . . .' This could be the *Saturday Review* on the detective of fiction in general: 'You allow him a few scraps of clothing, a lost hat, or the marks of a pair of shoes, and he constructs a theory, by a process generally described as an "inexorable induction", which infallibly identifies the murderer.' When these words of the *Saturday* were first quoted (p. 92) the point at issue was the basing of detective plots on circumstantial evidence and more especially the paradox of presenting such evidence, when it suited the author's purpose, as absolute proof of an individual's guilt. Now at one level this is Gevrol's objection to Tabaret's system—the old detective's juggling with circumstantial evidence to produce those inexorable inductions and the guilty party, and at this level it was suggested that the author can be judged by the degree to which he convinces the reader that his detective has made the only possible reconstruction. Gaboriau usually wins this round, and A. B. Maurice's words come to mind—'we take those [deductions] of Lecoq, because they convince beyond all question.' Gevrol's words can even be seen as Gaboriau's throwing down a challenge, Queen-fashion, to the reader to find fault with the deductions with which Tabaret is about to astound him.

At another level, however, the level of what Gaboriau himself is doing as opposed to the level of what he is making his characters do, Gevrol's protests raise the question of why Gaboriau should have felt it necessary at all to draw attention to the 'trick' he was about to make Tabaret perform. The answer is surely that Gaboriau was only too well aware that amateurs like Tabaret just do not happen and he therefore felt it necessary to try to smooth Tabaret's path and to forestall mutterings about salted mines; which he does by putting the complaints, rather cunningly, into the mouth of the objectionable Gevrol. Nevertheless, by doing it at all, Gaboriau seems to draw attention to the unreality at the back of the situation. 'Why, this is romance', it may be remembered is Gevrol's not unexpected exclamation during Tabaret's recital of events at the widow's cottage and his description of the assassin. And Maurice on Dupin and Holmes comes to mind—'The deductions of Dupin and Sherlock Holmes we are ready to accept, because we feel that it is romance, and in romance we care to refute only what seriously jars our sense of what is logical.' This must also apply to Tabaret and probably even to Lecoq, for when their deductions are analysed they are no more inexorable than Dupin's and Holmes'. Tabaret's version is of course correct in the story, but one sympathises with Gevrol, for in the sense of what happens in reality as against what is acceptable in fiction, this is *not* how crimes are solved. However well-qualified and however well-connected, amateurs do not in real life present themselves uninvited at the scene of a crime, much less by invitation, to indulge in quasi-philosophical by-play which amounts to obstruction of the police in the execution of their duty.

And so we come to a second paradox in detective fiction: the impossible character, the Great Detective, in the all too possible situation of a crime; a paradox which brings with it that problem of how to get this amateur or private professional into what we know for a fact is the professional's private stamping ground. All sorts of devices have been deployed to achieve this reconciliation which is but one aspect of the wider problem of verisimilitude in detective fiction. These devices will be looked at in more detail, but many of them, it seems to me, come down to variations and elaborations on what Gaboriau is doing through Gevrol in *L'Affaire Lerouge*. He is deliberately drawing attention to the impossibility of what is about to occur in the well-founded hope—for are we not casual loungers?—of lulling us into its acceptance on the principle that brazen display is more likely to succeed than devious concealment—what might be called the Purloined Letter Principle; for just as the villain in Poe's story 'concealed' the stolen letter quite openly in his card-rack, so Gaboriau is trying to fool us into believing that he has nothing to hide or problem to overcome by explicitly advising us beforehand of the impossible feats his impossible detective is about to perform. And notwithstanding previous suspicions and disappointments, we are so impressed, for the moment at least, by such transparent honesty that we walk gaily into the trap of accepting that this particular story at any rate must be possible.

Up to a point this device works. Common sense gives way to anticipation of the cryptic acrobatics of the amateur and the deserved discomfiture of the patently incompetent and jealous police. But only up to a point, and I would like to suggest—this is the reaction of addiction, not allergy—that it was the over-elaboration of this device that sabotaged, not perhaps detective fiction as such (whatever it is), but detective fiction of the Golden Age and detective fiction of the Great Detective.

The funeral oration of detective fiction has been read many times, but the gleeful morticians have never quite got the coffin to the graveyard, or if they have, the corpse has been found missing. The burden of these orations is usually some variation on the theme that the devices of detective fiction have become so hackneyed, so fatal to credibility, that burial, even burial alive, constitutes justified euthanasia—much the same arguments, really, as were used to foretell the doom of sensation fiction in the nineteenth century. But detective stories are still being written today and will go on being written. They differ very much from those of the Golden Age, sometimes to the point of non-recognition by those brought up on Holmes, Poirot and Wimsey, but the term can be quite legitimately applied to them. The principal difference is the absence today of the Great Detective. The indefatigable and brilliant private investigator is no longer always to hand when murder is committed. His place has been taken by the disgruntled professional, often indistinguishable from the criminal, by the disenchanted spy, by the part-time sex maniac, in a word by the modern anti-hero:

'. . . you were gone this morning, too.'
'All fucking day.'
'Why do they have to hassle?'
'Because they're shits. They just see you coming and they're against you. Fuck 'em.'
'Fuck 'em,' she said.
'Fuck 'em all. The shits.'

Thus *Fletch* (1976) by Gregory McDonald, in which the eponymous hero at the above point is undercover as dope addict and shop-lifter, 'hassled' by store detectives. Now this may be the language of dope addicts or shoplifters or both, and it may be mandatory for today's undercover agent to talk this way (though as literature the dialogue could be criticised as repetitive), but reading this, one begins to appreciate a remark by Barzun, in *A Catalogue of Crime*, that 'habitual vulgarity of speech is not "more real" than civil talk among educated people'. However, while we may agree with Barzun that the disappearance of the Great Detective, at least in his superior manifestations, is to be regretted, it is also a fact, and while the unreality or otherwise of his conversation was not a crucial factor in his going, unreality in a general sense was.

Many explanations exist for the demise of the Great Detective, ranging from the World War II through his monotonous infallibility to his lack of a sex-life. All these and more doubtless had a part to play, but all add up to a complaint of unreality, and ignoring social, sexual, political and such-like influences and considering solely the literary causes of the passing of the Great Detective, these also lie in unreality, specifically the unreality which Gaboriau was trying to combat through Gevrol's words, the unreality of cases built on circumstantial evidence and especially the unreality of the descent on the scene of the crime of the omniscient amateur.

The most common defence of detective fiction against accusations of lack of reality is that it does not aim at total reality and credibility at all, but only at the more negative achievement of that well-known state of suspended disbelief. A typical version of this argument is to be found in Cyril Hare's essay on 'The Classic Form':

> . . . a detective novel is not complete unless it is not only ingenious and surprising, but also, within its own sphere, lifelike and credible. Within its own sphere—that is an all important qualification. The detective story is no more a picture of real life than *Hamlet* is a picture of how people really talked and behaved at the court of Denmark in the Middle Ages. Murders have been committed from time immemorial and their perpetrators discovered and punished, but *never* in the ways that detective writers represent . . . You must take the detective story for what it is—for the wholly artificial picture of a wholly imaginary world. And, let me say at once, none the worse for that. In the theatre you accept Hamlet for a real person . . . though your commonsense tells you that no prince of Denmark ever soliloquised in blank verse. In just the same way, on our much humbler level, we detective novelists endeavour to create for you a world that seems real while you are reading it, to induce in you what has been so well called 'the willing suspension of disbelief'.

A statement like this leads one to wonder what Gaboriau would have thought of the development of the detective and detective stories since his day. With his panoply of society, high and low, its crimes, the perpetrators, the victims, as well as his detectives, Gaboriau, one feels, set out to achieve rather more than we have come to expect or demand from detective fiction. Given his success at producing something more than a wholly artificial picture of a wholly imaginary world, he would surely be disappointed that more had not been made of his lead than one fantastical character surrounded by 'half characters', as Hare admits them to be. As far as it goes, Hare's is a persuasive apology for detective stories—if we are willing to take them for what they are, but with its talk of spheres and levels it is essentially a revised and improved version of W. H. Wright's view of detective fiction as *sui generis*. To argue thus is to deprive the genre at the outset of any claim it might have to permanent literary excellence. Hare is honest enough to admit this: 'But is it literature at all? Not, let it be conceded at once, literature with a capital L.' This defeatist attitude is Chandler's basic gripe about the classic detective story—its admission of its own inferiority which must suborn any effort to improve its image. In 'The Simple Art of Murder' Chandler quotes Sayers' Introduction to *Great Short Stories of Detection:* ' "It (the detective story) does not, and by hypothesis never can, attain the loftiest level of literary achievement",,' and using Hammett as an example Chandler goes on to argue that 'the detective story can be important writing. *The Maltese Falcon* may or may not be a work of genius, but an art which is capable of it is not "by hypothesis" incapable of anything. Once a detective story can be as good as this, only the pedants will deny that it *could* be even better.' Now this could be Bennett on Gaboriau. The creator of Sam Spade is a far cry from the creator of Tabaret and Lecoq—almost as far as Bennett from Chandler—but both are being cited as examples of how it might be possible, using their leads, to write about detectives within the tradition of novel-writing as a whole; and Bennett and Chandler have in common the injunction to detective fiction not to snuggle in self-imposed and self-satisfied exile, as Hare in his wholly imaginary world and Wright with his unilateral permission to detective fiction to set its own standards would have it. It is easy to excel if you set your own standards.

Let us accept Hare's argument, however, and taking detective fiction as it did in fact develop let us see where we are led and where the Great Detective is left.

If it is essential, as Hare and Wright and many others maintain, that the reader should at least suspend disbelief in the characters and events of a detective story—a requirement whose importance increases the more one adheres to the fair-play principle whereby the reader is supposed to participate with and even anticipate the detective—then the credibility of that detective is crucial to the achievement of that suspension; however fantastic in ultimate terms, the Great Detective must be made at least temporarily real. For as Hare himself admits in so many words, crimes are not solved in life as they are in detective stories. However hard the blow may fall on The Baker Street Irregulars, The Speckled Band and the other battalions of fanatics, Holmes is an impossible creation, as are all others built to his specification.

But, it will be said, surely Holmes at least was and still is for many a real person, a claim borne out by the letters addressed to him at Baker Street, and is Ronald Knox not right to asseverate that Holmes is one of the people, so real are they, for whom we will ask when we get to Heaven? This is an opportune moment to make clear that what is here intended by 'real' and its derivatives (dangerous words all!) is that which we expect to happen, or even at a pinch that which we are willing to conceive of as happening in our day-to-day lives. Let me rush to add that I, too, have heard that fact is stranger than fiction. Even as I write the newspapers contain reports of a plan to steal a nuclear submarine and of murder by poisoned umbrella tip. There is a distinction, however, between what one can accept as having the ring of truth in a work of fiction, however untrue in fact, and what, however well-documented in fact, one still has difficulty in accepting when introduced into a story—Dickens' spontaneous combustion of Krook in *Bleak House*, for example. Mrs. Oliphant, writing in *Blackwood's* in 1863, puts it very neatly: ' . . . truth and fact are two different things; and to say that some incident [in a book] which is false to nature is taken from the life, is an altogether unsatisfactory and inadmissible excuse.' In other words, a basis in fact is no guarantee of a reader's belief in a story. At the risk of continuing to state the obvious, reality is not to be confused with credibility. The talent in an author for good lies may be of much more use to him than a predilection for facts. This is especially true of detective fiction where Holmes can now be seen as an unreal but very credible creation, while in the actual world the theft of submarines and the poisoned umbrellas become real but incredible events.

Unreality is a favourite criticism of detective stories, but as with the fallacy of basing plots on circumstantial evidence, it is up to the reader whether he accepts the infallible amateurs, the myopic Watsons, the long-suffering police, the coincidences and the whole impedimenta of the genre, just as it is even more up to the writer to persuade the reader that it all could happen. This is Hare's point, and it is a reasonable argument, especially when given the abandonment of detective fiction as Literature. Thus realism in my suggested sense of the actual, the probable or even the possible, is not proposed as an essential feature of detective fiction.

There remains the problem of achieving credibility. This problem is by no means peculiar to detective fiction, but detective fiction of the Great Detective kind was setting itself a particularly difficult exercise in verisimilitude not encountered by related genres. To take two grossly over-simplified comparisons, there is science fantasy where the author can be seen as making impossible characters do impossible things, and there is science fiction where possible characters do impossible (for the moment) things. But with tales of Great Detectives authors were setting themselves the awkward combination: the impossible character doing possible things. Hare mis-states the situation of the would-be detective story writer when he claims that he is trying to create 'the *wholly* artificial picture of a *wholly* imaginary world'. That is what Shakespeare did in *The Tempest* to such good effect that Coleridge argues for a state of 'negative reality', like dreaming, in which the audience 'simply do not judge the imagery to be unreal'. Coleridge, however, goes on to speak of *The Tempest* as 'a species of drama which owes no allegiance to time or space, and in which, therefore, errors of chronology and geography—no mortal sin in any species— are venial faults, and count for nothing. It addresses itself entirely to the imaginative faculty'.[4] And here detective fiction must part company with Coleridge and Shakespeare—not simply because errors of chronology and geography in a detective story are usually regarded as mortal sins; in 'The Simple Art of Murder' this was Chandler's case against A. A. Milne's *The Red House Mystery* where there are several pro- cedural slips, but in drawing attention to which Chandler proves only inaccuracy and not, as he claims, unreality, much less disappointment to the, like me, ignorant reader. The parting occurs because detective fiction does not address itself entirely to the imaginative faculty, for unless we regard the willing suspension of disbelief as common to all fiction (which is valid in a wide, but almost meaningless, sense), the detective writer has this peculiar difficulty of creating and maintaining a realistic setting inhabited by an unreal character—the Great Detective. Thus the author is faced on the one hand with events—a murder, or at least a crime, clues, an investigation, an inquest, a trial perhaps—of which his readers will have experience in at least a general way; and on the other hand he is faced with a character—a non-police detective—of whom his readers cannot possibly have any experience because he does not exist. The poisoned umbrella and the ice-dart, in fact or in fiction, can be explained, if sometimes only just, in terms relatively familiar to the average person. Even the overworked country house with the body in its library can be accepted from capable hands, for as Barzun points out in *A Catalogue of Crime*, *contra* Chandler, 'private libraries are still more numerous than private eyes.' But how does an author explain and justify the amateur investigator's presence on a case? Or more crudely, how many Great Detectives do you know?

Very awkward, then, but not insurmountable. Gaboriau succeeded. Doyle succeeded. Many others, too, succeeded, and the irony of the whole affair, as we shall see, is that so far from being unable to cope with the actual unreality of the Great Detective, writers coped with it too well.

NOTES TO CHAPTER 14

1 David Holloway, 'Strictly for the Seagulls', *Daily Telegraph*, 25 March 1978.

2 J. B. Priestley, 'On Holiday with the Bodies', *Saturday Review*, 3 July 1926.

3 The inevitable parody of the Campion/Fortune approach in which the simple police theory proves correct can be found for example in *Top Storey Murder* (1931) by, inevitably, Anthony Berkeley, and, better, Leo Bruce's *Case for Three Detectives* (1936); best of all, perhaps, are the Radford Shone stories by Headon Hill (F. E. Grainger) which first appeared in *Woman at Home* in 1905.

4 Samuel Taylor Coleridge, *Essays and Lectures on Shakespeare*, Dent, 1907 (reprinted).

15
CURTAIN

> On hearing Lecoq's recital, all the conflicting sentiments that are awakened in a child's mind by a fairy tale—doubt, faith, anxiety, and hope—filled Father Absinthe's heart. What should he believe? What should he refuse to believe?
>
> Emile Gaboriau, *Monsieur Lecoq*

The wonder of detective fiction, considered dispassionately, is that it ever got off the ground. Its main character was a theoretical impossibility, a contradiction in terms. Yet, in Tabaret and Holmes, there he was. He existed. Indeed, circumstances having so combined in the 1880s to enable this pig to fly, there seemed to be no means of recall. Doubts were expressed in the next decade or so about the life-expectancy of the detective of fiction. In 1890, A. Innes Shand in *Blackwood's Magazine* closed a generally sympathetic account of 'Crime in Fiction' with the words:

> But surely this sensation business must soon come to an end, or be suspended for half a generation or so. The public is getting familiarised with all manner of mysteries, in cabs, in black boxes, in garrets and in cellars; the detectives have been told off for such intolerably hard duty, that it is clear they must soon strike in disgust, and refuse to lend themselves to those stale combinations.

The author of 'The Passing of the Detective' in the *Academy* for 30 December 1905, is typical of the regular forecasters of doom: 'The detective in literature is hardly more than fifty years old, but already he is passing into decay.' The *Outlook* for 1910 contains an amusing article on the subject, called 'The Unromantic Detective', reminiscent of Chandler in a good mood, in which it tries to jerk the reading public back to reality:

> One ought . . . to remember that the detective of real life is a man who has only just escaped from being a policeman . . . The ordinary detective cannot look at the mud on a man's trouser-ends and tell to a yard where he keeps his country house . . . The ordinary detective is a man, and one step, a simple one, is enough for him at a time. Sherlock Holmes, on the contrary, is a wizard. He never lived a real life; he never solved a real crime; he never dogged a real criminal. He is just a shining ideal, so wonderful that even a slow-witted government recognised the merit of the mere act of creation and knighted the author . . . I have only known one detective. He looked almost as dull as I do, but he wore a better hat. He also smelt of rum, a penetrating fluid that does not necessarily promote acute reasoning. The criminal was in the house opposite to mine; the solution lay in watching; the only place of satisfactory vigil was my garden. When he asked permission to use my garden I granted it, disliking the man. For three nights he stood there watching. It was November, and it rained the misty, soggy rain peculiar to November each night. Nothing came of all this. The criminal, who was caught for another crime twelve months after, was arrested by an ordinary constable, with the help of a cabman, in fine weather. That seems to be all there is in being a detective. You wait round the corner and get wet. Or perhaps you get your head punched. Not a heroic life; it lacks in charm and variety, and is not uniformly successful. It is necessary the public should know these things . . . one can then give him real credit for sticking to a doleful task under dismal conditions, and occasionally succeeding despite the most depressing odds. If one judges him on the wet-feet basis instead of in the Baker Street manner, he really does begin to loom heroically.

Yet the heyday of the detective was still to come. The Jeremiahs saw only the difficulties of trying to perpetuate the omniscient sleuth, reckoning without the ingenuity of the enthusiasts. This is not to say that the problem of welding the impossible detective on to a down-to-earth chassis was not formidable. The histories of detective fiction show how the variety of detective types seems infinite, but behind the histories' rolls of honour it must be remembered that every time an author conceived a non-professonal detective he was faced with the problem of how to get his hero involved in a case, for he was well aware that his creation, if such existed in real life except as signatories to newspaper letters, would be given short shrift by the official police.[1] Linked to this problem was how to make *this* detective sufficiently different from his predecessors to avoid accusations of plagiarism, unoriginality and stereotyping, yet sufficiently close to the prototypes of Gaboriau and Doyle to afford a chance of similar success, for Lecoq and Holmes, the latter eventually more so, seemed to make the greatest appeal to readers.

The means used by authors to infiltrate their detectives into police territory were almost as varied as the types of detective. The problem had existed from the beginning—in *Henry Dunbar*, it will be remembered, Miss Braddon contrived to admit Clement Austin into partnership with Mr. Carter by the convincing means of money—but the situation of police and amateur working simultaneously on an inquiry, amicably or inimically, was rare between Poe and Gaboriau. Policeman against policeman, as we have seen, was the more common situation in sensation fiction. After Doyle, however, the amateur was the order of the day, and imaginations had to work overtime. At first the most common method and probably the least unlikely was simply to follow the master and give the amateur a room or an office and hence the semi-professional status of a private investigator; clients and cases could come to him and after all there were such things as private detectives. B. L. Farjeon in *The Last Tenant* could afford to be offhand about the employment of such an individual, but then it was only 1893: 'I therefore determined to enlist the services of a private enquiry agent . . . Looking through the columns of a morning paper, I saw Mr. Dickson's advertisement; and at eleven o'clock I set out for his office . . . I explained to him what I wanted done, and he undertook the commission for a specified sum . . . Two days afterwards I received his report.' As with most of B. L. Farjeon's detectives, Dickson is in the tradition of the detective in a supporting role, but Arthur

Morrison uses this same technique, giving us only the bare bones of his detective hero, Martin Hewitt, in the series of short stories which, beginning in 1894, the *Strand* used to fill the blank left by Holmes' 'death'. A successful investigation on behalf of the legal firm which employs him as a clerk and Hewitt 'determine[s] to work independently for the future'. This reticence was probably a deliberate move by Morrison to achieve a contrast with Doyle's flamboyant character. Hewitt is the plain man's detective, almost a plain clothes policeman. He is at pains to work with, not against, Scotland Yard, and as for the science of deduction—' "System?" said Hewitt . . . "I can't say I have a system. I call it nothing but common-sense and a sharp pair of eyes".'[2]

A variation on the private investigator who made a living from detection was the part-timer for whom detection was a hobby. Of independent means or self-employed (authors, particularly authors of detective fiction, were favourites), he was immediately available to the baffled police, who eventually presented themselves on his doorstep, reluctant caps in hand. Here we have the likes of Dr. Priestley, Roger Sheringham and Dr. Fell. As a retired professional still available for consultation, Poirot has a foot in both camps. Relationship with the police, by blood with Ellery Queen and by marriage with Wimsey, seems to have been enough for them to gain admission to police circles, though Dorothy Sayers betrays a qualm of conscience when in *Unnatural Death* (1927) she makes Parker tell Wimsey: 'I've no business to let you come with me on a job at all.' Another approach was to make the detective somehow connected with the police on an official or semi-official basis, without restricting his freedom by admitting him to the ranks. Doctors, lawyers and journalists were ideal, since each might have a legitimate role in an inquiry. This is how Philip Trent, representing the *Record*, started his last case, and how Mr. Fortune, as police-surgeon extraordinary, became an inextricable thorn in the sides of Lomas and Bell. These attempts came closest to possiblity perhaps, though not reality—not that anyone seemed to care when these gentlemen overstepped the recognised boundaries of their professional connections with the police. They were no guarantee of success, however, since the hugely improbable 'my-goodness-I've-just-fallen-over-a-body' school, mostly amiable bumblers, chalked up several hits and the authors had simply to strew down a few more bodies waiting to be stumbled over in order to continue their success. The permutations and cross-breedings of these devices were legion and the charisma of the amateur affected even those writers who ostensibly preferred truth and made their detectives policemen. Thus a favourite scheme of Crofts and the Coles, seen in the former's *Pit Prop Syndicate* (1922), was to devote the first part of a story to the amateur's efforts to solve the mystery, and then, when he has failed, to bring in the professionals to sort things out. Connington's variation on this, with his partnership of a chief constable, Driffield, and a would-be amateur, Wendover, was to make the amateur the dullard and the policeman the successful member of the pair. Yet this inversion of Doyle's division of labour indicates more the influence of that author than a break from his pattern.

Success in establishing an amateur on a criminal investigation seems at times to have been almost in direct proportion to the size of the lie, and the author who hesitated to quit the altar of truth could well find himself sacrificed thereon. The least likely creations could enjoy the greatest acceptance, and whatever hesitations and doubts authors may have had about their manoeuvrings to get their fantastic detectives into real settings, readers seemed willing to ignore them, for there were compensations, not least the fantastic detective himself. Readers, indeed, did not seem to care even in cases where no explanation would have made better sense; thus Margery Allingham's explanation of the presence of Mr. Campion in *Death of a Ghost* is unpersuasive in the extreme: 'There were some who insisted that he was in reality a member of Scotland Yard's vast army of unobtrusive agents whose work is done entirely behind the scenes, but Mr. Campion himself would have denied this vigorously', and later, more qualms: 'The inspector never quite knew why he always invited the pale young man to accompany him on this sort of expedition in defiance of edict and etiquette alike, but the fact remained and so did Mr. Campion.' Vague, indeed, but Mr. Campion did more than remain; he flourished.

Nevertheless, the overall unreality of the situations they had often cleverly and interestingly devised seemed to haunt authors. They were either not able or not content to leave the contradiction alone, but felt obliged to emphasise to the reader and perhaps to themselves, in much more elaborate ways than Gaboriau, that *this* particular story could have happened— that it is real however unreal other detective stories may have appeared. So aware were they of the essential inconsistency in what they were doing that this awareness comes out in their writing as, at best, self-reference, but more often as self-consciousness and eventually self-mockery as the absurdity of their situation became increasingly apparent. Introspection may make for excellence in other types of fiction but it somehow seems inappropriate to the extrovert process of the detective story where it led to such a shallow approach and presentation that credibility had to be a fatal casualty.

Traces of this feeling by authors of a need to give their detectives and stories a degree of verisimilitude beyond the normal devices of novel-writing can be found before the advent of Gaboriau. The obvious reason for this is that the detective of fiction was a cliché of Victorian sensation fiction, the apparent inevitability of his appearance being itself a cliché of Victorian criticism. Poe, Waters and McLevy all indulge to some degree; Collins felt the pressure of it when he came to introduce Cuff in *The Moonstone*, for, like Gaboriau, he adopted what became the standard form of self-exoneration for daring to introduce yet another detective: 'He might have been a parson or an undertaker—or anything else you like, except what he really was.' This procedure became so commonplace that one begins to wonder what a detective does look like since none look like one. Collins also made use of what developed into another time-honoured tactic to convey reality, when he has Cuff say that 'it's only in books that the officers of the detective force are superior to the weakness of making a mistake.' Subsequent variations on this theme were to prove a prime source of loss of credibility instead of its intended achievement.

It was argued earlier that sensation authors were attempting and succeeding in the presentation of realistic pictures of detectives, most of them actual policemen. If they felt the need to emphasise that reality, how much more must this have been a problem for Doyle and his impossible character. Yet the cliché of the detective had not progressed so far that Doyle could not manipulate it to his advantage. As long ago as 1913 Friedrich Depken, in his *Sherlock Holmes, Raffles und Ihre Vorbilder*, gave an extensive list of the means Doyle used to 'give the stamp of the obvious and an air of seeming reality to . . . stories filled with improbabilities'. Again, many of these already had or were soon to become common practice in detective fiction: the eye-witness accounts, with Watson repeatedly expressing the fear that what he is saying will not be believed and his dismissal of some of Holmes' more outrageous assertions as 'foolish prattle'; then there are the references to past cases, to forbidden cases, to real newspapers, the giving of almost specific dates and so on, all helping, as Depken says, 'to compel the reader into believing that the individual occurrences really did take place'. Interestingly, Depken adds: 'Finally, it must be mentioned that Gaboriau and Hornung rarely use any means to increase the air of probability in their stories.' Could it be that these two authors saw their characters as entirely possible creations and not embarrassments, so that self-defeating devices for credibility were not needed?

Doyle must be given his due, however; he succeeded beyond his own dreams in putting his detective over. I suggested earlier that the problem for those coming after Doyle was how to follow him, and nowhere is this more apparent than in the question of how to impart credibility to what was receiving the accolade of parody before the century was out. It is here, after Holmes, that the self-reference and the self-consciousness begin in earnest. Many an author must have cursed Doyle and his detective and his detective's world for their too great success. So enveloping was their shadow that writers seem continually to be looking over their shoulders, Tam o' Shanter fashion, wondering if they will be struck down for their impertinence in creating other detectives.

The method adopted to deal with Holmes *was* impertinent, though at the same time flattering; it was also, on the face of it, very astute. Thus there is scarcely a detective novel written in the Golden Age which does not refer to Holmes in some way or other; it may be to him by name or to him by implication as the Great Detective or the story-book detective, but select at random ten such novels and the reference—I mean this literally —will be in nine of them; at least. For example, all twelve of Dorothy Sayers' detective novels contain such a reference. The solution, then, was to take Holmes, a fiction, into the world of a story and use him to confirm the reality of that world; he is assimilated into the tricks of the trade used by Doyle himself— a tribute to his standing, even though the reference is usually disparaging. Occasionally the remark is an innocent, passing one, but more often there is a sting of varying toxicity in it. An early expression of disenchantment is the ambitious detective's in Burford Delannoy's *The Margate Murder Mystery* (1902):

> . . . the boots were of French make, worn at the heel, and the wearer limped or was lame in the right leg. That was easily read, and I need not trouble to describe how. The writers of detective stories—confound them—have long since let the public into these hitherto secrets. Mr. Sherlock Holmes was very interesting reading, but his revelations have enabled many an otherwise ignorant criminal to cover up his traces and make the real detective work the harder.

His detective's loss is of course the author's gain, for through the grievance he has managed to tell us that his is a real detective.

Another technique is to make a character at the scene of the baffling crime point out that if this were a story the Great Detective would have no difficulty in finding the vital clue that is eluding the police, to which another character, usually the baffled policeman, replies along the lines of Sir Clinton Driffield in Connington's *Murder in the Maze* (1927):

> 'What's wrong with your outlook on the business, Squire, is that you want to treat a real crime as if it were a bit clipped out of a detective novel. In a 'tec yarn, you get everything nicely sifted for you. The author puts down only those things that are relevant to the story. If he didn't select his materials, his book would be far too long and no one would have the patience to plough through it. The result is that the important clues are thrown up as if they had a spotlight on them, if the reader happens to have any intelligence . . . In real life . . . there isn't any of this kind of simplification. You get a mass of stuff thrown at your head in the way of evidence; and in the end nine-tenths of it usually turns out to be irrelevant. You've got to sift the grain from the chaff yourself, with no author to do the rough work for you.'

The implication of speeches like this is clear enough and is directed always at establishing the credibility of the story in which they figure; there is to be no concealment of clues here, they say, no detective fireworks, but only detective work as it really happens. In Carolyn Well's *The Onyx Lobby* (1920) we find the American version of Driffield's dissertation, expounded at the scene of the crime:

> 'That finding of tiny clues, such as shreds of clothing, part of a broken cuff-link, a dropped handkerchief, all those things are just story book stuff—they cut no ice in real cases.'
>
> 'I'll bet Sherlock Holmes could find a lot of data just by going over the floor with a lens.'
>
> 'He could in a story book,—and do you know why? Because the clews [*sic*] and things, in a story, are all put there for him by the property man. Like a salted mine. But in real life, there's nothing doing of that sort. Take a good squint at the floor, though, before you remove those stains. You don't see anything, do you?'
>
> . . . There was nothing indicative to be seen.

And when in *Murder in the Maze* the crime occurs, Wendover and Driffield find a clue but their conversation follows the same pattern as in *The Onyx Lobby*:

'Hullo! Look, Clinton! There's a bit of black thread lying on the ground.'

They stooped over it and examined the fibre.

'Ordinary sewing-silk off a reel, obviously,' was all that Sir Clinton vouchsafed . . . 'We may as well collect the specimen, though really there's nothing distinctive about it. One bit of thread's very much like another.'

'Sherlock Holmes might have made more out of it than that,' said Wendover.

'Doubtless. But as he isn't here, what can we do? Just bumble along to the best of our poor abilities . . .'

The burden of these extracts is identical, but—and this is where things begin to ring false—the reader knows very well that there are going to be fireworks. And sure enough along comes Pennington Wise, Great Detective, to the onyx lobby to find just that clue that everyone else has missed; and the thread in the maze is really a conclusive indicator to Driffield, who two pages later, that is just over half way through the book, is able to state in the best tradition that he knows the murderer, but, need I add, cannot prove it yet.

All of this may be necessary to make a detective story in the classic manner. It is, however, in the duplicity of the open derision of the Holmesian approach while actually using it that self-consciousness and overtones of insincerity can be seen. An interesting sidelight on Gaboriau is that on the few occasions when writers refer to him instead of Holmes, their comments, Doyle's apart, are ungrudgingly favourable.[3] Holmes, or rather the Holmes-complex, ruled the roost, however, so much so that the reader, inundated with references, soon fails to notice them, the use to which they are being put and their effects. It is only when an author tries a variation that the reader may realise the absurdity of what is happening, with the consequent loss of credibility:

'And,' [the inspector] barked at Merlini, 'you'd better snap out of it because all the amateur dicks in town are gunning for your job. When those papers hit the street, all hell broke loose at headquarters. Philo Vance has been crowding his friend the D.A. He wants to kick the case around. Says it's right up his blooming alley, don't you know. Ellery Queen's campaigning to get his old man assigned to it so he can get a look-see, and Malloy says that a while ago he saw Archie Goodwin circling the island in a speedboat . . . And if you don't stop being cryptic, I'll ——'

Merlini shook his head. 'I doubt it, Inspector. Your threat is toothless. You know very well that a clam is twice as informative as any of those gentlemen up until chapter twenty.'

Clayton Rawson, *The Footprints on the Ceiling* (1939)

Anything to defer the dénouement. To return to Holmes, yet another device was to make detectives perform openly in his manner. Here are Wendover and Driffield in *The Boat House Riddle* (1931):

'Perhaps you'll describe your supposed murderer,' [Wendover] suggested ironically . . . 'We might recognise him.'

"I don't much care for following in the footsteps of Sherlock,' Sir Clinton said mildly. 'But if you insist on it, I'll do my best. The murderer belongs, probably, to the middle-class or higher up the social scale. He's a person of fair physique at any rate. I should guess that he's got some knowledge of boxing. His boots and socks were thoroughly soaked last night. And I should think he has his wits about him on most occasions . . .'

That is innocuous enough, but look what Agatha Christie makes of the same approach in *Cards on the Table* (1936):

'If you had mentioned the object I had in mind [says Poirot] it would have been extremely surprising to me. As I thought, you could not mention it.'

'Why?'

Poirot twinkled.

'Perhaps—because it was not there to mention.'

Roberts stared.

'That seems to remind me of something.'

'It reminds you of Sherlock Holmes, does it not? The curious incident of the dog in the night. The dog did not howl in the night. That is the curious thing! Ah, well, I am not above stealing the trick of others.'

'Do you know, M. Poirot, I am completely at sea as to what you are driving at.'

'That is excellent, that. In confidence, that is how I get my little effects.'

The irresistible temptation to be oracular; quite open, very amusing, but utterly self-conscious on the part of the author and confusing to the willing reader trying hard to suspend his disbelief, especially as the habit of self-reference was refined as certain usages themselves become hackneyed and extended beyond Holmes to detective stories as a whole. In *The Eight of Swords*, for example, John Dickson Carr has a character, Morgan, who writes detective stories of the blatantly sensational type, involving usually the murder of at least one elevated personage by the most *outré* of means. Morgan, however, is obliged to admit that he is also another author, one William Block Tournedos, whose stories are 'written for the critics' benefit. You see [he explains], the critics, as differentiated from the reading public, are required to like any story that is probable. I discovered a long time ago the way to write a probable and real story. You must have (1) no action, (2) no atmosphere whatever—that's very important—(3) as few interesting characters as possible, (4) absolutely no digressions, and (5) above all things, no deduction'. On the face of it this is an entertaining digression—I use the word for obvious reasons —on the category of story for which Carr hopes *The Eight of Swords* will not qualify. What, then, is the reader to make of the last words of the book in which the characters sum it all up?

J.R. scowled. 'All the same,' he said, 'I'm glad the only detective plot in which I ever took part was not full of improbabilities and wild situations, like—well, like Morgan's *Murder on the Woolsack* or *Aconite at the Admiralty*. There are no fiendish under-clerks shooting poison darts through keyholes at the First Sea-Lord, or luxurious secret dens of the Master Criminal at Limehouse. What I mean by probability . . .'

'And you think,' Morgan inquired, 'that *this* is a probable story?'

'Isn't it?' asked Hugh. 'It's exactly like one of those stories by William Block Tournedos. As Mr. Burke says . . .'

Morgan sank back.

'Oh, well!' he said. 'Never mind. Let's have a drink.'

The slightly bewildered reader begins to need one. He is not helped in *The White Crow* (1928) where Philip MacDonald has his detective, Anthony Gethryn, investigate one Lennett, who turns out to be E. Tennel, author of numerous 'bloods', the hero of which is Carlton Howe, 'Prince of Investigators'. When, in the course of the story, MacDonald wants Gethryn to do Great Detectival things, he covers what can only be his embarrassment by making Gethryn play the part of Howe: 'Everything explained in a few words. The case fell to pieces under the masterly analysis, conveyed in shrewd, terse phrases of that Prince of investigators, Carlton Howe. Apply his methods, my dear Pike . . .' Which methods of course result in an unsatisfactory explanation of the murder, for Howe is storybook stuff and this is the real thing. Or is it? Gethryn and friend, Deacon, are attacked and wounded. As they lick their wounds, Deacon glances through a Carlton Howe adventure:

'Listen to this: "Immovable as a statue hewn from marble, Carlton Howe stood erect against the wall. Through the all-enveloping and malignant darkness he could hear the soft, sibilant hissing breaths of the Spaniard Pedro who crouched, deadly knife in hand, waiting for his arch-enemy the detective!" What about that, eh? . . . And they call this stuff pernicious nonsense. After tonight, I know it's Realism. With two big R's. J. Joyce is a fantasist beside our Tennel.'

And after another Howe-ish episode Gethryn sings the same song:

'Lucas,' he said, 'I once told Boyd [the official policeman in *The Rasp*] that the reading of detective stories would do him good. He sniffed. I then told him that detective stories were far more like life than life was like detective stories . . . Then I was thinking of Gaboriau and Poe and Bailey. But now'—he paused and opened the door—'now, by the beard of Père Tabaret, I'd tell him to read up Sexton Blake and Nat Pinkerton. To say nothing of Carlton Howe . . .'

These passages illustrate better than any argument the positive disadvantages of the attempt to sever detective fiction from the sensational. Sensational elements, everyone realised, were necessary to make a story go, but at the same time were considered so *infra dig* and *passé* that it was felt they had to be

specifically excused and justified, but this succeeded only in
drawing attention to the sensational episode and hence to the
author's self-consciousness at mentioning it:

> [Wimsey] put his arm round her, and felt her shrink.
> 'What's the matter?' he demanded. 'What's up, old girl? Look
> here, Mary, we've never seen enough of each other, but I am
> your brother. Are you in trouble? Can't I ——'
> 'Trouble?' she said. 'Why, you silly old Peter, of course I'm
> in trouble. Don't you know they've killed my man and put my
> brother in prison? Isn't that enough to be in trouble about?'
> She laughed, and Peter suddenly thought, 'She's talking like
> somebody in a blood-and-thunder novel' . . . 'You'd better toddle
> back to bed,' said Lord Peter. 'You're getting all cold. Why do
> girls wear such mimsy little pyjimjams in this damn cold climate?
> There, don't you worry. I'll drop in on you later and we'll have
> a jolly old pow-pow, what?'
> 'Not today—not today, Peter. I'm going mad, I think.'
> ('Sensation fiction again,' thought Peter.)
> Dorothy L. Sayers, *Clouds of Witness* (1926)

One could be shrewish and ask what Lord Peter is talking like,
but to confine the matter to Lady Mary's emotional outbursts,
since people do sometimes talk as she is doing, why not just
let her get on with it and leave the reader to judge credibility?
As it is, Dorothy Sayers is here virtually telling the reader to
discount Lady Mary as a credible character.

The same criticism applies beyond the obviously sensational
speech and action to the whole paraphernalia of detection.
Self-consciousness eventually made it *de rigueur* for an author
to produce a clue, a magnifying glass, a secret passage, a
Chinaman, a deduction, above all a detective, only if accomp-
anied by an emphatic flourish tantamount to an apology—
with consequences to credibility similar to poor Lady
Mary's:

> 'Hitherto,' said Lord Peter [in *Clouds of Witness*] . . . 'I have always
> maintained that those obliging criminals who strew their tracks
> with little articles of personal adornment—here he is, on a
> squashed fungus—were an invention of detective fiction for the
> benefit of the author . . .'

Or take B. L. Farjeon's description of the discovery of a secret drawer written in 1884 and compare it with Philip MacDonald's of 1924:

> It was a round table of Spanish mahogany, and was a contrast to the other furniture in the room, being old-fashioned and of ancient make. As he raised it, one of the lower surfaces on which he placed his hand shifted slightly, and the thought flashed through his mind that there might be a drawer beneath. He stooped and looked upward, and saw that his impression was a correct one. A drawer was there, evidently intended as a secret drawer; it was locked. With trembling hands he tried the key.
>
> B. L. Farjeon, *Great Porter Square* (1884)

> A desk more than a hundred years old! . . . 'A hundred to one on Secret Drawer!' thought Anthony, and probed among the pigeon holes. He met with no success and felt cheated. His theory of the essential reality of story-books had played him false, it seemed.
>
> Loath to let it go, he tried again; this time pulling out from their sheaves the six small, shallow drawers which balanced the pigeon-holes on the other side of the alcove containing the inkwell. The top drawer, he noticed with joy, was shorter by over an inch than its five companions. He felt in its recess with long, sensitive fingers. He felt a thin rib of wood. He pressed, and nothing happened. He pulled, and it came easily away. The Great Story-book Theory was vindicated.
>
> Philip MacDonald, *The Rasp* (1924)

MacDonald's version is undoubtedly the more amusing; it may even be the better written. But it is not the more convincing. The tricks of the trade aimed at achieving credibility have boomeranged and achieved the opposite effect. They pull the reader up short:

> 'I've always had a secret hankering to be a detective!'
> 'The real thing—Scotland Yard? Or Sherlock Holmes?'
> 'Oh, Sherlock Holmes, by all means.'
>
> Agatha Christie, *The Mysterious Affair at Styles* (1920)

'Where exactly am I?' the now thoroughly bewildered reader begins to ask. 'I started off reading a story, prepared to accept as real, at least for the moment, a world of mysterious murder and a brilliant detective, a world recognisable as the one I live in except for that detective, and even for him I was willing to do my best. But the author keeps reminding me that I am in a fictional world. Unreality is being thrust down my throat. I am being denied so much as the opportunity to suspend my disbelief.'

The reader has been brought to this pass by those twin paradoxes of infallible conclusions from circumstantial evidence and impossible amateurs doing the work of the police. Stemming partly from the inherently argumentative and supposititious nature of what they were writing—remember Berkeley's advertisement of how authors select evidence—but mostly from the incongruity of a character moving parallel to, but outside, the regular police, authors, noticeably better authors, became so aware of their God-like position and the unreality of what they were writing that they not only ceased to believe in it themselves—that is neither new hat not necessarily fatal—but went out of their way to advise the reader of their disbelief. And that is fatal. The reader may be willing, in Maurice Richardson's phrase, to 'garrotte his disbelief', but even the privilege of self-inflicted injury is being denied him.

W. H. Wright, in his article on 'The Detective Novel' in *Scribner's Magazine* (1926) wrote that 'the objective of a detective novel . . . would be lost unless a sense of verisimilitude were constantly maintained—a feeling of triviality would attach to its problem, and the reader would experience a sense of wasted effort', and detective fiction has often been accused of cheapness and unprofitability on several counts—contrived settings, technical jargon, technical inaccuracies, disappointing endings, snobbery, farcicality, humdrumishness. Yet good writers could and did cope with these problems successfully, and the best writers could afford to ignore them. The trouble came when the writers themselves could not accept the monstrous lie on which all else was based—the lie of the Great Detective. The fruits of this failure have been seen, and here, for me, is the one major inescapable source of that feeling of triviality and wasted effort of which Wright wrote. And here in self-parody is the literary cause at least of the death of the Great Detective, and this is why parodies of detective stories are rarely successful: they are indistinguishable from the—dare I say it?—real thing.

The detective of fiction was thus allowed to slip from the world of Lecoq into a fairy tale realm. 'Enter Fairy Godmother' is Anthony Gethryn's explicit view of his role, but the idea of the detective as dispenser of justice and guardian of the weak is inherent in many commentaries after Holmes. G. K. Chesterton, for example, writing 'A Defence of Detective Stories' at the turn of the century, argues that 'by dealing with the unsleeping sentinels who guard the outposts of society, [the detective story] tends to remind us that we live in an armed camp, making war with a chaotic world'. This view of the detective story as symbolising the struggle between good and evil and sublimating middle-class neuroses by bringing order to a chaotic world—what might be called (if it were not so long) the 'Holmes-is-in-Baker-Street-and-all's-well-with-the-world' theory—has been repeated, elaborated and refined over the years, reaching its best, and most mystical, exposition in W. H. Auden's essay 'The Guilty Vicarage':

> The magic formula is an innocence which is discovered to contain guilt; then a suspicion of being the guilty one: and finally a real innocence from which the guilty other has been expelled, a cure effected, not by me or by my neighbours, but by the miraculous intervention of a genius from outside who removes guilt by giving knowledge of guilt.[4]

Another version is to be found in Eric S. Rabkin's *The Fantastic in Literature* (1976). It is particularly relevant as it combines a discussion of the present issue of what I call self-consciousness but Rabkin calls self-reflection. He quotes an example of this from Agatha Christie's *The A.B.C. Murders* (1936):

> 'Well?' I demanded eagerly . . .
> 'The crime,' said Poirot, 'was committed by a man of medium height with red hair and a cast in the left eye. He limps slightly on the left foot and has a mole just below the shoulder-blade.'

'Poirot!' I cried.

For a moment I was completely taken in. Then the twinkle in my friend's eye undeceived me . . .

'*Mon ami*, what will you? You fix upon me a look of dog-like devotion and demand of me a pronouncement à la Sherlock Holmes! Now for the truth—*I do not know what the murderer looks like, nor where he lives, nor how to set hands upon him.*'

'If only he had left some clue,' I murmured.

'Yes, the clue—it is always the clue that attracts you. Alas that he did not smoke the cigarette and leave the ash, and then step in it with a shoe that has nails of a curious pattern. No—he is not so obliging.'

Rabkin then says:

> This little speech demonstrates Christie's great skill at manipulating reader affect within the confining conventions of her genre. By making light of Holmes, Christie subliminally tells us that hers is no simple fairy tale word. However, by using this speech to further build Poirot's good sense in comparison to those around him, Christie lets us know at a deeper level that, however complex it may be, this is still a fairy tale world after all with Poirot the presiding genius.

Very deep, indeed. What has always worried me slightly about this and similar approaches to detective fiction is that anyone should choose to write or read a detective story in order to achieve such complex ends as the exorcism of guilt complexes, the allegorical continuation of the quest for the Holy Grail or even this simpler one of Rabkin's—the maintenance of order in a fairy-tale world. I have this recurring suspicion that they are written for our amusement and that that is why we read them. This does not mean that they cannot be or should not be serious, but the plots are complicated enough without reading subconscious knots into them. Stripped of their psychology, however, Rabkin's words make exactly my point, rather more succinctly. His statement may be generalised thus: by using Holmes and references to detective stories at large, authors tell us that theirs is no unreal, fairy-tale world, but at the same time manage to convey the opposite. Rabkin sees this achievement as a success, attributing it, in Agatha Christie's case, to her skill in affirming and conveying Poirot's good sense. I see it, on the other hand, as a failure, a failure to convey at least the semblance of a world in which a crime could conceivably take place. Is there crime in fairyland? In Agatha Christie's case of course, this was a deliberate failure, but nonetheless a failure. She has given up the unequal struggle to achieve that elusive but vital combination of the unreal detective in a real situation and, tongue in cheek, she has settled for poking fun at the genre, the reader and, to be sure, herself. But when in *Dumb Witness* (1937) she has Hastings say to Poirot, 'Oh, you're *serious* enough. But this business seems to be of the academic kind. You're tackling it for your own mental satisfaction', she is being honest to the point of dishonesty. Rabkin is complimentary in calling this self-reflection, for unfortunately this verdict on Christie applies to many of her contemporaries. They do not have the excuse of writing deliberate fantasy and must therefore be branded guilty of amusing but fatal cynicism.

All this must give us pause and make us wonder what we have come to since Lecoq and Tabaret came down from Paris to La Jonchère. The foregoing assessment of detective fiction of the Golden Age and the reluctantly unfavourable verdict on it are based on what happened to the detective story *after* Gaboriau. Which is only realistic. The detective story did come, as Rabkin says, to be predicated on an ordered world. Its conventions did force it into fantasy and, as with sensation fiction, its sheer quantity smothered any intimations of quality. The fantasy and the self-consciousness must now be accepted and in accepting it there is still much to be enjoyed. But to accept what we have come to since Gaboriau does not prevent us from regretting just a little what might have been.

In fairness, however, it must be remembered that Gaboriau himself seems to have recognised the dangers of the amateur detective with his deductions out of a hat, for after giving Tabaret one long run in *L'Affaire Lerouge*, he relegated him to an advisory capacity (and that only in one other book, *Monsieur Lecoq*) and developed Lecoq along much more practical and realistic lines. I have suggested that Gaboriau gave sensation fiction the opportunity for improvement which Doyle took up at one level, but it is tempting to agree with Bennett and the writer in *The Times Literary Supplement* who go beyond this to see Gaboriau's example as an opportunity for sensation fiction to move from the second-rate level to which it had been condemned, and to see Gaboriau himself as coming at least very close to combining secrets, mystery, detection and detectives with mainstream literature. In his combination of practicality with deduction, Lecoq is seen, not as the inferior contrast to the pipe-puffing, dressing-gowned Great Detective who followed him, but as the ideal presentation of the detective, which, if it could be followed, would allow great books to be written about detection. Quite how one combines the realities of detection with the fantasy of the Great Detective and how one rides the narrow track between the dullness of Inspector French and the non-detection of psychological crime stories is to ask what songs the Sirens sang; it is also to ask if there are any classic 'classic' detective stories. The answers may not be beyond all conjecture, but they would require another book and a better hand. The fact also remains that whatever the merits of individual stories, the Golden Age did not meet the challenge, for instead of broadening its horizons in the manner of Gaboriau, it indulged, as we have seen, in an orgy of inbreeding.

In fairness again, it is possible that when Bennett and others made their protests and suggested their remedies, they were already nearly half a century too late, forlorn echoes of that forlorn cry by R. L. Stevenson and Lloyd Osbourne in that postscript to *The Wrecker* (1892):

> We had long been at once attracted and repelled by that very modern form of the police novel or mystery story, which consists in beginning your yarn anywhere but at the beginning, and finishing it anywhere but at the end; attracted by its peculiar interest when done; repelled by that appearance of insincerity and shallowness of tone, which seems its inevitable drawback. For the mind of the reader, always bent to pick up clews, receives no impression of reality or life, rather of an airless, elaborate mechanism; and the book remains enthralling but insignificant, like a game of chess, not a work of human art.

It seems that if anything was to be made of Gaboriau's example, it had to be done hard on his heels and based on Lecoq rather than on Tabaret, for here, very close to the event, are Stevenson and Osbourne concerned about reality in what they see as a new form, but critical of it in terms reminiscent of the objections to earlier sensation fiction and anticipatory of the strictures about detective fiction that were to come; and while few of their criticisms apply to Gaboriau, indeed their intentions could be said to coincide with Gaboriau's achievements, their reference to 'insincerity and shallowness of tone' could be applied to Gaboriau's mild device to render Tabaret credible, and their words are altogether too accurate and damning a description of what was to come by way of elaborations on that device.

I ought now to end pessimistically with Evelyn Waugh's account of the fate of Ronald Knox's last venture into detective fiction, as a sad epitaph on the classic detective story. Knox had become friendly with Lady Acton as a potential convert to Roman Catholicism and in 1937 they found themselves together on a Hellenic cruise:

> Lady Acton was the first person (so far as can be ascertained) to whom he confided his yearning for privacy and his ambition to write something of permanent value. She was certainly the first person to give him full-hearted and practical encouragement. Cardinal Bourne had disapproved of Ronald's detective stories and he had gone on writing them. She threw *Double Cross Purposes* overboard (after her own lipstick, of which Ronald had expressed dislike), and he never wrote another.[5]

But I will in fact end selfishly with Rose's words in Mrs. Humphry Ward's *Richard Meynell* (1911). Rose's sister, Catherine, is suffering, so Rose believes, from too many books on 'the lives of bishops and deans and that kind of thing', and Rose advises Catherine's daughter: 'Your mother would be well in a week if we could only stop it and put her on a course of Gaboriau.'

NOTES TO CHAPTER 15

1 Doyle's involvement in the Edalji and Slater cases was *after* the arrest, trial and conviction of these gentlemen; and in the Pearl Robbery case of 1913, the police were reluctantly obliged to use lay assistance.

2 Arthur Morrison, 'The Lenton Croft Robberies' in *Martin Hewitt, Investigator* (1894).

3 'Have you ever read *Gaboriau*? Ah, you have missed a treat, indeed.' (Mary Roberts Rinehart, *The Man in Lower Ten*, 1909); 'Tell me, have you ever read a book called 'The Detective's Dilemma'? [a variant title for the first part of *Monsieur Lecoq*] . . . there is a great deal to be learned from detective fiction of the right kind.' (Francis D. Grierson, *The Zoo Murder*, 1926). '. . . I feel as futile as if I were Sherlock Holmes trying to solve a case of Lecoq's.' (Philip MacDonald, *The Rasp*). Apart from those given earlier these three quotations are the meagre result of vast research!—indicative, granted, of the relative obscurity of Gaboriau, but surely also of genuine respect for his achievements.

4 W. H. Auden, 'The Guilty Vicarage,' in *The Dyer's Hand* (1963), Given the popularity of this theory, it is mildly surprising to find Christopher Booker enunciating it in the *Daily Telegraph* in December 1977 and claiming that he has thereby 'solved the last great detective mystery', though I am obliged to agree with his conclusion: '. . . we comfort ourselves with endless stories in which we know from the start that we can play the God-like role and the villain will always be someone else. It is frustrating because, deep down, we know that this is not what proper, grown-up, life-giving literature is about.'

5 Evelyn Waugh, *Ronald Knox* (1959).

APPENDIX 1

(see page 17)

Some Notes, Corrections and Comments on *Victorian Detective Fiction*, A Catalogue of the Collection made by Dorothy Glover and Graham Greene, Bibliographically Arranged by Eric Osborne and Introduced by John Carter. Bodley Head, 1966.

Ignoring the semantic question of what constitutes a detective story, and accepting the system in *Victorian Detective Fiction* of naming the detective or detectives in each book as a useful bibliographical and historical exercise, the catalogue's accuracy and consistency in this respect are less than impressive. Ostensibly in the cause of scholarship, then, but probably from subconscious jealousy of such a splendid collection, I hazard below a list of corrections and additions to detectives' names.

I fear this list is not exhaustive, as *Victorian Detective Fiction* contains around four hundred different titles, of which I have read only about one-fifth, and it would be too optimistic to hope that the errors are confined to these eighty or so books.

For the present purpose, debatable detectives such as James Short of *Mr. Meesom's Will* are accepted, and this list refers solely to what I believe are errors of fact or misleading omissions. Though perhaps merely the result of bad proof-reading, mis-spellings are included on the grounds that even they cannot be excused in a prestigious publication such as this.

No.	VDF No.	VDF Author, Title and Detective(s)
1	23	Bangs, John Kendrick *The Dreamers: A Club* Famous fictional detectives parodied
2	373 (but see between 41 & 42)	Boothby, Guy *A Prince of Swindlers* Kimo the famous detective alias Simon Carne, Prince of Swindlers.
3	58	(Braddon, M. E.) *The Trail of the Serpent* Sergeant Jo Peters
4	59	(Braddon, M. E.) *Wyllard's Weird* Edward Heathcote
5	109	Dickens, Charles *The Mystery of Edwin Drood* Mr. Grerigious, lawyer
6	118	Donovan, Dick *The Mystery of Jamaica Terrace* Howel Walter, private detective
7	152	Du Boisgobey, Fortuné *The Matapan Affair* Albert Doutrelaise, young astronomer
8	172	Farjeon, B. L. *Great Porter Square: A Mystery* Crime reporter from 'The Evening Moon'

Only one fictional detective is parodied—Holmes, in the chapter entitled 'The Adventure of Pinkham's Diamond Stud'.

Klimo.

Peters is not a Sergeant and is not referred to as Jo, but as Joseph. However, this is the one definite instance with these detectives where an author is known to have changed at least his name. This book was written in 1854 and published as *Three Times Dead: or, The Secret of the Heath*. In an interesting article on Miss Braddon in *The Times Literary Supplement* of August 29th 1942, Montague Summers tells us that this book re-appeared in 1861, and often thereafter, as *The Trail of the Serpent*, with several changes to names of places and characters, including that of the detective from 'Joe Waters' to 'Joe Peters'. I have not seen the 1861 edition. When Summers wrote it was the only known copy, but it is unlikely that there were further changes in the reprints, though this might account for 'Jo', 'Joe', and 'Joseph'. The edition consulted is the 'Author's Edition' of the same vintage as the VDF copy and likewise published by Simpkin, Marshall. See also Michael Sadleir, *Things Past* (1944), pp. 81–83.

Heathcote certainly, but also Distin, Trottier and Drubarde must be mentioned, if *VDF* is to distinguish *Nicholas Nickleby* by naming Newman Noggs, Frank Cheeryble and a police officer as detectives therein.

Grewgious, and even if correctly spelled, the designation of the lawyer as the detective could be queried as begging some of the major questions of Dickens' unfinished story—who is the detective, who is Datchery, even, is there a detective?

Walter is not a private detective, but 'one of the quiet but active representatives of Scotland Yard'.

Doutrelaise is a young man-about-town, not an astronomer, despite a tendency to gaze at the light in his lover's window.

One of the *Evening Moon's* articles states: 'Our reporter . . . was not acting the part of detective . . . it is not in his nature to give offence.' This is accurate. The reporter plays a passive role, and the detective of this book is an un-named one employed by the hero and whose use the hero finds 'revolting'!

No.	VDF No.	VDF Author, Title and Detective(s)
9	175	Farjeon, B. L. *The Mystery of M. Felix* Robert Agnold, crime reporter on 'The Evening Moon'
10	181	Ford, Paul Leicester *The Great K. & A. Train Robbery* Narrator
11	190	Gaboriau, Emile *The Gilded Clique* Lecoq
12	192	Gaboriau, Emile *In Peril of his Life* Gondar, 'one of those agents whom the authorities employ for specially delicate tasks'
13	196	Gaboriau, Emile *The Little Old Man of Batignolles and other stories* J. B. Casimir Godeuil
14	208	Green, Anna Katherine *The Circular Study* Ebenezer Gryce
15	216	Green, Anna Katherine *7 To 12. A Detective Story* Byrd, New York Police
16	264	Hume, Fergus *The Chinese Jar* Octavius Fanks, private detective
17	279	Hume, Fergus *The Mystery of a Hansom Cab* Samuel Gorby
18	280	Hume, Fergus *The Mystery of Landy Court* Inspector Dove, Scotland Yard
19	296	Le Fanu, Joseph Sheridan *Checkmate* David Arden, art collector

This is correct, but on the *Nicholas Nickleby* principle, Bob Tucker, whose 'fad lay in the detective line', is worth a mention.

The narrator has a name, Richard Gordon, and since narrators of other books are named (e.g. Rissler, the narrator of Coulsan Kernahan's *Captain Shannon* (292), consistency is called for.
I wish it were Lecoq. The nearest one can come to detectives in this book are Papa Ravinet and an un-named magistrate.

The *VDF* edition is the first English edition, published by Vizetelly in 1881. An American edition by Belford, Clarke of about the same time gives 'Goudar'.

Godeuil, a medical student, narrates 'The Little Old Man', but his detective work is under the tutelage of Méchinet, whose example causes him to take up detective work in place of his medical studies.

Gryce's *bête noire*, Amelia Butterworth, is worth a mention as the authoress put them together regularly.

The *VDF* edition, the first English edition, 1887, should also contain two other stories, *One Hour More* and *X.Y.Z.* The first is not a detective story, but the latter is—with an un-named detective as hero.
Fanks is a Scotland Yard man, interesting as a precursor of the Appleby type: 'Fanks was a man of good family, and followed the profession of detective, as one for which he was particularly adapted by nature . . . In Scotland Yard he was known solely as Octavius Fanks; but in clubland he assumed the role of Octavius Rixton, idler and man-about-town.' His rival, Crate, is also worth naming.
Gorby's rival, Kilsip, is as prominent as Gorby and actually identifies the murderer.

Dove is but the 'local Dogberry' and plays a Seegrave role; the main detective is Drage, the 'Vidocq of London'.

David Arden is not an art collector. He has a splendidly-furnished house, but he himself 'did not care for finery; no man's tastes could be simpler or more camp-like'.

No.	VDF No.	VDF Author, Title and Detective(s)
20	324	M'Govan, James *Hunted Down: or Recollections of a City Detective* Hugh M'Indoe, thief turned detective
21	338	Martel, Charles [pseud. Thomas Delf] *The Detective's Note-Book* Bolter, ex-Bow Street Runner
22	378	Phillpotts, Eden *A Tiger's Cub* Tarrant Tinkler
23	443	[Warden Florence] [pseud. Florence Alice Price] *The House on the Marsh* Maynard, Scotland Yard
24	467	Wood, H. F. *The Englishman of the Rue Cain* Toppin, Scotland Yard representative at the Sûreté

CORRECTION/COMMENT

This is misleading. The detective, as always in a McGovan book, is McGovan himself. While McIndoe coincidentally assists the police by turning in criminals in the course of his search for the man who caused the death of his wife and child, the book is essentially episodic and several of the stories do not involve McIndoe at all.

Bolter is not an ex-Bow Street Runner, but a nightwatchman who transfers to the New Police. Some of the stories in this book contain other detectives e.g. Hallett and Tinman; others have no detective.

Not so; Tinkler is simply a lay character (see p. 16).

Maynard figures briefly as the 'pretty fellow' who allows himself to be drugged by the villain. The little detective work in this book is done by the hero, Laurence Reade.

M. Renaud of the Sûrete looms at least as large as Toppin.

APPENDIX 2

(see page 74)

In each pair, the first quotation is the older:

1 (a) 'The Decay of Murder', *Cornhill Magazine*, December 1869

  (b) T. J. Hardy, *Books on the Shelf* (1934)

2 (a) H. F. Chorley, review of *Armadale*, *Athenaeum*, 2 June 1866

  (b) W. Somerset Maugham, 'The Decline and Fall of the Detective Story', in *The Vagrant Mood* (1952)

3 (a) Review of Miss Braddon's *The Trail of the Serpent*, *Athenaeum*, 23 March 1861

  (b) Robert J. Casey, 'Oh, England! Full of Sin', *Scribner's Magazine*, April 1937, quoted from *The Art of the Mystery Story*, ed. Haycraft

4 (a) Review of *The Woman in White*, *Saturday Review*, 25 August 1860

  (b) Edmund Wilson, 'Why Do People Read Detective Stories?', *New Yorker*, 14 October 1944

5 (a) 'Miss Braddon', *Eclectic Review*, January 1868

  (b) Howard Spring, *Evening Standard* 1939, quoted from *London Mercury*, February 1939

6 (a) 'Miss Braddon', as 5 (a)

  (b) Q. D. Leavis, 'The Case of Miss Dorothy Sayers' (a review of *Gaudy Night* and *Busman's Honeymoon*). *Scrutiny*, December 1937

7 (a) Review of T. W. Speight's *In the Dead of Night* (1874) (published anonymously), *Saturday Review*, 26 December 1874

  (b) Clayton Rawson, *Death from a Top Hat* (1938), edition quoted: Stacey, 1971

SELECT BIBLIOGRAPHY

This list consists of the most helpful and relevant books, articles and reviews on the various topics discussed. Other sources are given in the footnotes and text.

The Bibliography is arranged alphabetically by authors' and editors' names. Where an item is anonymous, it has been listed alphabetically by the first word of the title in the case of articles and the first word of the title of the book reviewed in the case of reviews.

Names in square brackets denote authors originally published anonymously, now identified.

All full-length books published in London unless otherwise stated.

Unpublished Material

Curry, Nancy Ellen. *The Life and Works of Emile Gaboriau*, unpublished Ph.D. thesis, University of Kentucky, 1970

Edinburgh Town Council Records, Vol. 280, Minutes of the Watching Committee, 29 May 1860

Public Record Office, 'Memorandum relative to detective power of Police', Commissioners to Sir James Graham, 14 June 1842, in Home Office 45/292

———. Phillipps to Commissioners, 16 June 1842, in Home Office 65/14

Published Sources

L'Affaire Lerouge. Review, *Saturday Review*, 15 December 1866

'Amateur Detectives'. *Saturday Review*, 22 February 1868

Armadale. Review, *Westminster Review*, October 1866

Auden, W. H. 'The Guilty Vicarage', in *The Dyer's Hand*, Faber & Faber 1963. First published *Harper's Magazine*, May 1948

Autobiography of an Emglish Detective. Review, *Saturday Review*, 19 December 1863

Aydelotte, William O. 'The Detective Story as a Historical Source' in *The Mystery Writer's Art*, ed. Nevins, q.v. First published *Yale Review*, Vol. XXXIX, 1949–50

Aylmer, Felix. *The Drood Case*, Hart-Davis, 1964

B-J, G. *Memorials of Edward Burne-Jones*, 2 vols. Macmillan, 1906

Barzun, Jacques. 'Detection and the Literary Art', *New Republic*, April 1961

———. 'Detection in Extremis' in *Crime in Good Company*, ed. Gilbert, q.v.

———. 'Not "Whodunit?" But "How?"', *Saturday Review* (American), 4 November 1944

——— and Taylor, W. H. *A Catalogue of Crime*, New York, Harper & Row, 1971 (2nd impression corrected)

Bennett, Arnold. 'I Take Up the Challenge of Detective Fiction Lovers' in *Arnold Bennett: The "Evening Standard" Years*, ed. Andrew Mylett, Chatto & Windus, 1974. First published *Evening Standard*, 17 January 1929

———. 'No Really First-Rate Detective Stories', *ibid.* First published *Evening Standard*, 27 December 1928

Bentley, E. C. *Those Days*, Constable, 1940

Bleiler, E. F. Introduction to *Monsieur Lecoq*, New York, Dover, 1975

Browne, Douglas G. *The Rise of Scotland Yard*, Harrap, 1956

Carr, John Dickson. *The Life of Sir Arthur Conan Doyle*, John Murray, 1949

Carter, John. 'Collecting Detective Fiction' in *The Art of the Mystery Story*, ed. Haycraft, q.v. First published in *New Paths in Book Collecting* (1934), ed. Carter

———. Introduction to *Victorian Detective Fiction*, q.v.

Chandler, Raymond. 'The Simple Art of Murder' in *The Art of the Mystery Story*, ed. Haycraft, q.v. First published *Atlantic Monthly*, December 1944

Chesterton, Cecil. 'Art and the Detective', *Temple Bar*, 10 October 1906

Chesterton, G. K. 'The Best Detective Story' in *Detection Medley*, ed. Rhode, q.v.

———. 'A Defence of Detective Stories' in *The Defendant*, Dent, 1901 (reprinted)

———. Introduction to W. S. Masterman's *The Wrong Letter*, Methuen, 1926

[Chorley, H. F.] Review of *Armadale*, *Athenaeum*, 2 June 1866

Cobb, Belton. *The First Detectives*, Faber & Faber, 1957

Cole, G. D. H. and M. Introduction to *The Moonstone*, Collins, 1953

Coleridge, Samuel Taylor. *Essays and Lectures on Shakespeare*, Dent, 1907 (reprinted)

Collins, Wilkie. Preface to 2nd edition of *The Dead Secret*, 1861 (first published 1857)

——. Preface to *No Name*, 1862

[——.] 'The Unknown Public', *Household Words*, 21 August 1858

Colum, Padraic. Introduction to Edgar Allan Poe's *Tales of Mystery and Imagination*, Dent, 1908 (reprinted)

'Contemporary Literature'. *Westminster Review*, October 1864 and November 1887

Crispin, Edmund. 'Is the Detective Story Dead?', see Symons

Critchley, T. A. *A History of Police in England and Wales, 1900–1966*, Constable, 1967

Curiosities of Crime in Edinburgh during the last Thirty Years. Review, *Athenaeum*, 23 February 1861

——. Review, *Saturday Review*, 2 February 1861

Depken, Friedrich. *Sherlock Holmes, Raffles und Ihre Vorbilder*, Heidelberg, Carl Winter's Universitätsbuchhandlung, 1914

'Detection Club Oath' in *The Art of the Mystery Story*, ed. Haycraft, q.v.

'The Detection of Crime'. *Saturday Review*, 22 September 1860

'Detective Fiction'. *Saturday Review*, 4 December 1886

'Detectiveness in Fiction'. *Nation*, 15 August 1912

'Detectives'. *Saturday Review*, 5 May 1883

'Detectives'. *Saturday Review*, 21 December 1878

'Detectives in Fiction and in Real Life'. *Saturday Review*, 11 June 1864

'The Detective's Rescue'. *Punch*, 20 October 1888

'The Detective System'. *Saturday Review*, 1 December 1877

Dilnot, George. *The Story of Scotland Yard*, Geoffrey Bles, 1926

Donaldson, Norman. Introduction to *Lady Audley's Secret*, New York, Dover, 1974

[Donnelly, Thomas]. 'Crime and its Detection', *Dublin University Magazine*, May 1861

Doyle, Sir Arthur Conan. *Memories and Adventures*, John Murray, 1924

East Lynne. Review, *Saturday Review*, 15 February 1862

'Edgar Allan Poe'. *Saturday Review*, 19 December 1874

'The Efficiency and Defects of the Police'. *Saturday Review*, 15 February 1868

Eliot, T. S. 'Books of the Quarter, *New Criterion*, January 1927
———. Review of *The Mystery of Orcival* (Gollancz, 1929) in 'Books of the Quarter', *Criterion*, July 1929
———. Introduction to *The Moonstone*, Oxford University Press, 1928
'Emile Gaboriau: The Detective Novelist's Dilemma'. *The Times Literary Supplement*, 2 November 1935
The Englishman of the Rue Cain. Review, *Athenaeum*, 23 February 1889
'The Enigma Novel'. *Spectator*, 28 December 1861
Les Esclaves de Paris. Review, *Saturday Review*, 6 June 1869
'Fine Knacks'. Review of *Victorian Detective Fiction* (q.v.) in *The Times Literary Supplement*, 8 December 1966
Freeman, R. A. 'The Art of the Detective Story' in *The Art of the Mystery Story*, ed. Haycraft, q.v. First published *Nineteenth Century and After*, May 1924
'The French Police System'. *Saturday Review*, 8 February 1862
Gilbert, Elliot L. 'The Detective as Metaphor in the Nineteenth Century' in *The Mystery Writer's Art*, ed. Nevins, q.v. First published *Journal of Popular Culture*, Winter 1967
Gilbert, Michael, ed. *Crime in Good Company*, Constable 1959
Gilbert, W. S. *A Sensational Novel in Three Volumes* (1871) in *Gilbert before Sullivan*, ed. Jane W. Stedman, Routledge and Kegan Paul, 1969
Graham, Kenneth. *English Criticism of the Novel, 1865–1900*, Oxford, Clarendon Press, 1965
Griest, Guinevere L. *Mudie's Circulating Library and the Victorian Novel*, Newton Abbot, David & Charles, 1970
Hagen, Ordean A. *Who Done It?*, New York, Bowker, 1969 (So incomplete and inaccurate is this work that the *Armchair Detective*, the American magazine devoted to detective fiction, published regular lists of corrections for a time; see also Jacques Barzun's review of Hagen's book in *American Scholar*, Winter 1969.)
Hardy, A. E. Gathorne. 'The Examination of Prisoners.—Emile Gaboriau', *National Review*, July 1884
Hare, Cyril. 'The Classic Form' in *Crime in Good Company*, ed. Gilbert, q.v.
Hatherill, George. *A Detective's Story*, Andre Deutsch, 1971
Hawthorne, Julian. 'Riddle Stories', Introduction to *American Stories* in *The Lock and Key Library*, 10 vols., New York, Review of Reviews, 1909
Haycraft, Howard, ed. *The Art of the Mystery Story*, New York, Grosset & Dunlap, 1946
———. *Murder for Pleasure*, Peter Davies, 1942 (first published 1941 in U.S.A.)

Henry Dunbar. Review, *Saturday Review*, 9 July 1864

'How to Make a Novel'. *Blackwood's Magazine*, May 1864

[James, Henry]. 'Miss Braddon', *Nation*, 9 November 1865

John Marchmont's Legacy. Review, *Athenaeum*, 12 December 1863

Keating, H. R. F. *Murder Must Appetize*, Lemon Tree Press, 1975

Knox, Ronald, ed. Introduction to *Best Detective Stories of the Year 1928*, Faber & Gwyer, 1929

———. 'Studies in the Literature of Sherlock Holmes', in *Essays in Satire*, Sheed & Ward, 1928 (originally given as a paper to the Gryphon Club, Trinity College, Oxford in 1911)

La Cour, Tage and Mogensen, Harald. *The Murder Book*, Allen & Unwin, 1971 (first published 1969 in Denmark)

Lady Audley's Secret. Review, *Athenaeum*, 25 October 1862

Lady Flavia. Review, *Athenaeum*, 22 July 1865

'Law and Police'. *Guardian*, 10 January 1855 and 26 July 1865

Le Fanu, J. S. 'A Preliminary Word' to *Uncle Silas*, 1864

Levine, Stuart. *Edgar Poe: Seer and Craftsman*, De Land (Florida), Everett, Edwards, 1972

'Literary Activity in England'. *Saturday Review*, 12 January 1867

'Literary Policemen'. *Saturday Review*, 15 August 1874

'Literature of the Month'. *Sixpenny Magazine*, September and December 1861

Man and Wife. Review, *Saturday Review*, 9 July 1870

[Mansel, H. L.] 'Sensation Novels', *Quarterly Review*, April 1863

Mason, A. E. W. 'Detective Novels', *Nation & Athenaeum*, 7 February 1925

———, Introduction to *Inspector Hanaud's Investigations* (omnibus volume containing *At the Villa Rose*, *The House of the Arrow* and *The Prisoner in the Opal*), Hodder & Stoughton, 1931

Matthews, Brander. 'Poe and the Detective Story', *Scribner's Magazine*, September 1907

Maugham, W. S. 'The Decline and Fall of the Detective Story', in *The Vagrant Mood*, Heinemann, 1952

Maurice, A. B. 'The Detective in Fiction', *Bookman* (American), May 1902

[McCarthy, Justin]. 'Novels with a Purpose', *Westminster Review*, July 1864

Meason, M. Laing. 'Detective Police', *Nineteenth Century*, May 1883

———. 'The French Detective Police', *Macmillan's Magazine*, February 1882

Messac, Regis. *Le "detective novel" et l'influence de la pensée scientifique*, Paris, Champion, 1929
(Undeservedly, this work has not yet been translated into English)

'The Metropolitan Police'. *Saturday Review*, 20 April 1867

Milne, A. A. Introduction to *Detection Medley*, ed. Rhode, q.v.

'Miss Braddon. The Illuminated Newgate Calendar'. *Eclectic Review*, January 1868

'Modern Novels'. *Saturday Review*, 18 May 1878

The Moonstone. Review, *Spectator*, 25 July 1868

——. Review, *The Times*, 3 October 1868

Moylan, Sir J. F. *Scotland Yard*, Putnam's, 1929

'Mr. Sala on Sensationalism'. *Saturday Review*, 15 February 1868

Murch, A. E. *The Development of the Detective Novel*, Peter Owen, revised edition 1968 (first published 1958)

'The Murders of the Day'. *Saturday Review*, 17 October 1857

Nevins, Francis M. (Jr.), ed. *The Mystery Writer's Art*, Bowling Green (Ohio), Bowling Green University Popular Press, 1970

'The New Police', *New Monthly*, November 1829

Nicolson, Marjorie. 'The Professor and the Detective' in *The Art of the Mystery Story*, ed. Haycraft, q.v. First published *Atlantic Monthly*, April 1929

[Oliphant, Margaret]. 'Novels', *Blackwood's Magazine*, August 1863

[——.] 'Novels', *Blackwood's Magazine*, September 1867

[——.] 'Sensation Novels', *Blackwood's Magazine*, May 1862

Ousby, Ian. *Bloodhounds of Heaven*, Cambridge (Mass.), Harvard University Press, 1976

Palmer, Jerry. *Thrillers*, Edward Arnold, 1978

Page, Norman, ed. *Wilkie Collins: The Critical Heritage*, Routledge & Kegan Paul, 1974

'The Passing of the Detective'. *Academy*, 30 December 1905

'The Perils of Sensation'. *Saturday Review*, 5 November 1864

Phillips, W. C. *Dickens, Reade, and Collins: Sensation Novelists*, New York, Columbia University Press, 1919

'The Police'. *Graphic*, 11 August 1877

'The Police and Mr. Speke'. *Saturday Review*, 8 February 1868

'Police Detectives'. *Leisure Hour*, 29 October 1857

Priestley, J. B. 'On Holiday with the Bodies', *Saturday Review*, 3 July 1926

Quayle, Eric. *The Collector's Book of Detective Fiction*, Studio Vista, 1972

Queen, Ellery, ed. Foreword to *Rogues' Gallery*, Faber & Faber 1947
——. *Queen's Quorum*, Gollancz, 1953

Rabkin, Eric S. *The Fantastic in Literature*, New Jersey, Princeton University Press, 1976

[Rae, W. Fraser]. 'Sensation Novelists: Miss Braddon', *North British Review*, September 1865

'Recent Popular Novels'. *Dublin University Magazine*, February 1861

Rhode, John, ed. *Detection Medley*, Hutchinson, 1939

Richardson, Maurice, ed. Introduction to *Novels of Mystery from the Victorian Age*, Pilot Press, 1945

Robinson, Kenneth. *Wilkie Collins*, Davis-Poynter, 1974 (first published 1951)

Routley, Erik. *The Puritan Pleasures of the Detective Story*, Gollancz, 1972

Sadleir, Sir Michael. *XIX Century Fiction*, 2 vols. Constable, 1951
——. *Things Past*, Constable, 1944

Sayers, Dorothy L., ed. Introduction to *Great Short Stories of Detection Mystery and Horror*, Gollancz, 1928
——. ed. Introduction to *Great Short Stories of Detection, Mystery and Horror, 2nd Series*, Gollancz 1931
(A 3rd Series appeared in 1934; all three were published in U.S.A. under title *Omnibus of Crime*)
——. Introduction to *The Moonstone*, Dent, 1944
——. ed. Introduction to *Tales of Detection*, Dent, 1936
——. 'The Present Status of the Mystery Story', *London Mercury*, November 1930

Seaborne, E. A., ed. Introduction to *The Detective in Fiction*, Bell, 1931

'Sensationalism'. *Saturday Review*, 16 May 1874

'Sense v. Sensation'. *Punch*, 20 July 1861

Scott-Moncrieff, George, ed. Introduction to *The Casebook of a Victorian Detective*, Edinburgh, Canongate, 1975

[Shand, A. Innes]. 'Contemporary Literature: IV. Novelists', *Blackwood's Magazine*, March 1879

[——.] 'Contemporary Literature: VI. French Novels', *Blackwood's Magazine*, June 1879

[——.] 'Crime in Fiction', *Blackwood's Magazine*, August 1890

Shrapnel, Norman. 'The Literature of Violence and Pursuit', *The Times Literary Supplement*, 23 June 1961

The Silver Cord. Review, *Saturday Review*, 21 September 1861

'The Sin of Light Reading'. *Saturday Review*, 2 September 1865

The Sliding Scale of Life: or, Thirty Years' Observations of Falling Men and Women in Edinburgh. Review, *Athenaeum*, 24 August 1861

———. Review, *Saturday Review*, 7 September 1861

Steeves, Harrison R. 'A Sober Word on the Detective Story' in *The Art of the Mystery Story*, ed. Haycraft, q.v. First published *Harper's Magazine*, April, 1941

[Stephen, Leslie]. 'The Decay of Murder', *Cornhill Magazine*, December 1869

Steinbrunner, Chris and Penzler, Otto. *Encyclopedia of Mystery and Detection*, Routledge & Kegan Paul, 1976

Stern, Philip Van Doren. 'The Case of the Corpse in the Blind Alley', *Virginia Quarterly Review*, Spring 1941

Stevenson, B. E. 'Supreme Moments in Detective Fiction', *Bookman* (American), March 1913

Stevenson, R. L. and Osbourne, Lloyd. Epilogue to *The Wrecker*, 1892

[Story, W. W.] 'In a Studio', *Blackwood's Magazine*, December 1875

Summers, Montague. 'Miss Braddon', *The Times Literary Supplement*, 29 August 1942

Sutherland, J. A. *Victorian Novelists and Publishers*, Athlone Press, 1976

Symons, Julian. *Bloody Murder*, Faber & Faber, 1972 (Title in U.S.A. *Mortal Consequences*)

———. Introduction to *The John Franklin Bardin Omnibus*, Penguin, 1976

———. and Crispin, Edmund. 'Is the Detective Story Dead?', *The Times Literary Supplement*, 23 June 1961

Taylor, W. H. *A Catalogue of Crime*, see Barzun

Thomson, Sir Basil. *Queer People*, Hodder & Stoughton, 1922

Thomson, H. D. *Masters of Mystery*, Collins, 1931

Tillotson, Kathleen. 'The Lighter Reading of the Eighteen Sixties', Introduction to *The Woman in White*, Boston, Houghton Mifflin, 1969

Trollope, Anthony. *Autobiography*, Oxford University Press, 1950 (first published 1883)

Uncle Silas. Review, *Saturday Review*, 4 February 1865

'Undetected Crime'. *Saturday Review*, 29 November 1856

'The Unromantic Detective'. *Outlook*, 3 December 1910

Van Dine, S. S.—pseudonym of W. H. Wright, q.v.

Victorian Detective Fiction. A Catalogue of the Collection made by Dorothy Glover and Graham Greene Bibliographically Arranged by Eric Osborne and Introduced by John Carter, Bodley Head, 1966. (Limited edition of 500).

Wagenknecht, Edward. *Edgar Allan Poe*, New York, Oxford University Press, 1963

Waugh, Evelyn. *Ronald Knox*, Chapman & Hall, 1959

Welcome, John, ed. Introduction to *Best Crime Stories 2*, Faber & Faber, 1966

Wells, Carolyn. *The Technique of the Mystery Story*, Norwood (Pa.), Norwood Editions, 1976 (first published Springfield (Mass.), Home Correspondence School, 1913; the Norwood edition is a reproduction of this first edition)

[Williams, D. E.] Review of *Poor Miss Finch*, *Athenaeum*, 17 February 1872

Williams, Valentine. 'Gaboriau: Father of the Detective Novel', *National Review*, December 1923

Wolff, R. L. 'Devoted Disciple: The Letters of Mary Elizabeth Braddon to Sir Edward Bulwer-Lytton, 1862–1873', *Harvard Library Bulletin*, January and April 1974

Woodruffe, W. L. 'Detectives', *Graphic*, 3 July 1880

Wrong, E. M., ed. Introduction to *Crime and Detection*, Oxford University Press, 1926 (reprinted)

Wright, W. H. 'The Detective Novel', *Scribner's Magazine*, November 1926

——. 'Twenty Rules for Writing Detective Stories' in *The Art of the Mystery Story*, ed. Haycraft, q.v. First published *American Magazine*, September 1928, under pseudonym S. S. Van Dine)

[Wynter, Andrew]. 'The Police and the Thieves', *Quarterly Review*, June 1856

INDEX

INDEX

351